ABOUT THE AUTHOR

Bob Jackson, born in Carlisle in 1941 and the oldest of three brothers, spent his life at sea in the Merchant Navy, trading around the world's major, and minor, ports. He is now retired and lives in Carlisle with his wife, also a writer, and their three dogs.

Cover image by Bob Jackson: Heavy weather in the North Atlantic.

I think I'll go to sea

Bob Jackson

First Published in 2010

Copyright © Bob Jackson

2nd Edition

British Library C.I.P.

CHAPTER ONE

I think I'll go to sea

South Shields
August 1957 – September 1958

I had just turned sixteen and finished taking my 'O' Levels at Carlisle Grammar School. I hated school and most of the teachers although I didn't dare admit it to my parents as they were both teachers – Dad a primary school headmaster; Mum taught secondary school English. They, of course, hoped I'd do quite well in my exams but I was extremely pessimistic about the results. I had no idea what I was going to do but one thing was for sure: I was going to leave and find myself a job and not continue into the sixth form. I had toyed with joining the Royal Navy as a helicopter pilot but after a bit of research decided it was way beyond my capabilities and I'd need at least six decent 'O' Levels to get in which was not going to happen.

Earlier in the year one of my mates, John Bannister, had been going to join the Merchant Navy but had failed the medical and decided to become a mechanic instead. He gave me all the literature about joining which included a book called *The Merchant Navy Today*. I idly picked it up and leafed through it. There were pictures of various types of ships and also they showed the officers' accommodation on some. I thought it looked pretty impressive. It seemed a really good life at sea. I did a bit more research and found the best way to go to sea was to do a year's pre-sea training. There were some really high class establishments like *HMS Worcester, HMS Conway* and Warsash College near Southampton but these were really expensive so I looked around at the various Nautical Colleges. I sent away for some prospectuses from colleges in South Shields, Liverpool and Glasgow. South Shields looked the best bet as it was nearest to home in Carlisle and seemed to have better facilities. They had a course starting in August. The requirements were four 'O' Levels or there was an entrance exam which happened to be in a couple of weeks. After reading *The Merchant Navy Today* I had decided I would like to be an engineer as it seemed a lot more interesting than being

1

on deck. I briefly talked about it with Mum and Dad and they seemed quite enthusiastic so I applied to take the entrance exam and was told to present myself at the college the following Monday.

I caught an early train over to Newcastle then changed to a local train to take me to South Shields. I sat opposite a bloke in his forties who turned out to be a ship's engineer going to the college to study for his Second Engineer's Certificate. I told him what I was intending to do and he said I must be mad to want to be an engineer. He painted a picture of long hours sweating away in grubby enginerooms being deafened by the noise of the engines. He reckoned being on Deck was the best life, swanning around in uniform in the sunshine and open air, chatting up the female passengers.

When we got to South Shields he showed me the way to the college and pointed me towards the reception desk. There were about forty of us sitting the exam which turned out to be three papers in Maths, English and Physics. We were all finished by two in the afternoon and were told to wait in the canteen and they would mark the papers and give us the results straight away. The other blokes were a real mixed bunch with several a couple of years older than me. Everyone seemed to get on really well despite having just met.

After about an hour the Tutor re-entered with the results and I was surprised to find I'd passed with flying colours and got nearly a hundred per cent in Physics which was my worst subject usually. Only about four or five people failed. It turned out the exam was the same one for both deck and engineers. The Head Tutor told all those for the deck course to follow him and those wanting to be engineers to remain with the other tutor. I thought "what the hell" and got up and followed him imagining how smart I'd look in uniform tapping up the girls.

We filled in some forms and were advised to take the Ministry of Transport eye test to ensure we were able to see reasonably well but mainly to ensure we weren't colour blind which was a definite no-no for navigating officers. I then headed off home to tell Mum and Dad the good news. They were really pleased that I'd got in. I have a feeling they expected me to fail knowing my academic ability. We travelled over to Newcastle the following week and I passed the eye test no problem so I was going to go to sea! I then had about six weeks with nothing to do but at least I felt I knew where I was going now.

One day I happened to meet up with Mike Cavaghan, who lived

along the road, and he was just finishing off his pre-sea training at Warsash. He was really enjoying it though he made me feel a bit inferior. They seemed to spend most of the time learning how to march, which knife and fork to eat with and even how to dance. He had at least three different dress uniforms whereas it was come as you are at South Shields. Looking back I think I managed to cope without being able to march and used my cutlery reasonably proficiently though I never have mastered dancing!

We were able to organise a grant from Carlisle Education Authority that would at least pay for my digs over in Shields but it would still cost Mum and Dad a fair bit as I needed money for food and clothes and various books. I was surprised at the cost of the text books I needed and I also had to lash out for paper and files. I got my 'O' Level results and I'd managed to pass four though I somehow failed Biology which was by far my best subject but at least I had Geography so I'd be able to find my way around the world.

A week before I was due to start Mum and Dad took me over to look for some digs. We had been given a list of 'recommended' places and I don't think they were very impressed with any of them but I was dying to get started and would have lived in a tent if necessary. We chose a place on Madeira Terrace mainly because there were four other blokes staying there that would be on the same course. It turned out to be an excellent choice as it was just down the road from a girls' school so we used spend most of our free time trying to get off with the sixth formers though with very little success I have to admit.

The following Sunday Mum and Dad ferried me over in the car with my bags and Mum said afterwards she felt really tearful leaving me there, but I was happy enough.

The other blokes arrived later on and turned out to be a really good bunch of lads. We were all the same age and all in the same boat with no money to spend. There was an old radiogram in the lounge though we only had one record, *Heartbreak Hotel* by Elvis, for the first couple of weeks until we brought some of our own from home.

We presented ourselves at the college the following morning and met up with the rest of the class. I think there were twenty eight of us budding Ship Masters. There was no messing about – we were given our timetable and a quick briefing on the course and it was straight into the first lesson which was basic navigation.

It was completely different from the Grammar School as all the lecturers had been at sea and obtained their Ship Master's Certificates and took a keen interest in drumming their knowledge and expertise into us. The subjects were seen in a different light too and it dawned on us that there had been a reason for learning trigonometry and there was a purpose in finding out the relative density of an object (it meant the difference between sinking and floating). I couldn't believe I was actually enjoying being educated. We got masses of homework which we all completed without complaining too much. I think we could all see an end goal.

Our digs were only from Sunday night to Friday breakfast. We could stay if we wanted but there was no food or facilities to cook so we all went home on Friday evening clutching a large bag of dirty laundry. The train fare was my greatest expense every week and I became a dab hand at hitch hiking though a couple of times I had to phone Dad to pick me up from odd places when it got too late. Most weekends I would manage to meet up with my old school mates and we would nip into the Lake District for a spot of rock climbing, usually in Borrowdale, if we could get transport. Some weekends I actually stayed in and did my course work much to Mum and Dad's amazement and I couldn't wait to get back over to Shields.

The course was hugely diverse ranging from stellar navigation to boat handling, ship construction and learning the international rules for navigating and avoiding collisions. The course was made so that we should have all the knowledge necessary to pass our Second Mate's Certificate at the end but we had to have four years sea service before we were allowed to sit the exam. We had to become proficient in all the forms of signalling so we spent hours learning the international code flags and practising semaphore and the morse code. Some of the stuff was a bit old fashioned and irrelevant but still formed part of the exam. One such subject was called "How's she heading?" We were told we were on a vessel heading in a certain direction and given the direction of the wind. We were then told we had sighted a single red or green light on a certain bearing. The single light meant it was a sailing vessel and from this information we had to work out what course the sailing ship would be on. It was hard enough when we had to work it out in degrees but the devious bastards insisted we work it out in compass points and quarter points. Alan Clish, who sat next to me, could do them in seconds whereas I would still be struggling ten minutes later.

The subject I enjoyed most was boat handling. The college had a boat house down on the Tyne where they kept an old lifeboat, a whaler and some Cadet Class sailing dinghies. We used to have a whole afternoon messing about and the only downside was when the tide was right out we couldn't launch the boats so had to learn all the different knots and practise rope and wire splicing. We practised boat handling up and down the Tyne and I often noticed Port Line ships undergoing their annual dry dockings at Wallsend and was impressed by how smart they always looked with their immaculate grey and white paintwork and streamlined bridges. Our instructor said it wasn't worth applying to them as they only took cadets from the elite establishments like Warsash and Conway. I decided it was worth a try and in my final term at the college I applied to Port Line for an apprenticeship. The staff at the college were surprised when I was invited to London for an interview.

I travelled up from Carlisle on a Monday wearing my best, and only, suit. It was bright green tweed and I wince even now when I think how I must have looked. Anyhow, I presented myself at the Port Line office in Leadenhall Street in the heart of London. I was interviewed by a couple of the Marine Superintendents for nearly three hours. They gave me a real grilling and I was sure I'd have to look elsewhere for a job but at the end they both complimented me on my knowledge and offered me an apprenticeship provided I got good results in the final exams. I left the office about three o'clock and grabbed a bite to eat in a Lyons Cornerhouse and then went off to do a bit of sightseeing. I had no idea where I was but I had a wander down The Mall and stood outside Buckingham Palace before heading back to the city centre. I found myself in Leicester Square and decided to watch a film. I can't remember what I saw but it was rubbish and I was really disappointed as it hadn't been cheap. I then headed up to King's Cross Station and got myself a ticket for the night train up to Newcastle arriving there at about six o'clock in the morning. I got back to the digs just in nice time for breakfast and was told off by the landlady as she hadn't been expecting me and hadn't cooked enough. When I got to the college I told the lecturers that I'd been accepted and that the company had been impressed by how much knowledge they had managed drum into me they were over the moon.

The last term ended with us sitting 'O' Level exams in Navigation and Seamanship but the big test was to get good results in my Certificate of Proficiency from the college which should not only get me a job with Port Line but would also reduce the amount of seatime I had to do before the next exams by six months. Somehow I managed to get third highest in the class in the Proficiency Certificate and obtain good passes in the 'O' Levels. I posted off all my reports and certificates and crossed my fingers. I think it was a week later when Dad got a letter with my indentures for his signature. He had to pay a £35 bond on me which he was supposed to get back when I completed my apprenticeship but I have a feeling it went in my pay packet and got spent on beer! Sorry Dad.

I'd really enjoyed my year at Shields and when I came to pack my bags it was quite a wrench leaving all my mates. I couldn't believe how much course work I'd done and how much stuff I'd accumulated. I had to ask Dad to come and pick me up otherwise it would have meant at least a couple of trips on he train.

Now all I had to do was wait to be appointed to a ship. Easy!!

CHAPTER TWO

My First Trip

m.v. Port Phillip
9th September 1958 – 13th March 1959

After a week at home Port Line returned my indentures all signed and sealed with a proper wax seal so I was now officially indentured to them as an apprentice. The next thing to arrive was a list of uniform and essentials I would need. It seemed a hell of a lot and included things like white uniform shoes, white silk scarf and a Number One white uniform, none of which were ever worn. After my first trip I left most of it at home – I have no idea what eventually happened to it – to make room for the really essential things like radios and record players.

Thinking back it must have cost Mum and Dad quite a bit to kit me out but they never said anything. We went across to Newcastle for my reefer (everyday) uniform but the rest came by mail order from the Red Ensign Club in London. There seemed to be a mountain of stuff to take. Everything was really heavy duty – the tropical white shirts and shorts could quite happily stand up by themselves the material was so thick!

I then had a couple of weeks trailing around Carlisle like a lost sheep waiting for joining instructions. I'd just got my provisional driving licence so used to pester Dad to take me out driving all the time. I must have driven him mad but he never complained. Another package arrived with my Port Line insignia and buttons. Mum had to change all the buttons on my uniform and sew three small buttons on the sleeves to show I was an apprentice. There was a lot of discussion as to where exactly they had to be sewn but eventually it was done. They used to say the sleeve buttons were there to stop us wiping our noses on our sleeves.

A week later at the beginning of September, my joining letter arrived instructing me to go up to London for a pep talk in the head office and be welcomed by a couple of the directors. I had to travel in uniform and I felt a bit of a prat in my new cap. When I got to the head office in Leadenhall Street I met up with Brian (known as Ears for reasons obvious to anyone who saw him) Stephenson from Hull who was also just joining the company. We spent the morning being shown round the office and were introduced to some of the directors. We were told we had to join the *Port Phillip* in Liverpool the following day. We had the afternoon off and went sightseeing then met up with Brian's family who took us out for a meal in a really suave restaurant. I ordered pigeon breasts as I couldn't understand anything else on the menu. I had a terrible time eating them as it seemed to be all bone. Anyhow…

We left our most of our luggage at Euston Station and went down to King George V Docks and spent the night on the *Port Vindex* and met up with some other apprentices on there. Next morning Ears and I travelled up to Liverpool to join the *Port Phillip*. We pooled our resources and got a taxi down to the docks. It was bedlam on board as the ship had just docked from Australia and most of the crew were paying off. The two other apprentices had also just joined but they were both old hands so at least we got a bit of guidance. We were issued with clean linen and shown our cabin and left to unpack our cases and have a look around. Our cabin was close to the galley and there was a really strong smell of curry permeating everywhere – for some reason the galley always smelt of curry on that ship even though we rarely got any. The *Port Phillip* had been built by Swan Hunter on the Tyne in 1942 for the Australia trade. She could carry 11,000 tons of cargo and most of the holds were capable of being refrigerated. She also carried a few passengers so the food was going to be good. I was really impressed when we went in for the evening meal to find it was silver service and we had our own steward to look after us. I thought I could get used to this!

The discharge was already in full swing using the ship's derricks. Slings of frozen lamb, butter and parcel mail were hauled up from the holds, swung across the deck and onto the quay. You really had to keep your wits about you when walking along the deck. Bales of wool were being discharged from two holds and these were even more dangerous as regularly one would fall from its sling and bounce around the deck. I spent most of my time tallying the mail bags off which kept me out of harm's way. The first couple of weeks were a very steep learning curve as although we'd learnt quite a few nautical terms and definitions at sea school it seemed a whole different language once we got on board. For start there were all the different ranks and how they fitted into the pecking order. Obviously the Captain or 'Old Man' was in overall command. The Deck Department was easy with the Mate known colloquially as 'Harry Tait', in charge and the Second, Third and Fourth Mates under him and us Apprentices below them all. The Bosun was in charge of the deck crew with the Lamptrimmer or 'Lampey' as his deputy. The deck crew consisted of a core of trained seamen known as Able Seamen or ABs of which four were designated Quartermasters and were on watches all the time. Below them came the Senior Ordinary Seamen and Junior Ordinary Seamen who had been at sea for some time but hadn't got any qualifications. Bottom of the pile were the Deck Boys or Peggies who were usually on their first trip to sea like myself. They were called Peggies as they had to serve in the crew mess and keep their accommodation clean and this was known as peggying. The Engineering Department was relatively easy with the Chief Engineer in charge of the department followed by Senior Second, Junior Second, Senior Third etc all the way down to Fourth after which came the Junior Engineers. There were usually two or three electricians as well under the Chief Electrician. The Engineroom Storekeeper was in charge of the ratings who were divided into Donkeymen and Greasers. The Donkeymen did the watches while the Greasers did all the cleaning and greasing. The Catering Department was overseen by the Chief Steward or Purser with all the stewards and cooks under his control. The only other department was the Radio which was a one man band usually consisting of the Radio Officer or 'Sparks'.

The other huge change I encountered was having to do my own washing (or dhobi) and ironing. We had to wear uniform most of the time and keeping a stock of clean white shirts was a major problem. We wore shirts that had detachable collars and I could usually get away with the shirt lasting two days and just changing the collars. There were a couple of knacks to wearing the collars – we used a cuff link instead of the front stud which made it a lot more comfortable to wear and for some reason used a front stud in place of a back stud. There would have been a good reason for this. On my first day off I nipped up the road spent all my spare cash on another dozen white collars so I had a reserve. We all had a dhobi bucket and a supply of dhobi powder and I seemed to wash something every day just to keep ahead. Ironing wasn't too big a problem as we only ironed the bits that would be visible from under our reefer jackets.

I was just starting to get the hang of things when we sailed. Then it was a whole new ball game. We sailed at eleven o'clock at night just to make things more difficult and the deck lighting left a lot to be desired. As we were being manoeuvred into the lock there was a tremendous bang and the wire connecting the stern tug parted. Everybody dived for cover as the wire whipped across the deck. It smashed a couple of light fittings and damaged the railings. Luckily nobody was hurt. The result of the wire parting was that we backed heavily into a lock wall and damaged the rudder and the stern plating. I hadn't a clue what was going on and had to keep relaying messages which I didn't understand but I seemed to manage. There was a lot of muttering about whether we should sail because of the damage but we eventually got away about two in the morning. We sailed down to Avonmouth where we continued to unload the frozen meat and wool for three days.

My first foreign port was Antwerp but I didn't see much of it as we were kept on watches as they discharged cargo round the clock. I didn't have any money anyhow. It was then on to Bremerhaven but we arrived at four in the morning and sailed late in the afternoon so I didn't set foot ashore. So much for seeing the world. Then it was back to London to finish discharge which took about ten days. We then moved down the river to Tilbury to drydock and repair the damage to our stern. We seemed to spend all our time in boiler suits crawling around in tanks with surveyors but it was certainly interesting and I think I learnt more about ship construction in those few days than the whole year at sea school. I also was able to draw some money so had a couple of good nights out ashore.

After Tilbury it was time to begin loading for Australia so we sailed up to Immingham to load railway lines. As Ears lived in Hull he managed to get home for the night. I think we were both surprised that we weren't homesick – I don't think we had time to be.

From Immingham it was across to Hamburg for some heavy plant and machinery. I think it took longer to secure it all than it did to load it. I was taken ashore by Len Taylor, the Senior Apprentice, and I got completely legless. He took me down the Reeperbahn which was a small street with prostitutes sitting in windows plying for trade. It certainly opened my eyes! I had a terrible hangover the next day but had to work anyhow. Then it was back to King George V Dock in London to complete loading. I was very impressed with the expertise of the dockers. They managed to squeeze huge crates into impossible corners. I had a quiet time there because I had very little money.

We sailed deepsea on 30th October. It was nice to get away and settle down to sea routine. As first trippers Ears and I had all the usual tricks played on us. I spent quite a while hanging about waiting for a 'long stand' one day until it dawned on me. Once the ship cleared the Channel we went on day work. This entailed starting at six in the morning, cleaning the bridge and our accommodation and polishing an awful lot of brass. One of us had to spend the two hours steering which was a doddle in calm weather but a real workup in bad weather. Then we had an hour for breakfast and turned to again at nine, working with the crew overhauling the cargo gear or painting. We got an hour again for lunch and then worked until half past four. We then had to study for an hour before the evening meal at half past six. I was surprised how quickly the days went as everything was new to me.

We got Sundays off although there always seemed to be something to do. It was linen change day and one of us had to go down to the linen room and get our change of bed linen and fresh towels from the Second Steward. It must have been quite a problem organising the laundry as there were forty odd crew and also twelve passengers so after a four week sea passage there was a huge amount of dirty laundry to send off to be washed as soon as we docked. It would all be returned a couple of days later and had to be carried down to the linen room. We always used to volunteer to help as the Second Steward would get our white uniforms done for free.

Our first stop was Las Palmas in the Canary Islands for fuel. We were only there for six hours and then on our way again down into the South Atlantic. When we crossed the equator there was a 'Crossing the Line Ceremony'. There were three of us who hadn't crossed the line before – a Deck Boy, Ears and myself. The Chief Engineer dressed up as Neptune with various people as his attendants. Two of the stewards turned up dressed as women in long ball gowns and it was very hard to tell they weren't blokes. We were tried and convicted of various heinous crimes and then we were liberally coated in some diabolical mixture of grease, tallow and fish oil. We also endured very dodgy haircuts. Luckily we had a week at sea for it to grow back a bit.

We had to stop off in Walvis Bay on the South African coast to land an engineer who got some steel fragments in his eye. We then berthed in Durban where we discharged mail and loaded some general cargo and frozen fish before setting off eastwards across the

11

Indian Ocean. I seem to remember the weather was ideal with blue skies and the sea like a mirror for the most of the passage. I was the bridge messenger for this bit of the voyage which meant I had to run up to the bridge when they blew three blasts on a whistle. I also had to take the 'clock book' around after lunch so everybody knew how much the clocks were changing that night. It was quite a cushy number as it was easy to skive off if we were doing a difficult job on deck.

A couple of days out I was returning the clock book to the bridge and found the Second and Third Mates trying to repair the echo sounder which had packed in. I stuck my nose in to see what they were doing and the Second Mate announced that the Rendall's Pessary was broken and sent me down the engine room to get a new one. After being sent from pillar to post looking for one I was told that the Radio Officer would definitely have one. I found him playing deck golf with the Captain and a couple of lady passengers. The Old Man spotted me lurking around and asked what I wanted. I told him that I wanted a Rendall's Pessary from the Sparks. The two lady passengers seemed to take quite an interest in my request and started giggling when I said the Second Mate needed it to fix the echo sounder. The Old Man sent me back to the bridge with a message that he'd told me they would have to wait until Adelaide to get one. What I didn't know was that a Rendall's Pessary was an old-fashioned form of female contraception and they were winding me up. The two mates nearly had a fit when they heard I'd asked the Old Man so I won that round in the end.

Our first port in Australia was Adelaide where it surprised me how hot it was. We only discharged from eight in the morning until five o'clock so had plenty of time to get ashore and look around. Then it was on to Melbourne and Geelong. We discharged the heavy machinery here – it was a complete panel-pressing plant for Ford.

We got to Sydney in time for Christmas. I was invited out for Christmas dinner by some relatives of Mum's. It was a bit of a disaster as I didn't know anyone. They took me back to the ship about midnight and to my surprise there was still a huge party going on with some nurses from the local hospital. I ended up with a lovely nurse called Fay and things got even better when she asked to see my cabin. When we got there I couldn't understand why the door was locked as we never bothered usually. I retrieved the key from its hiding place and opened the door. We were confronted by the sight of Ear's white bare bum bouncing up and down between a pair of knees. We quickly retreated with some strongly worded suggestions ringing in our ears. The sight seemed to have put us both of any thoughts of sex and we ended up sitting cuddling on the boat deck looking at the Harbour Bridge. So my Christmas turned out all right in the end. I didn't get to see Fay again as she had to work the next couple of days and we didn't return to Sydney that trip. Pity.

After Sydney we went up to Brisbane to complete discharge, then to Gladstone to clean the holds and prepare them for loading frozen meat. It took over a week. After that we were back down the coast loading frozen lamb and beef and butter. We finished off in Adelaide and Melbourne filling every available corner with bales of wool. The ship was completely full in the end so it must have been really profitable for the company.

We sailed from Australia on the 6th February – two months after arriving – and headed home via the Suez Canal. We stopped off in Aden for fuel and I bought a little Japanese transistor radio and was amazed to pick up Radio Luxembourg in the Red Sea. We transited the Suez Canal without problem, headed up the Mediterranean, through the Straits of Gibraltar and into the Channel. Our first port was Dunkerque where we discharged for a day or two then off to Liverpool. The day before we got there I was told I was paying off but Ears had to stay on round the coast. When we docked there were two more first trip apprentices joining – wandering around looking lost. I knew exactly how they felt. I had to go up to the officers' mess and sign off and receive the balance of my wages. I had earned the princely sum of £56 for the six months work but by the time they had deducted the money I'd withdrawn abroad and what I'd spent on board on booze I think I was left with about a fiver to last for my entire leave! I got off the ship about noon and caught the train home to Carlisle. I felt really sad leaving the ship and all my mates. It had been a great first trip! Mum and Dad picked me and all my bags up at Carlisle station. It felt great to be home again though I don't think Mum and Dad were too impressed when Mum asked if was hungry and I replied, "I'm fucking starving". It went quiet for a while.

CHAPTER THREE

New Zealand this time

m.v. Port Napier
28th April 1959 – 28th September 1959

After the *Port Phillip* I had about six weeks leave which turned into a bit of a downer. I couldn't seem to mix with my friends as I wasn't interested in the same things as they were and I rapidly got fed up so I was glad when a telegram came telling me to join the *Port Napier* in London. I joined her in the King George V Dock where she was nearly finished discharge. She was built in 1947, slightly bigger than the *Port Phillip* and a couple of knots faster. The apprentices' accommodation was a self-contained deckhouse on the boat deck which was nicely set out with a study and our own bathroom. It was really good to be back on board and with a bunch of blokes with the same interests. I hadn't realised, until I was at home on leave, how noisy ships were. There was always a generator running and various pumps starting and stopping and the constant hiss from the ventilation system. It was always there but I only noticed the silence when I was home without it.

We had a couple of days in London then up to Liverpool to finish off. Dave Arnold was the Senior Cadet and he was a real character. He seemed to know every seedy bar in Liverpool and I think we must have visited most of them in the few days we were there. We inevitably ended up in a pub on the Dock Road called Mabel's where the girls were very free with their favours. Our main problem was getting back to the ship before eight o'clock as the flags had to be hoisted exactly at eight or all hell let loose. There was also a clause in my indentures which said I should not frequent alehouses or taverns or houses of ill repute – mmm least said!

We sailed up to Glasgow for repairs and the annual drydocking which lasted about a week. Again we gravitated to the roughest bars but I was running out of money so stayed on board quite a bit. I visited a friend from school – Jock Anderson – whilst there. He was already married with a baby and living in a tenement and still had

14

two years to do at college. Rather him than me!! I really began to appreciate the life I was leading.

Port Line ships always looked smart but I was really impressed when we undocked with the hull all nicely painted. I was proud to say I was on board whereas later on in life I had to admit to sailing on some really scruffy ships. After drydock we loaded some heavy lifts using a floating crane built by Cowans Sheldon in Carlisle. We also loaded an awful lot of whisky – tons and tons! I'd never heard of half the brands and I think some were really special. We spent most of our time trying to stop the dockers from pinching it.

Then it was down to Liverpool to finish off loading. I was amazed at the variety of cargo. I remember there was a huge amount of toilet pans and wash basins etc. The company must have been in a hurry to get the ship out because we worked round the clock and finished loading in a week. I drew the short straw and had to work the night shift from ten at night until six in the morning. It all turned out for the good in the end as I'd run out of money so wasn't able to go ashore anyhow. The other perk was our breakfast. The cooks would leave out a mountain of eggs and bacon and things to fry and the duty mate and engineers and myself would have a huge fry up about three in the morning. We could hardly move afterwards. Ears joined just before we sailed – he'd been round the coast on the *Port Phillip* and then taken his leave.

As the cargo was for New Zealand we set off across the Atlantic to Panama. The Mate was a tremendous bloke called Ian North. He was later killed in the Falklands War when he was Master of the *Atlantic Conveyor* which was sunk by an Exocet missile. He took a real interest in our training and he had us doing everything from overhauling the cargo blocks and winches to painting the masts. He also taught us a lot about loading different cargoes and stability which came in very useful when I was promoted to mate myself.

We stopped off at Curacao for fuel. I went ashore with Dave Arnold and ended up in the biggest brothel I've ever seen. It was called Happy Valley. Just as well I was broke but it opened my eyes to say the least. Then it was a couple of days to Panama. The canal was very impressive after Suez. The Mate had us filling up tanks as we went through the Gatun Lake so he had loads of fresh water to wash the ship down with. We then had a couple of weeks across the Pacific to New Zealand.

When we berthed in Auckland the dockers were on strike so we

15

thought we'd get a few days off but the Mate had other ideas and set us chipping and painting over the bow on stages which didn't endear him to us very much. Eventually they started discharge and after a couple of days we sailed for Wellington. We had about a week there and the Mate organised for us to go 'sea-gulling' which meant working on the wharf and driving cranes in the evenings. We earned loads of money which we promptly spent on beer. The Mate had gone up considerably in our estimation.

After Wellington we sailed to Lyttleton on the South Island. I went up to Christchurch one evening to see Jock Anderson's brother and family. Again it wasn't very good as I didn't know them at all. I went up again the following night with Dave Arnold to meet a couple of nurses but got stood up and ended up boozing. The pubs used to shut at six o'clock but we managed to get a 'lock in'.

We missed the last train and tried to walk back beside the railway line. We thought we'd cracked it when we found a railway hand cart – the sort you see in silent movies that two people had to pump a handle to make it go. We manoeuvred it onto the rails and off we jolly well went. We'd only gone a mile or so when we were spotted by the police. They followed us in a car on a road running alongside the line shouting for us to stop. Dave reckoned we could outrun them but lost concentration and the handle came up and hit him on the chin and catapulted him into the bushes. I eventually got the cart stopped and went back with the police to extricate Dave from a particularly prickly bush. I think they were sorry for us as the booze was beginning to wear off and we were all scratches and bruises. They made us take the cart back to where we found it and let us off with a warning but it was about five in the morning when we got back to the ship feeling very sorry for ourselves.

We sailed from Lyttleton down to Port Chalmers to finish discharge and then went empty down to Bluff which is about as far south as you can go in New Zealand. It took a week of really hard work to clean and prepare the holds to load frozen lamb. The Mate gave us the weekend off and organised for me and Mike Smithson (another apprentice) to go out on an oyster trawler and Dave Arnold and Ears went on a wild boar hunt. Mike and I were both horribly seasick for the first few hours until they started trawling and the boat steadied up. It was fascinating seeing what came up in the trawl. There were squid, sea urchins and all sorts of crabs but they were only interested in the oysters and we seemed to get a pretty good haul. When we got back the Skipper gave us a sack of oysters each which, as neither of us liked oysters, we promptly swopped for a couple of cases of beer back aboard our ship. The other two also had a good time though they were completely knackered from tramping through the undergrowth. They got two boars and we all went to a huge barbeque the next night where they roasted one. It was a fantastic night.

We then loaded frozen lamb for a week before sailing up to Wellington to finish off with even more lamb and butter and bales of wool. There was a consignment of lamb for Callao in Peru as a trial but I don't think they liked it as we never went back.

Wellington to Callao took nearly three weeks and there was a rumour we were going to stop at Pitcairn Island but although we sailed pretty close we never stopped. When we got to Callao it was like stepping back in time. They unloaded the lamb into fantastic old steam lorries which chugged off into the town and as the weather was pretty warm the lamb must have just about been cooked by the time they got it to the warehouse.

After discharge we sailed up to Panama and through the canal. We stopped off for fuel at Curacao again and then across the Atlantic to London. It was thick fog in the Channel and it was really tiring doing bridge watches, staring for hours into the grey wooliness. We eventually berthed in King George V Dock and I was paid off on arrival. Poor old Ears got stuck with the coastal again.

Two trips under my belt and I was getting to be an old hand!

CHAPTER FOUR

Australia again

m.v. Port Pirie
14th October 1959 – 2nd May 1960

Thinking back I think these were the best times of my life. I loved the sea life and the camaraderie. I couldn't wait to get back on board and life seemed one big happy adventure. I suppose part of it was that I had no responsibilities to worry about and I couldn't understand how the Senior Officers and Skippers were always worrying about something or other. All problems seemed to resolve themselves sooner or later. After only two weeks leave it was off again to Liverpool to join the *Port Pirie*. She was the same size as the *Port Napier* and the same age but a different design. Our cabins were down on the main deck beside the engineers which wasn't as good. She had come from New Zealand and had been discharging for a week or so. The discharge was very slow as there was some sort of labour dispute. We sailed after a week to Dunkerque. There was a complete contrast here with everything going very quickly. We were only in a day then to Antwerp and Hamburg with less than a day in each before sailing to London to finish off at a more leisurely pace.

From London we went up the coast to Newcastle where we laid up at Spillers Quay before dry docking for a week at Swan Hunters, Wallsend. We lay in the river for a couple of days after coming out of dock. The ship looked immaculate with the hull all newly painted and I remember looking over the side one afternoon and seeing the pulling cutter from the Sea School rowing past with my old tutor, Captain Proudlock, sitting in the stern. I gave them a whistle and a wave and got an acknowledging wave back. I wondered if any of the cadets were thinking that it looked a good company like I had done. We loaded some steel products and bags of flour for a day and then it was back down to London to complete loading. Two new apprentices joined here and I found I was second in seniority so I was moving up the ladder already. I think they were a bit short of cargo as we sailed quite light. We carried six dogs and a cat as cargo and it was our job to look after them which I enjoyed though mucking out was a bit of a chore.

I was put on the eight to twelve watch with Ray Mitchell, the Fourth Mate, until we cleared the Channel. I really enjoyed being on watches though it could get boring if the mate didn't let you do anything. The last half hour of the watch was always pretty hectic, though, as I had to call the next watch, wash up all the tea things, go to the stern and take a reading from the log register to see how far we had gone and then make some fresh tea for the new watch. On my third watch I got back to the bridge at ten to midnight with the reading and Ray was writing up the log in the chartroom. When I went into the wheelhouse I became aware that it was thick fog and visibility was just about zero. I stuck my head in the chartroom and asked Ray if he knew it was foggy and he came running out muttering "Fuck. Fuck. Fuck." There is a standard procedure when the visibility becomes reduced which involves putting the engines on 'stand by', calling the Old Man, putting the radar on, calling extra lookouts and start sounding the whistle. It wasn't the most popular thing to do at midnight when everyone was asleep but Ray did it all by the book and within minutes he had everything organised. I was sent out on the bridge wing to keep a lookout and when I got there I was amazed to find a lovely cloudless night with great visibility. When I went back inside to report this phenomenon I found Ray still setting up the radar. I also found the reason for the 'fog'. I'd put the kettle on before I went to call the watch and forgotten about it and it was boiling away merrily filling the wheelhouse with steam. Once I'd switched it off the condensation on the windows rapidly cleared and we were left with unlimited visibility. Just then the Old Man arrived on the bridge in his dressing gown grumbling about being woken. I thought I was due an enormous bollocking but Ray quickly told the Old Man that we'd passed through an isolated fog bank and now we were out of it. He even convinced the Old Man he could see the fog bank astern. The Old Man brightened up as it meant he could go back to bed and we quickly got the ship back to normal running. After we'd been relieved by the next watch Ray bought me a couple of cans of beer and warned me that he would personally kill me if I ever mentioned it to anyone. Of course I was dying to tell the other cadets but somehow managed to keep quiet.

We stopped off at Las Palmas for a few hours for fuel then continued on our way to Capetown. We had a day loading frozen fish and crayfish tails then off to Durban where we docked on Christmas Eve. There was no work Christmas or Boxing Day and we had a great Christmas dinner followed by a party at night with the nurses from the local hospital. On Boxing Day the electrician hired a car and we had a tour inland to a Zulu kraal and afterwards went swimming in some huge surf.

We loaded drums of chemicals and chrome ore before setting off for Adelaide. It was about a fortnight's voyage and I remember we had some fantastic weather on the way across the Indian Ocean with some unbelievable sunsets. We spent most of our time cleaning and painting the lifeboats. They looked really smart afterwards.

I had dropped a large shackle on my toe when I was on the *Port Napier* and ended up with an ingrown toenail which was really sore. The ship's doctor tried to operate on it and made it worse. I later found out he was pissed as a newt and the Second Mate, who was helping, had made him stop before he really did some damage. The Old Man decided it should be sorted so I was sent off to a private hospital the day after we berthed in Adelaide. I had sixteen days in the hospital recuperating! It was really good with great food and a private room looking out over the beach. I got on really well with one of the nurses but she nearly got caught by the Matron in my room late one night and she was scared of losing her job so she stopped coming in. The company flew me up to Sydney to rejoin the *Port Pirie*. It was the first time I'd flown and I really enjoyed it. Eventually I began to absolutely loathe airports and planes especially when I was joining ships. I thought I would have an easy time after the operation as I wasn't supposed to walk around much but the Mate got me sewing canvas covers as I didn't need to walk to do that. I think I made a canvas cover for every bit of deck machinery on the *Port Pirie*.

We sailed for Tasmania the day after I rejoined where we finished off discharge in Beauty Point and Hobart. We didn't get much of a chance to go ashore in Hobart as we were cleaning the holds in preparation for our next load. The upper deck of Number Six hatch was a nightmare as we had carried some huge drums of talcum powder and unfortunately one of the drums had split and the powder had gone everywhere. It was just plain talcum powder with nothing added and had been bound for a cosmetics company in Melbourne. When we tried to sweep it up the dust would go up in the air and then settle again when we stopped sweeping so it looked no different from when we had started. Eventually we got it clean enough to satisfy the Mate and knocked off about midnight. He gave us a case of cold beer for our efforts so we sat out on deck still covered in the talc and looking like ghosts drinking the beer. We had saved quite a bit of the talc in empty containers so at least we wouldn't need to buy any talc for the next few years. After a couple of beers someone had the bright idea of playing a joke on the Carpenter who was always winding us up. We crept along the deck and tipped a big tin of the talc down the ventilator into his cabin. We then went to the end of the alleyway to await the results. We waited for ages but nothing happened so we sent Mick Jupp, the junior apprentice, along the alleyway to find out what was happening. He glanced into the Carpenter's cabin and said something to whoever was inside and carried on walking. When he passed the next cabin he hesitated then shot off down the alleyway at a rate of knots. He came back round the outside and we could tell by his face that something was wrong. It appeared we had miscounted the ventilators and had tipped the talcum powder into the Bosun's cabin next door. The Bosun was sitting at his desk fast asleep completely covered in the white powder. It had settled on his moustache so when he breathed it looked like puffs of smoke coming from his nostrils. He also had a glass of beer sitting on his desk with the talc floating on top. Now this was pretty bad news for us as the Bosun was known as "Mad Macgasgill". He was a huge hairy bear of a man who came from the Shetland Isles. He could have killed us all with one hand tied behind his back. We quietly slipped back along the deck to our cabins and had a council of war while finishing off the beer. We could either keep quiet and profess ignorance or own up and volunteer to clean his cabin. In the end we decided to risk our luck and keep quiet. We had quick showers and retired to bed locking our doors. When we woke up next morning nothing was said and we kept well out of the Bosun's way. The odd thing was that we never did hear anything more about our escapade and we didn't dare ask anyone as they would have know it was us. I often wondered how the Bosun cleaned up all that talc.

Once the holds were clean we then headed back to Beauty Point to load ingots and billets of zinc in the bottom of two holds. The Old Man let us take the lifeboat off up a river for a jaunt. We went for ages and saw all sorts of birds and animals on the banks. We thought we saw a Tasmanian Devil at one stage though it was probably an otter. When we turned around to go back we found the tide had gone out and we had to wait four hours on a sandbank until the water came back. The Old Man went mad when we eventually got back especially as we'd sneaked some beer on board and were slightly the worse for wear. He stopped our shore leave for a couple of weeks.

After Beauty Point we went up the coast to Newcastle where we prepared the holds for frozen meat and butter. It took about a week and then we started loading frozen lamb. We weren't allowed ashore but it worked out all right as the Mate had us helping the carpenters at night and we got paid extra for it.

After Newcastle we sailed down to Sydney then Melbourne loading meat and butter and topping off with bales of wool and barrels of hides. We completed loading in the middle of March and set off across the Indian Ocean for the Suez Canal. We did the usual stop off for bunkers at Aden for a few hours then on up the Red Sea to Suez. When we got to the north end of the Canal at Port Said we moored alongside and loaded bales of cotton for a day. A couple of us got ashore for a few hours in the afternoon but we never felt very safe there. We found a huge department store called Simon Artz which catered to tourists and people going on Safari. There were pith helmets, mosquito nets and even elephant guns. It was an amazing place to wander around though it seemed to be going into decline. Everything was really expensive so we didn't buy anything.

Early next morning we sailed for Liverpool. It was always ten days sailing to Liverpool or London – five to the Straits of Gibraltar and five to the home port. It always seemed to be ten days whatever ship I was on, even the faster container ships I was later to sail on. I never could figure that out.

We arrived in Liverpool on 12th April and discharged a fair bit of the wool but mostly it was cartons of butter. For once I had to stay on round the coast. After five days we sailed for the continent and discharged in Dunkerque, Antwerp and Bremen in quick succession with only a day in each port. Then it was across to London where we finished off discharge in the King George V Dock which took a further week or so. I enjoyed the time there as there were several other Port Line ships in dock and we got a chance to meet other apprentices. We had some really good nights ashore in the Round House, a pub just outside the dock gate.

I paid off on the 2nd May and took the train home for leave.

CHAPTER FIVE

Right round the world

Port Melbourne
30th May 1960 – 1st March 1961

I'd only had about three weeks leave when I got orders to join the *Port Melbourne* in London on the 30th May. The *Port Melbourne* was something special. She was only five years old and of really modern design with a streamlined bridge and even had one electric crane. All my previous ships had been equipped only with derricks. She was bigger than the others and could carry nearly 14,000 tons of cargo. Everything was clean and nicely painted so she was a pleasure to sail on.

She was nearly finished loading when I joined and we sailed a week later for Melbourne via Suez. It was an uneventful trip out though we were kept pretty busy. We were carrying twelve dogs and keeping them clean and exercised took up quite a bit of our time. There were four pedigree Bloodhounds for the Australian Police and they were lovely dogs though they used to drive everyone mad when they started baying at meal times. We also had a tiny Yorkshire terrier which came into season so we had to keep it in our cabin because the other dogs would howl all night trying to get to her. I dread to think what a Bloodhound/Yorkie cross would look like! One of the Bloodhounds fell overboard when we were at anchor off Melbourne. We had to lower a gangway to get it back on board. The Old Man really tore us off a strip for letting it escape. We got a really good bonus from the owners when they collected the dogs, though, because they were in such good condition. It went straight on a couple of cases of cold beer.

There were two cadet ships in Melbourne from other companies. I think they were P&O and British India. I was glad Port Line didn't have cadet ships because life seemed very regimented on board and the senior cadets were very full of themselves. We were challenged to a lifeboat pulling (rowing) race and we came in last despite Percy Hayball our Third Mate surreptitiously starting the engine. It turned

23

out the other boat crews had been practising so we didn't feel too bad.

We had the Sunday off and Percy organised a lifeboat trip up the River Yarra. We went for miles and were away most of the day and got pretty sunburnt but it was a cracking day. After a week in Melbourne we sailed up to Sydney and Brisbane to finish discharge. They must have been in a hurry for the ship because we were cleaning and preparing the holds for frozen meat as we discharged. We started loading in Port Alma which was a tiny port with only one wooden jetty, a wooden Pier Master's house and a railway line disappearing into the distance. The dockers all arrived on the first train with the frozen lamb and left on the last one without it. It was really isolated there and we were warned not to wander ashore at night because of poisonous snakes. They got a surprising amount of cargo on board in three days then we sailed up the coast to Bowen to continue loading. We had a week there, though, as loading was a fair bit slower.

I ended up in hospital for most of the time we were there. I had been noticing blood in my stools for a while and decided I had to do something about it so I asked to see the local doctor. He promptly booked me into a private hospital with my own private room. I then had a not just one but two enemas so I was beginning to wish I'd kept quiet. I had a couple of investigations and a barium enema but they never found anything. He kept me in for observation for several days but I think that was just to get more money from the company. Anyhow the bleeding stopped so it sorted itself. Of course everybody seemed to know about my problem and I got fed up with people saying they hadn't realised I was 'queer' and all the other innuendos. At least I had a nice few days with pretty nurses and good food and no work.

The day after I was back on board we sailed down to Brisbane to continue our loading. The Mate organised a trip around an abattoir for us. I didn't enjoy it at all – in fact I think a few of us went vegetarian for a week or so. After Brisbane it was Sydney then Melbourne and we finished off loading wool bales in Fremantle. I liked Fremantle and especially Perth. They seemed nice clean towns with lovely parks and gardens. From there it was off across the Indian Ocean to Aden for fuel. We sailed up the Red Sea and stopped off in Port Sudan to load bales of cotton for a day. I found it fascinating. It was the first real port I'd been to that wasn't European or English speaking. I had a couple of hours ashore wandering around the bazaar though I felt pretty intimidated by the beggars and traders. I made the mistake of taking my camera ashore and ended up having a serious altercation with some locals who thought I was taking their pictures. Everything was resolved amicably, though, when I gave them some money. After Port Sudan it was up through Suez and back to Liverpool. I was back to my old routine as they paid me off on arrival and I took the train home to Carlisle.

After another three weeks leave I got a letter telling me to rejoin the *Port Melbourne* in Falmouth. I had a hell of a train journey down to Falmouth – it seemed to take forever. When I got there the ship was in dry dock just finishing her annual survey. We floated out the next day and the ship looked really fantastic with the hull all newly painted. It was really good going back on the same ship because I knew where everything was and how things worked. The officers were all the same, too, but the other three apprentices were new so I was the 'old hand'. We had one night ashore to sample the local scrumpy and we sailed next morning for the United States in ballast with no cargo.

Port Line's main trade was between the UK/Continent and Australia/New Zealand but they were also part of another group called the MANZ (Montreal Australia New Zealand) Line. When ships were put on the MANZ run they could be away for eighteen months before they got home instead of the usual five to six so there was a fair bit of conjecture as we sailed across the Atlantic about when we would eventually get back. Mind you, in those days very few people at sea seemed to be married so it didn't make that much difference.

Our first port in the States was Wilmington, North Carolina, and on our way up the Cape Fear River we passed hundreds of Liberty ships from the Second World War all laid up. There were line upon line of them just tied up to buoys and rusting away. When we got into Wilmington we spent a day loading agricultural machinery and tractors then it was on to Baltimore for tinned food and loads of Lucky Strike cigarettes. Again we were only in a day then we went through the Chesapeake Canal into Delaware Bay and up to New York.

I hadn't realised the United States has a canal system but they reckoned you could get from New York all the way to Florida without having to go out to sea. We didn't actually berth in New

York but in Newark which was several miles to the south. We were quite close to the airport so it was easy to catch a bus up to New York itself. I seemed to get quite a bit of time off because I got up there three or four times. I visited Times Square and went up the Empire State Building though, to tell the truth, I can't remember getting to the top. Percy Hayball organised a trip to Radio City to see a show and we met up with some of the Rockettes in a bar, though I think they were a bit out of my league!

We had about a week in New York loading general cargo (tinned food, clothes and crates of machinery) then we went off down the coast stopping at Philadelphia, Pennsylvania; Newport News and Norfolk, Virginia; and Savannah, Georgia. We had about a day in each so I didn't get much of a chance to get ashore. We had a night ashore in Savannah, though, and I nearly got arrested for under age drinking. The legal age was twenty one which no one had thought to mention and we were in a bar when it was raided by State Troopers. The Electrician lent me his ID card and I got away with it, but the Electrician nearly got arrested because he reckoned the Troopers were a load of posers and told them so. I had to sneak his card back to him just in case. The ship was just about full leaving Savannah and we even had some John Deere tractors on deck. I was amazed by the size of them after the ones I was used to in the UK.

Our next stop was Kingston, Jamaica, for bunkers. I bought a couple of bottles of Appleton Estate rum which I fully intended to take home but I found it was very pleasant sitting on deck as we crossed the Pacific drinking rum and Coke so they didn't even last a week! Then it was on to Panama and off across the Pacific to Australia.

Just north of New Zealand we hit a tremendous storm. It was the first real storm I'd been in and I couldn't believe how far over we rolled. We had to go out on deck with the Bosun checking the lashings on the tractors because they were all moving about. After a couple of hours we had them all secured again and went back to the safety of our cabins. The storm died away after a few hours but I began to realise that the sea could be a dangerous place. Things improved that night, however, when a steward arrived with a case of beer from the Mate as a thank you for the work on deck.

We arrived at Brisbane to begin the discharge on the 9th December. There wasn't much cargo to unload so we only had a day there before we set of southwards to Sydney. We had about a week discharging what should have taken a couple of days. It was very hot and the dockers stopped work when it got to 100°F. This was good for us as the Mate let us off when there was no cargo work so we used to catch the ferry from Circular Quay over to some lovely beaches on the north side of the harbour. I think Sydney Harbour is one of the most beautiful natural harbours in the world. I used to really enjoy the ferry ride.

Eventually we sailed and headed off to Melbourne where we arrived on the 21st December. Again discharge was very slow especially with the days off for Christmas. It seemed really odd eating a full Christmas dinner in the heat. The pudding just about finished us off. In the evening we were invited to a barbecue on the beach with some nurses. We supplied the booze and they organised the food. It was a fantastic barbecue with huge prawns and steaks. Somebody had a record player but there only seemed to be one record. I must have listened to Bobby Darin singing *Dream Lover* twenty times. It was there I learnt that sex on a beach wasn't all that brilliant as we ended up with sand in places sand shouldn't get to and bitten by some kind of sand fleas which only come out at night. Still, I wouldn't have missed it.

After Melbourne it was south again to Adelaide to complete discharge. I was on watch as we approached and the Old Man sent me down to organise the pilot ladder with the quartermasters. The *Port Melbourne* had gun port doors which were big watertight doors cut into the hull on either side so the pilot didn't have a long way to climb. We thought we had loads of time so we had a mug of tea before we opened the door. Unfortunately it was jammed solid. It took us ages to lever it open and when we did we saw the pilot boat was right alongside. I leaned out to tell them we'd only be a minute and as I did the huge door started to swing shut behind me. It was either stay put and have my legs chopped off or go for a swim. I chose the latter. The Old Man was leaning over the bridge wing fuming at the delay and was not amused to see one of his apprentices catapulting into the sea in full uniform complete with cap! When I landed in the water I realised that it wasn't the best idea in the world as the water was all churned up and swirling around me and I had no sense of which way was up. I could also hear the propellers chomping through the water towards me until the Old Man stopped the engines after what seemed like a lifetime. I eventually popped to the surface behind the pilot boat and was picked up, still clutching my cap, by the highly amused crew. Once back on board I had to report to the Old Man who seemed to think I'd done it on purpose and gave me a real bollocking. I had to stay on the bridge still dripping wet until we docked. The Fourth Mate told me later that the Old Man daren't look at me because he'd have cracked up laughing.

We finished off unloading in Adelaide then moved along the coast to load zinc ingots in Port Pirie. The ingots were put in the bottom of the holds and it was important that they were stowed properly so we could load frozen meat on top later. The Mate had an apprentice in each hold overseeing the stowage. The temperature was way into the hundreds, the dockers were bolshie and it was dirty and dusty so we had a miserable four days there. We all went ashore on the last evening for a few drinks and on the way back to the ship we were nearly run down by an express train travelling down the middle of the street. The main railway line went right through the centre of town. I couldn't believe we didn't hear it coming but I suppose we had rather over-imbibed. Once we'd recovered from the shock I had to admit it was really impressive with all the noise and steam. I was beginning to see why going to sea was classed as a high risk occupation.

We sailed from Port Pirie up to Port Melbourne where we started to load frozen meat and butter. It was a real work up as it was really hot and we had to keep sealing the holds up between wagons just to keep the cold in. The good bit was that they only worked from eight in the morning to five so we had every evening off. One evening Percy, the Third Mate, dragged three of us up to town to see an amateur production of My Fair Lady. We were dreading it and would much rather have stayed on board but it turned out to an absolutely ace performance and we thoroughly enjoyed it. The crew thought us a bit odd the next day as we kept singing the songs but we didn't care.

After Melbourne it was Adelaide and Fremantle to finish off loading. We got a week in Fremantle this time and again really enjoyed going ashore. All the pubs shut on Sunday and the only way you could have a drink was to buy a meal. We all ordered baby chicken which turned out to be a tiny chicken with hardly any meat on it which was inedible, anyway. I think they collected all the meals up at the end of the day and refroze them until next week but at least we could have a beer. The local brew was Swan Lager and I thought it was one of the best lagers made.

After Fremantle it was off across the Indian Ocean again to Suez with the obligatory stop at Aden for bunkers. Ian Nicholson was the Senior Apprentice and he was on his last trip so, for the passage home, he went on watch with the Mate and I was promoted to Senior Apprentice. I had moved up the ladder another rung!

It was a good voyage home with lovely weather all the way. As we were coming up the Bay of Biscay we got a radio message to say about half of us were paying off in Falmouth and I was on the list. As we didn't have any cargo for Falmouth the ship anchored in Falmouth Bay and the reliefs came out in a launch. We got off at about nine o'clock at night and were transported up to a hotel. When we got there they had laid on a huge spread and the bar was still open so it developed into a party. The waitresses were all French girls on work experience and they joined the party so it was a great end to the trip. I had to get up at six o'clock the next morning to catch my train home and I was really ill. I think it must have been the worst train journey ever. I found out later that a couple of the Mates and an engineer booked themselves into the hotel and spent a week there instead of going home. I wished I'd have thought of it but I couldn't afford it, anyhow, so it was back to Carlisle.

CHAPTER SIX

Fourth Mate

m.v. Port Alma
18th March 1961 – 26th July 1961

This time I didn't even get three weeks leave before they called me back. It was to join the *Port Alma* in Liverpool. It was from the sublime to the ridiculous. The *Port Melbourne* was one of the most modern ships in the fleet and the *Port Alma* was the oldest – built in 1925 on the Tyne but she could still manage a respectable fourteen knots most days with a following wind. It was really interesting seeing how things had evolved and improved. She had been really well maintained over the years and still looked pretty smart. She had just started loading in Liverpool for New Zealand when I joined. I reported to the Mate, John Webber, who didn't know anything about me joining so I found the apprentices' cabins and started unpacking my things and settling in. After meeting the other lads I found out I was Senior Apprentice again so after a mug of tea went off to find the Mate to see what I should be doing. He told me there was a shortage of Fourth Mates in the company and I was to sign on as uncertificated Fourth Mate and to move into the Fourth Mate's cabin. I couldn't believe my luck.

In a single stroke my wages tripled, I had my own single berth cabin with a steward to clean for me, I would be on watches – no painting and greasing – I could wear decent epaulettes with one stripe instead of buttons and I could order cases of beer from the bond. The *Port Alma* originally carried twelve passengers but when she got a bit long in the tooth they stopped carrying them and the officers moved up into the passenger accommodation. I had a huge cabin with a three-quarter bed and a large window. This was the life.

We spent ten days loading general cargo in Huskisson Dock. As Fourth Mate the job wasn't all that different from an apprentice when on cargo operations. I had to make sure things were securely stowed and lashed and keep our cargo plan up to date. Cargo plans were drawn up showing what items were stowed where and for which port and indicating their weights and sizes. We used to keep them as apprentices but they were for our own benefit so it didn't matter if there were mistakes. Now it was for real. Every morning the Second Mate would get a list of what had been loaded the previous day and we would all gather round and agree, or argue, as to where exactly it had been stowed. I found the plan fascinating with all the different hieroglyphics and colours for the different discharge ports. I wish, now, I'd kept some copies to look back on.

We sailed from Liverpool on the 28th March across the Atlantic to Panama. As I didn't have a certificate Dave Sinclair, the Old Man, put me on the four to eight watch with the Mate to supervise me. John, the Mate wasn't too happy about this as usually he would be on day work supervising the deck crew. One of the duties on the four to eight watch is to take star sights at dawn and dusk. John would take the actual sights and then leave me to work them out. I must have driven him mad because I was always making mistakes and he had to rework them to find out where I'd gone wrong. We got there in the end though. The Old Man gradually relaxed about my watch-keeping and John would only come to the bridge to check things a couple of times a watch.

We got to Panama on the 5th April but had to anchor off for a day as the Canal was unusually busy. We eventually went through on the 7th and stopped off in Balboa for bunkers. We sailed in the evening and I found to my delight that the Old Man trusted me enough to have my own bridge watch so we sailed from Panama with me doing the eight to twelve watch in charge of 11,000 tons of ship ploughing along at fourteen knots.

At about eleven o'clock I wandered out onto the bridge wing to chat to the lookout. It was flat calm with a full moon just setting and we were both agreeing how quiet it was when we both saw a ship's lifeboat with people sitting up in it drifting past. It went from peaceful tranquillity to mad panic in a moment. There were set procedures for encountering fog, fire on board, man overboard, collisions, but nothing in the book for finding a lifeboat. I told the lookout to try and keep an eye on it and ran into the wheelhouse and rang Standby on the engine room telegraph. I then blew down the voice pipe to the Old Man's cabin. Thankfully he answered straight away so I told him about the boat. He told me to ring the general alarm for boat stations. All hell let loose. When I rang Standby on the engineroom telegraph the duty engineer sounded the engineroom alarm to get the engineers down below to start pumps and generators. Just as they got to the bottom of the engineroom the signal went for boat stations so they didn't know whether to prepare the engine for manoeuvring or rush to the lifeboats. On the bridge it was equally chaotic with people arriving in various states of undress demanding to know what was going on. Things calmed down when the Old Man arrived and took charge. He turned the ship around and we steamed slowly back to where we'd seen the boat. There was a huge searchlight on the bridge top which was a relic of the wartime convoys. I think that must have been the last time it had been used. The Second Mate and a couple of others went up to switch it on. It went on all right but was pointing vertically upwards and was seized solid. They set about it with hammers and spanners. When we got back to the position we'd seen the boat there was no sign of it.

We steamed up and down for what seemed like ages but it had vanished. There were mutterings from all and sundry who were coming to the conclusion that I'd imagined it. After another couple of sweeps up and down even the Old Man was getting sceptical when all of a sudden there it was in the moonlight. I was going to be a hero!

At this moment the team on the bridge top managed to free the searchlight and it creaked and squeaked its way down. When it was finally in position it revealed a huge floating log with three large pelicans sitting on it. The silence was deafening. The searchlight was switched off and everybody wandered back to bed muttering derogatory remarks about me and my parentage. The Old Man made me feel a bit better saying I'd done all the right things and it very well could have turned out differently. For my troubles I ended up with the nickname 'Pelican Jackson' and I met up with a bloke thirty years later who remembered me as 'Pelican'.

After that things could only get better and they did. It was a great trip across the Pacific albeit a slow one. The Doxford main engines had a design fault. Each cylinder had two pistons and the top piston was water-cooled, fed by heavy rubber hoses. These had a habit of bursting at regular intervals, spraying the engineroom with scalding water. The engine had to be stopped and the hose renewed which took a couple of hours each time.

The weather was great and we eventually arrived in Wellington only to find there was a dockers' strike and the whole port was at a standstill. We went alongside and tied up at Aotea Quay which was a little way out of town but we didn't mind. For some reason – possibly the previous crew – the *Port Alma* was renowned for parties so as soon as we docked the phone started ringing with girls wanting to come to our parties. The parties were held in the officers' bar which had been the passengers' lounge in the old days. It came complete with a fitted-out bar and there was even a small dance floor. Initially we had loads of beer from the bond, which was duty free, but that ran out surprisingly quickly so we organised kegs of beer to be delivered from the local brewery and as we were such good customers they even lent us a cooler to chill the beer down. Things always seemed well organised with the cooks laying on a buffet supper for the price of a few beers. The girls even had their own toilet facilities as the company had left the lady passengers' washroom intact when they converted the accommodation.

The Third Engineer played a great trick one night. He got a couple of packets of ginger snaps and mixed them with water in a bowl until it was a brown mess and put it heaps on the floor in the girls' toilet. He then appeared at the party complaining about the state of toilet so everyone wandered in to see what the fuss was about. It looked horrible. He started to clean it up with his bare hands. "Yeah, it's definitely shit," he said. His final gesture was to lick his hand and announce it tasted like shit, too. A few people nearly threw up.

After five days our enthusiasm for partying began to wane as it was costing a fortune in booze. Luckily a couple of days later the dockers went back to work and started the discharge and we had to do some work so we reduced the parties to the weekends only and even then we were quite pleased when we came to sail after more than three weeks in port. We met some fantastic girls and I think at least one of the engineers got married later and emigrated to New Zealand.

We completed our discharge in Wellington and prepared the holds for refrigerated cargo. We sailed to Nelson on the north coast of the South Island. It was my first visit there and it was a lovely little port and really picturesque. After a few days loading cases of apples we shifted to Picton which was another tiny port with only one jetty. We tied up on one side and the ferry to the North Island berthed on the other. They were starting to enlarge the port to make it into the main ferry port for the South Island so there was a huge amount of construction going on which seemed to be spoiling the tranquillity of the place. We loaded more apples and some frozen lamb and then sailed down to Timaru to continue loading frozen lamb and bales of wool. It is exposed to easterly swells so as a storm was forecast we spent ages securing the ship with huge ropes made from coir. No sooner had we got them rigged than the forecast changed so we had to remove them. I think we had to rig them about five times in the fortnight we were there so we were pretty expert in the end.

We had a weekend off so on the Saturday I hired a car with two of the apprentices, Dave Wilson and Pete Reseigh, and we set off to see Mount Cook. We had no real plan or decent map but just set off in a westerly direction and by good luck arrived at a resort called Hermitage. It was a lovely clear day and Mount Cook looked really impressive and somewhat larger than the fells of the Lake District back home. We soon found out it was really expensive in the resort and we couldn't afford a meal so we just turned around and headed back. We stopped off for something to eat halfway back at a little café. We all had a huge steak and chips with battered oysters on top. It turned out really cheap and we could hardly move when we'd finished. We got back to Timaru about two in the morning having got lost a couple of times and at that time of night there was no one around to ask the way.

We got up late on Sunday and as we still had the car we had a drive south along the coast. It was really dramatic with huge rollers breaking on the beaches. It was very wild and unspoiled and we just sat on the beach watching the waves for ages. Looking back, I should have made more of an effort to take opportunities to get ashore and see places but I rarely got further than the first bar. I returned the car on the Monday morning and the garage gave me half the money back because I hadn't realised it was a deposit so we could probably have afforded a meal at Hermitage after all. Bugger!

We finished loading and sailed for the UK via Panama on the 9th June. It was an uneventful trip home apart from one day, off the Isles Rapa in the middle of the Pacific, when we spotted a large waterspout. The Old Man decided to go for a closer look. As we got nearer it started moving towards us and passed down the port side less than half a mile off. As it was hot weather everyone had their windows open and the wind sucked all sorts of things out of the cabins. I lost a white shirt that was hanging up to dry but the Old Man lost some quite important papers and certificates. He didn't do it again! Afterwards there was a really fishy smell in the air and a fine sand coating the decks which must have come from the cloud above the waterspout.

The passage was pretty slow with numerous main engine breakdowns but we eventually arrived in London on the 25th July and I paid off next day and went on leave.

CHAPTER SEVEN

Last trip with Port Line

m.v. Port Fairy
8th August 1961 – 5th March 1962

After another short leave of only twelve days I joined the *Port Fairy* in drydock on the Tyne. This time my joining letter said I was to sign on as Fourth Mate so it was good to know I wasn't dropping back to apprentice for my last trip. The ship was nearly finished her overhaul and was floating out of the dry dock so I had to hang around for a couple of hours before I could get on board. One of the apprentices was Matt Harger who I'd sailed with on my third trip. I had also sailed with quite a few of the crew before.

The *Port Fairy* was another old-timer built in 1928 and virtually identical to the *Port Alma* so I had no trouble finding my way round. She had been chartered on the MANZ run trading between Australasia and the States so everyone was expecting to be away quite a while. The Old Man was Dave Cloke who was doing his first trip as Skipper. He was a really good bloke and had been working for the company supervising the loading and discharging of our ships in the London docks so I'd met him quite a few times. He decided to put me on the four to eight watch with the Mate until he saw how I performed which was a bit of a downer as I'd got used to being in charge of a watch on the *Port Alma*. Mick O'Byrne, the Mate, wasn't happy about this at all as he was quite a senior mate and wanted to be on daywork. We sailed the following day on the 10th August in ballast for the States. There wasn't a good atmosphere on the bridge with Mick wandering about grumbling so I wasn't looking forward to the trip at all. We set off around the north of Scotland and through the Pentland Firth. This far north the sun hardly seemed to set and it felt odd to be having lovely warm weather. After we cleared Cape Wrath the Old Man decided I was experienced enough so he allowed me to do the watch on my own with instructions to call Mick if I ever had any problems. This was brilliant as the four to eight was the best watch with all the sunrises and sunsets and most of the day free. My big problem was that I had to do star sights by myself but I soon became pretty expert and produced accurate positions. I'd bought my first sextant in South Shields before we sailed and felt like a proper navigating officer now. Just after we passed Rockall I was standing on the bridge wing just after dawn having a mug of tea when there was a tremendous roar and an aircraft flew past so close I felt I could touch it. All I could do was wave my mug of tea at the pilot. The plane was a Royal Navy Gannet which must have come from an aircraft carrier somewhere near. After it passed it did a turn and came around for a second run. I thought for a moment it was going to land on the water as the flaps were deployed but he swept past really slowly with the cockpit canopy open and held his hand out for the tea! I could very nearly have given it to him! It was amazing.

All the way across the weather was fantastic but as we approached Newfoundland we met with thick fog on the Grand Banks. Every day the Radio Officer received a list of the positions of all known icebergs and it was my job to plot them so we could take avoiding action. As we cleared the Banks and came out of the fog we were confronted with a huge iceberg. I had a bit of a panic because I thought I'd missed plotting one but it wasn't on the list, thank goodness. It was quite an experience passing it and the air temperature dropped considerably when we got close. After we'd safely passed it we reported its position to the Coast Guard.

The first port was Newark again but this time I only managed a couple of outings to New York. The Third Mate, Bruce Watts, and I visited the Merchant Navy Club as we'd been assured by the Mate it was the place to meet girls. We had to take out membership which cost us $10 each which seemed a lot of money. When we got inside it was full of middle-aged American women on the lookout for husbands. Bruce was all for staying as they kept buying us drinks but we eventually escaped and headed for the downtown area, vowing to kill the Mate when we got back.

The loading was a repeat of the voyage on the *Port Melbourne* and the ports were the same as well. There wasn't as much machinery this time and we filled up with tinned fruit in the southern ports. I liked loading round the States as most places felt pretty safe to go ashore and everything seemed so cheap. We all bought jeans and t-shirts and stocked up on Fruit of the Loom underpants. It was dead cheap for meals ashore too and we were always nipping up to the nearest hamburger bar. They always tasted so good. I'd tried burgers in

Wimpy Bars in the UK but the ones over there were something else, especially with a really cold bottle of Coke. We always had to be careful in bars in the States as every State seemed to have different laws and in most of them the legal drinking age was twenty one. We sailed loaded from Savannah on the 6th September and after bunkering in Curacao passed through the Panama Canal and set off across the Pacific to New Zealand.

I was put on the eight to twelve watch once we sailed from Savannah and was getting to feel pretty confident on the bridge. I was back to taking sun sights again and began to realise that I'd bought the wrong sextant as it had a huge telescope which was brilliant for stars but not too good for looking through at the sun. I vowed to change it as soon as I could afford it. I found out much later that I had damaged the retina in my right eye staring at the sun through it. It was an uneventful passage across the Pacific apart from the regular stops to replace the cooling hoses on the main engine.

I was really enjoying life as an officer. We had a steward assigned to look after us so every morning I was woken up at quarter past seven with a cup of tea and some toast. After a leisurely shower I would get into uniform and wander down for a full English breakfast in the saloon. Then I'd go up to the bridge to start my watch at eight o'clock. While I was on watch the steward would clean the cabin and make my bunk and at half past ten he would bring a pot of coffee to the bridge. When my watch finished at noon I would nip into the bar for a couple of cold beers and then it was down to lunch which was usually a four course affair. After lunch I'd either sun bathe or have a kip for a couple of hours to be woken by the steward bringing a cup of tea usually with a tabnab (cake). I would then mosey around for an hour and even maybe do some studying and then I had to relieve the Second Mate for his dinner at six o'clock. When he returned to the bridge I went down for my meal which would be at least five courses. I then had an hour to kill before my evening watch began at eight. It was brilliant and I could have carried on for ever but we arrived on the New Zealand coast on the 3rd October and we had to actually do some work. The discharge round Kiwi proved to be uneventful with no unusual ports.

Although I really enjoyed Australia and New Zealand I was beginning to feel I'd seen it all and needed to see the rest of the world which meant I'd have to change companies once I'd got my certificates as Port Line only traded to Australia and New Zealand.

After completing discharge in Port Chalmers on the South Island we sailed through the Cook Strait and across the Tasman Sea to Brisbane arriving on the 5th November. We had to clean the ship and prepare the hold for frozen meat. As Fourth Mate I wasn't really involved so I took a bit of time to look around Brisbane itself. I got to the zoo a couple of times to see the koalas and kangaroos and things but couldn't find much else to do.

It took a week to prepare the ship for loading and then we loaded frozen beef. It was quite a work up as the regulations seemed stricter and the meat was loaded in ten to twenty ton lots. We had to mark on the cargo plan where each lot was and make sure it was separated from the adjacent lot by tape and marker pen. The temperature was up into the nineties on deck but minus eighteen in the hold so it's a wonder we didn't get frostbite working down there but we seemed to survive.

After Brisbane we went north up the coast to load in the Queensland ports of Bowen, Gladstone, Cairns and Townsville. These were small ports up inside the Barrier Reef and they were great places. Although the loading was hard work it was real fun to go ashore at night to the bars as they seemed to have more than their fair share of local characters. As we moved from port to port we went between the islands of the Barrier Reef which were really spectacular. Whoever surveyed them must have come from Cumbria – or Cumberland as it was in those days – because there were lots of features with names such as Penrith, Troutbeck, Penruddock etc. I spent ages poring over the charts trying to spot them. We had nearly a month loading chilled and frozen beef in these lovely little ports before sailing down to Sydney to finish off with some general cargo.

We got there on the 19th December and there was a mad rush to finish the loading and to sail before Christmas. It was going according to plan until the dockers went on strike on the 22nd so we ended stuck there until the 31st December. Yet another Christmas in Australia. It was very quiet with not too many parties for some reason but the Christmas dinner was up to the usual standard and the evening party must have been really good because I can't remember anything about it.

The passage across the Pacific was uneventful although we continued to have numerous stops to replace the main engine cooling hoses.

The first port in the States was New Orleans and what a great place that turned out to be. We only had two days there but I managed to get ashore both nights. I got to visit Al Hirt's jazz club and hear him playing, though it was quite expensive to get in. I also got to see Clarence Frogman Henry performing live. The atmosphere was electric and I really enjoyed the music. It was a good job we sailed or I'd have spent all my wages there. After New Orleans it was all the way up the coast to Boston arriving there on the 5th February. They put the pilot on board with a sailing pilot cutter and it was tremendous seamanship for them to sail precisely alongside us and put the pilot onto the ladder. It impressed me a lot.

We had a couple of days there but nobody went ashore much as it was bitterly cold. I bought myself a fantastic fur hat with ear flaps and everything. The first time I wore it the Old Man told me to take it off because it wasn't uniform. I think I only got to wear it twice and I left it on the ship when I paid off a month later so it was a bit of a waste of money. After Boston it was down to Newark again. We discharged the bulk of the cartons of frozen beef here. After all our work separating and marking the different consignments as it was loaded they took no notice and just discharged it as they came to it. Then they had to sort it all out on the quay. It took ages and the Second Mate was incensed because his cargo plan really had been a work of art.

We carried on discharge in the usual east coast ports then it was up to Halifax, Nova Scotia, to finish off. I remember the discharge was really miserable as it was always cold and we could never seem to keep warm. I'd have been all right if I could have worn my fur hat!

We then went back to New York to commence loading another cargo for Australia and I got a nice surprise when we arrived as there was a message that I was to pay off and travel home on the Cunard liner, *Corinthia*. I had completed my indentures so they were sending me home to sit my Second Mate's Certificate. I had assumed I would have to stay on for the full voyage which wouldn't have been too bad as Fourth Mate's wages were pretty good.

I was to travel with three or four other officers from other ships who were also due leave. We were booked to travel First Class and someone suggested that we change to Second Class and have the balance of the fare to spend on board. I couldn't believe it when the company agreed. We had a terrific trip over and by some oversight we had been left on the First Class list so we got invites up to the Captain's cocktail parties before the evening meal so got even more free drink. It took five days to cross the Atlantic and if the truth was known I was glad to be getting off. There was so much excellent food and free booze that it was just too much. I also won a bingo prize on the last night so I left the ship with more money than I joined and considerably fatter.

My ticket was to Liverpool but the ship called at Greenock first so I decided to get off there. I later found out that the company had arranged for one of the directors to present me with my completed indentures at Liverpool so I wasn't too popular but I would have stayed on if they had told me.

CHAPTER EIGHT

Back to Shields to study

South Shields
10th March 1962 – 14th September 1962

After a week at home I went over to South Shields and booked myself onto the Second Mates' Certificate Course. The term was already into its second week but the girl in reception said it was all right to start any time. To sit for a Second Mate's Certificate it was necessary to pass an eyesight test so I went down to the Mercantile Office on the quayside to book an appointment but luckily one of the examiners was doing nothing so he did the test there and then. He projected coloured dots onto a screen and I had to call out the colours. The light source for the projector was an oil lamp which was supposed to make it more authentic but I had a problem distinguishing the reds from the whites as the white colour was virtually orange due to the poor light source. I passed with no problem in the end but it was a bit worrying. I vowed to take my next eyesight test at Newcastle where they had progressed to an electric light. As I was coming out of the Mercantile Office I met Ken Pykett who had been a term ahead of me on the Pre-Sea Course. We adjourned to the nearest pub which happened to be The Locomotive and had a couple of pints and caught up with each other's travels. He told me of some good digs in Wood Terrace right beside the college so I went straight there and was able to organise myself a room. Not only was it close to the college but it was two doors away from a really good pub called The County. I had a quick wander around the town and nothing much seemed to have changed so I caught the next train home. I had a couple more days at home then packed some gear and moved over to Shields.

Two other lads in the digs were also on the same course so I tagged along with them the next morning. When I entered the class I found I knew at least three quarters of them from my previous time at the college so it felt like I'd never been away. At lunch time we adjourned to The County for a couple of pints and to reacquaint ourselves. It was really interesting comparing adventures and experiences. Needless to say it extended well past the lunch hour and quite a few of us never made it to the afternoon classes. This didn't bode well at all but it didn't develop into a habit as most of us were skint as we had to live off our savings. I was better off than the majority because my last year had been as Fourth Mate but most had finished as apprentices on very poor money. By some quirk we were allowed to sign on the dole even though we weren't available for work so that helped. The first class on Thursday mornings was always quiet as we had to collect our dole money from the labour exchange and Thursday afternoons could also be quiet as the money was promptly passed over the bar in The County.

After I'd been there a month I figured I needed some transport and my money seemed to be doing all right so I bought an old Ford Anglia. It was described by my mates as 'shit-coloured drab' and didn't do my image much good but at least I was mobile.

I found the coursework really easy as we had covered it all Pre-Sea. It was supposed to be a six month course but after I'd been there a couple of months I felt I wasn't learning anything so I put my papers in to take the next exam before the college broke up for the summer holidays. Luckily I passed everything first time and now had a shiny new Second Mate's (Foreign Going) Certificate with my name on it.

I didn't particularly want to go straight back to sea so when I contacted Port Line to tell them I was told that unless I joined a ship the following week I would be out of a job. I decided that I would stay home a while longer and try my luck elsewhere. I heard later that if I'd have gone back I'd probably have got promoted to Third Mate and got a bonus, but never mind.

After a few days at home I felt I should be earning some money so went down to the Labour Exchange and got a job as a Fitter's Mate installing central heating with a local Carlisle firm. I only stuck it for a few weeks but it was good experience learning how to use different tools and doing basic plumbing. I ended up installing liners in old chimneys and rapidly got disenchanted with being covered in soot or sitting on top of unstable chimneys trying to pull the liner up. I missed the camaraderie of ship life though as I didn't seem to have much of a social life in Carlisle any more.

I decided to go back to sea but realised I didn't know how to go about getting a job, so I travelled over to Newcastle to the Union office for some advice. The representative was totally useless and his main preoccupation was to get into the nearest pub before they closed. I picked up some magazines from his office and left. There was an address for a Glasgow company called Denholms inside so I banged off a letter and they phoned up two days later offering me job as Third Mate on an ore carrier, so off I went to sea again.

CHAPTER NINE

Up to Third Mate

m.v. Craigallian
14th September 1962 – 28th December 1962

I joined the *Craigallian* on the 14th September in Port Talbot where she had just arrived with a cargo of iron ore from Narvik. She was lying on a lay-by berth waiting to move to the discharge berth. The ship was completely different from the Port Line vessels having no cranes or derricks and also quite a bit smaller as she was built to get in and out of the locks. I was pleased to see she was looking in good condition all nicely painted and clean. The bloke I was relieving shot off as soon as I set foot aboard without handing over anything which didn't seem the best of starts. I'd just begun sorting the cabin and unpacking when it was announced we had to shift across the dock to start discharge. Whereas in Port Line there would have been five or six people on the bridge manning the telegraphs, wheel and telephones I found myself alone on the bridge with the pilot trying to figure out how all the equipment worked. Even the Old Man didn't bother to appear and shouted up the stairs to call him if we were going to hit anything. It certainly was a baptism of fire but we managed all right. They then started to discharge the ore with huge grabs banging and clattering in the holds. Cargo duties consisted of wandering around in a hard hat making notes of any damage that was incurred by the grabs. I was feeling that I'd made the wrong choice leaving Port Line.

The discharge was very quick and we sailed in ballast the next day up the Irish Sea to Narvik for another load of iron ore. Unlike my previous ships, the holds were just huge spaces with all the frames exposed, and sloping sides to help the discharge. She was only two years old and the navigation equipment was the best I'd seen. The only trouble was she used to vibrate terribly in ballast so the electronic stuff was always breaking down. The Radio Officer, Colin Hall, was really switched on and usually managed to repair stuff quickly

45

We sailed through the Minches inside the Hebrides where the scenery was fabulous. I even stayed on the bridge after my watch was over to take it all in. There were loads of seals and even a huge basking shark. Once we cleared the Islands we were really exposed to the weather and we had an uncomfortable three days rolling around violently. It was heaven when we got into the fjord and up to Narvik. We arrived at two in the afternoon and as I was off watch I had a wander into town but it was a miserable sort of place – very quiet and cold – though the scenery over the fjord looked pretty good. I was glad to get back on board into the warm.

The loading was really quick – they loaded 9,000 tons of iron ore in less than seven hours – and we sailed back out into the bad weather. I was seriously thinking of handing my notice in but the weather eased up and we had a pleasant trip back to Port Talbot.

We nearly ended up sunk in the harbour on the first night. We were supposed to start discharge at six in the evening and the Carpenter thought he would get ahead of the game so started filling the ballast tanks and then went up the road for a pint. Unfortunately they didn't start discharge for some reason and I was sitting in my cabin when the Cook came running in saying there was water in his cabin and we were sinking. It was quite a panic until we figured out what was happening and pumped the water out again. The Carpenter got his fortune told when he bowled up a few hours and a few pints later

We sailed again for Narvik the following day. I decided if the ship did another trip to Narvik I would definitely pack my bags. It actually turned out to be a lot better trip as the weather was good and we didn't have to go at full speed so the vibration was bearable. The trip was a repeat of the previous one except we loaded in Narvik during the night and it seemed even colder. As we were approaching Scotland the orders came through that our next two trips would be to Bône in Algeria so I decided I could cope with a couple of voyages to the sunnier climes. After discharging in Port Talbot we set off southwards for a change and took about a week to wander down to Bône. It was a bit dodgy going ashore in Algeria as the OAS were blowing things up and trying to kill anybody that looked remotely French. Somehow we got an invite up to the French Foreign Legion's Sergeants' Mess and had a really good night. The place was a glorified knocking shop really, with a gallery around two sides where all the girls would sit. There were some quite good looking girls but we were told they all had syphilis so we got drunk on pastis instead. We got a lift back to the ship in an army lorry which impressed us until the driver told us they were the OAS's favourite targets.

The loading took a bit longer than Narvik and the ore was completely different being extremely dusty and red as opposed to the grey damp Narvik ore. It was still a very quick load compared to the month it used to take with the type of cargoes Port Line carried and we sailed for Port Talbot the following day. It was quite a rough trip up through the Bay of Biscay but because it was warmer it didn't seem quite as bad as the Narvik trips. When we got to Port Talbot we found we couldn't enter because of the low neap tides so had to anchor off for two days and then it was a quick turn around and off back to Bône again.

I went ashore by myself in the afternoon and ended up in the Sergeants' Mess drinking pastis. I was slightly under the weather by the time I set off walking back to the ship and was mugged by some youths who tried to pinch my watch and wallet. Somehow I beat them off and returned to the ship complete with watch and wallet. Looking back I must have been mad because I could have easily ended up knifed and dumped in a back alley. I can't believe I didn't just give them my valuables.

I got back on board just in time to start my cargo watch and was trying desperately to appear sober but not too successfully, I gather. The Mate asked me to read the midship draft so I jumped over the rail onto the jacob's ladder only to find it hadn't been secured so I ended up falling into the dock still holding on to the ladder. Nobody could help me for laughing and I was really getting worried that I would drown as there was nothing to grab hold of and the ladder wasn't very buoyant. Eventually someone threw me a line and I was able to climb back on board. I changed into some dry clothes and as I re-emerged onto the deck a wire that the crew were using to close the hatches parted and whistled just over my head. I was beginning to feel it wasn't my day but Colin, the Radio Officer, reckoned things happened in threes so I should be all right for a while. Still I was really pleased when we sailed without further mishap.

It was back to Port Talbot again and when we docked we were told the next trip was down to Monrovia in West Africa which was something different. I was beginning to see the world, now, although I hadn't got much further than the dock gates in a few of the ports. We stopped in Freetown in Sierra Leone for bunkers then on to

47

Monrovia. It came as a bit of shock to see so much poverty and filth. A few of us had a walk into town but it wasn't pleasant as we were constantly surrounded by beggars. In the main street we were confronted by this huge naked man running down the road waving a machete. We dived into a bar till he went past. We only had one beer, drinking out of the bottle because the glasses were filthy. When we came out we were met by the naked bloke coming back still waving the machete but he didn't bother us so we retired to the ship. The loading was quite slow as things ashore kept breaking down but eventually we sailed after forty eight hours.

When we were in port we got to mix with the crews of the other ore carriers and I found out that most of the Third Mates in Denholms didn't have certificates and the Second Mates were sailing on Second Mate's Certificates. Our Second Mate, Willy Graham, was set to stay for another few months so I asked to be relieved when we got back to Port Talbot hoping that when I rejoined I would be promoted. We arrived just before New Year after spending Christmas Day bouncing around in a tremendous storm off Spain. The Old Man ended up with a full dish of tomato soup in his lap so the meal didn't start off too well and we couldn't drink too much because we were on watches. Still, the meal was up to the usual standard and it was a good laugh.

I got home on the 29th December intending to be home a week at the most but I found out an old school mate, Adrian Todd, was around so I had a social life for once. It was a terrific winter for snow so we did a fair bit of snow walking and tried to learn to ski without much success. I hired a Mini from the Crown & Mitre garage for a fortnight so at least we were mobile. We got stuck in the snow quite a few times and I don't think the garage would have been impressed if they knew where we'd been with their car. I was hoping Denholms would ring offering me a Second Mate's job but no such luck. I found out later I was expected to ring them when I was available.

Whilst talking to other officers when I was on the *Craigallian* I found out there was an agency called the Merchant Navy Establishment, known as the Pool, down on the quayside in Newcastle, so I travelled over to see what was on offer. They had notice boards all around the room listing the ships, where they were trading, the expected length of trip and what ranks were needed. There was an amazing variety of ships to choose from but just my luck nobody wanted Second Mates. I decided to sign on as Third Mate with a ship called the *Camellia* belonging to Stag Line of North

Shields. She was doing one trip across to the Great Lakes and back to UK for dry dock so I'd be able to get off quite soon.

CHAPTER TEN

A quick trip to Canada

m.v. Camellia
23rd March 1963 – 7th April 1963

I got home from Newcastle to be told that Stag Line had already been on the phone and I was to phone them back for my travelling instructions. I was to join the *Camellia* in Cork and had to catch the ferry from Liverpool to Dublin the following night. It all seemed a mad panic finding my kit and getting packed after my nice relaxing leave. I travelled by train to Liverpool the next day and met up with the other officers who were joining in the bar at Lime Street Station. The Second Mate was supposed to be in charge and he had all our tickets for the ferry and the train from Dublin to Cork. He also had some cash to buy us meals en route but they'd already spent most of it on beer when I met them. We spent most of the trip across the Irish Sea in the bar on the ferry and I was extremely unwell when we arrived in Dublin. I managed to sober up a bit on the train journey down through Ireland and remember it was a lovely journey with miles of green fields and nice scenery. We arrived in Cork about noon only to find the ship wasn't berthing until the evening. Naturally we adjourned to a bar to wait. We were all very much the worse for wear when we eventually got on board and the Old Man was distinctly unimpressed with his new officers. I took over from the Third Mate and then promptly went to bed as they didn't start discharge until the next morning. It was quite an eventful discharge as it was a cargo of coal from Poland and half an hour into the discharge there was a loud bang from number two hold. It appeared there were unexploded detonators in among the coal so the dockers refused to unload it. They came to an agreement, which involved extra pay, but they refused to work at night as they couldn't see the detonators so we had an easy time. Thankfully no more exploded.

I really enjoyed my time in Cork and developed a real taste for the Guinness. We went to some of the dances with the Irish Show Bands and they were really good. It was worth going just for the music. I met a really nice girl called Maeve. I took her out for a meal of fish and chips one night (dead romantic) but got caught in a torrential downpour on the way home which somewhat dampened my ardour. We couldn't have been wetter if we'd gone swimming and I had a couple of miles to walk back to the ship afterwards. I promised I'd write but never did.

The *Camellia* was another bulk carrier like the *Craigallian* but only carried 7,000 of cargo. She was ten years old but still in pretty good nick. The navigational equipment was a real disappointment after Denholms but things seemed to work all right. We sailed in ballast on the 28th March for Canada. It was a great trip across with lovely weather all the way until we hit the fog off Newfoundland. I made a bit of extra money on the trip over working overtime cleaning the holds of the remains of the previous cargo of coal ready for grain.

The radar packed in as soon as we hit the fog and I was dead nervous about icebergs but the Old Man didn't seem bothered as he reckoned it was too early in the year for them. We had to navigate using the radio direction finder which was like something out of the Ark. I actually got quite good with it in the end and when we emerged from the fog we were where I'd hoped we would be.

We hit some quite heavy ice on our way up the St Lawrence but it didn't slow us down too much as the *Camellia* was specially strengthened for going through ice. I slipped up when I forgot to take the log in as we entered the ice. The log consisted of a rotator towed astern on a long piece of rope which turned as it travelled through the water and registered on a dial how many miles we'd done. Obviously I should have taken it in as when I looked astern it was bouncing along on top of the ice. When I retrieved it there was nothing left of the blades as the ice had broken them off. At least I would remember next time.

We went quite a way up the St Lawrence and were supposed to go to Montreal but the berth was iced up so they diverted us to Sorel which is halfway between Quebec and Montreal. We had to wait a couple of days anchored in the river as the berth was occupied by another ship. It was pretty impressive with huge rafts of ice coming down the river and we had to be alert in case they caused us to drag anchor. When we did berth they loaded us with 7,000 tons of wheat in about ten hours and we set off back to the UK. It was an uneventful trip back apart from the radar breaking down for the much of the time. Also on one occasion the engine stopped suddenly and when we rang down to find out the problem we were told the washing machine had broken. It turned out that the engineers had fixed a washing podger to the end of the main engine cam shaft and it used to go up and down in a drum of soapy water and wash their boiler suits very effectively. It seems it had come adrift and was flying around on the end of the engine threatening to decapitate the engineer. It was repaired in five minutes and we were on our way again.

The cargo was destined for Ipswich which surprised me as I thought we were far too big to get up the River Orwell. It was a bit a squeeze but we managed and berthed on the 26th April. Discharge was pretty slow as the local silo was full and we had to discharge into lorries. It took over ten days and I was glad to sail as I found it a boring place with not much to do. We set off in ballast up to the Tyne to dry dock in the Mercantile Drydock in South Shields. On the way up the river we passed the Stag Line office in North Shields and all the staff came outside to wave as we went by. We seemed to merit more interest than usual from people on the river bank who were all waving and cheering, which somewhat intrigued us. Only when we got in were we told that some of the crew had painted some oversize genitalia on the stag on the funnel during the night. The Superintendent was doing his nut when he got on board. The Mate, Jim Young, came and asked the Second Mate and me to paint it out as the crew were all finished and refused to do any more work. As a favour to him we got a ladder and some red paint and painted out the offending appendage. When we got finished and cleaned up the Old Man called us up to his office. We thought a nice thank you was in order but we ended up with a bollocking because he had decided that we'd done it in the first place. It ended up with a real shouting match with the Superintendent joining in. I had intended to work-by in the dry dock for a few days but in the end I left as soon as I was paid off. It wasn't a good way to leave a ship.

I took a couple of weeks leave then travelled over to Newcastle to see what jobs were on offer on the Pool. My luck was in as there were loads of jobs for Second Mates. Most of them turned out to be on tankers and I wasn't sure I wanted to sail on them. A company called Eagle Oil were really keen and the wages were exceptionally good but I decided to stick to the cargo boats. I sometimes regret it because Eagle Oil was a first class company and the wages were the best around. Instead I went for a Second Mate's job with Chapman and

Willan who were renowned as one of the meanest companies but the ship was down for world-wide tramping, which really appealed to me, and could be away for eighteen months. I had to go for interview in their office on the Quayside and it was like stepping back in time. Some of the clerks were sitting on high stools at enormous desks. I expected them to be using quills. My interview was with a surprisingly pleasant superintendent who offered me the job straight away and actually put me on pay even though I didn't need to join for a few days. When I got home there was a call from Stag Line offering me a Second Mate's job on the *Camellia* so someone must have put the Captain straight about the funnel painting. I also got a call from Eagle Oil offering even better conditions so it was nice to be wanted. I later found out that there was a huge shortage of certificated junior officers and ships were actually being delayed because there was no one to sail them.

CHAPTER ELEVEN

Second Mate on a Geordie tramp

m.v. Clearton
1st June 1963 – 6th April 1964

I joined the *Clearton* in dry dock in Cardiff where she was undergoing an overhaul. She was a typical tramp, trading around the world with no fixed contracts. She was only a couple of years old and everything was very basic though it was tried and tested – and it worked. She had six holds and could carry virtually anything from bulk cargoes to general. My duties as Second Mate were to look after all the navigational equipment and keep the charts up to date. The *Clearton* carried a full worldwide folio of charts and I must admit to being somewhat overawed by the task. Anyhow I set to checking through and very quickly discovered that the previous Second Mate had done virtually no corrections even though he'd claimed the overtime for it. After four days I presented the Superintendent with a list of over a hundred charts that needed renewing which didn't please him. It was an education sailing on a proper tramp ship. There was always a great deal of secrecy about the next voyage in case another company jumped in and took the charter. We never got to know where we were going to until the last minute so it was a bit of a give away when my new charts arrived but only the ones for South America, Japan and Australia were supplied.

We sailed for Argentina on the 8th June. We stopped off at Funchal in Madeira for bunkers and I had a bit of a wander around the port. It was a quaint little place and their power station consisted of two Second World War tankers tied up in a corner of the port connected to the local grid. It seemed to work well. My intention was to buy some bottles of Madeira wine purely because I'd heard of it but it proved to be really expensive so I settled for a couple of bottles of plonk. Thinking back I'd also heard of Madeira cake but I made no attempt to buy any! The day after we sailed was my birthday and we had a hilarious party with all sorts of wine flowing much to the Old Man's disgust, but I had to stay sober as I was on watch at midnight.

The Old Man came up to the bridge at half past twelve for a cup of coffee – he normally went to bed at ten – so it was really obvious that he was checking to see if I was sober – which indeed I was.

It took two weeks to reach the River Plate. As we passed Montevideo on the way in I was amazed see the remains of the infamous German battleship *Graf Spee* sticking out of the water. It looked in surprisingly good condition. We picked up a River Plate pilot at a place called Recalada where there was an old warship anchored in the middle of the estuary and the pilots lived on board until they were needed. I came on watch at midday after we'd been going up the river about four or five hours. I took over from the Third Mate who said he had no idea where we were as there were no recognisable landmarks. I wandered out onto the bridge wing and was puzzled to see that we were stationary in the water and yet that engine was thumping away at full ahead. It baffled me and I had visions of us losing the propeller or something. I went back inside and pointed this phenomenon out to the Old Man and the Pilot who were deep in conversation about the war or something. It certainly produced some action as it appeared we were hard aground on a sand bank and probably had been for an hour. It took ages to get off as the tide was going out and the Old Man was getting worried in case we had to call for tugs but we pumped out some ballast and eventually floated off with no damage to our hull.

Our first port was Rosario which was about 180 miles up river. We started loading bags of fertiliser and expellers (the residue from soya after they removed the oil) from lorries using a clever system of conveyors to get the bags on deck and then chutes to put them into the holds. It was pretty slow even though they worked round the clock. The cargo watches were really boring and the Third Mate took to oiling the conveyors as he had nothing else to do.

I met up with a pretty little barmaid called Hildaku who was Japanese. I never did figure out why she and her family lived there. She seemed to speak pretty good Spanish but was keen to learn English and insisted on visiting museums and things which wasn't really my scene. We also went to the pictures a couple of times – the films were in English – and I had to spend most of the time explaining the plot so I ended up losing the plot myself. The Third Mate and I organised the cargo watches so that we did twenty four hours on and twenty four hours off changing at eight in the morning. I'd go to bed at eight and get up at one o'clock, have some lunch and wander ashore to meet up with Hildaku. She started work about five so I went back to the ship then, for a meal and a couple of hours kip. I went back ashore about ten to meet her in the bar, had a couple of drinks and retired to a hotel. I thought I could get used to this life.

A couple of days before we sailed I got back at eight o'clock to find the Third Mate had been arrested during the night. A woman had been found murdered on the dockside and the body was left, lying there, covered with a sheet. About one in the morning he got curious and went over and had a look under the sheet. He was promptly arrested for her murder. It took ages to get him released and all sorts of bribes to the local police. I was really pissed off as I had to do all the cargo watches and couldn't get ashore. I managed to sneak Hildaku on board one evening and thought things were going well until the Old Man caught us in bed. He didn't say much but I felt really guilty for some reason.

I was really sad to leave Rosario but we sailed on the 16th July down the river to Buenos Aires to finish off loading. It was a completely different place and I think it was one of the liveliest places for nightlife I've ever seen. Nothing seemed to start until midnight. It was just as well we had only three days there or I'd have spent all my money. I bought a leather jacket because they were supposed to be good value and a picture made from butterfly wings but the seams on the jacket soon came apart and all the colours faded on the picture so I'd have been just as well buying beer.

We finished loading at about four in the afternoon and had to wait until seven o'clock for the tide to come in. There was a local barber on board offering his services and the Chief Engineer decided he was having all his hair shaved off as we would be at sea for at least a month. We all thought this was a good idea so the majority of the officers had their heads shaved. It felt really odd and we looked like a bunch of convicts. Just after tea the Old Man announced that there were no pilots and we wouldn't sail until the next morning and we could have another night ashore. We all looked at one another's bald heads and decided that we'd just have an early night. Then Tom Willey, the Mate, appeared with a huge wad of Argentinean pesos which he'd been given as a bonus. He shared it all out and then told us it could only be spent in Argentina – it was getting worse by the minute. In the end we sent one of the engineers up to a local bar to buy booze to drink on board. It turned out to be quite a party and we all staggered to bed in the early hours. When we woke up the next morning we found that thieves had ransacked all the engineers' cabins and stolen most of their belongings. They had emptied drawers and cupboards and taken just about everything. We had some of the bonus left so they got a chance to buy some clothes and boiler suits before we sailed but they had lost a lot of personal stuff. We eventually sailed at noon and headed out to sea.

Once we dropped the pilot and secured the ship for sea we went down to the Chief Steward for the bond issue (to buy beer and cigarettes) only to be told there was no beer on board. We all thought he was joking but the Old Man had decided we were drinking too much and hadn't taken any with the stores. It was a seven week trip to Japan with no beer! There was very nearly a mutiny and it didn't help with the Old Man saying, "It's only beer."

There was usually no hurry for the types of cargo that tramp steamers carried so they tended to amble around the oceans at a leisurely pace. Whereas the Port Line ships used to travel at fifteen/sixteen knots the *Clearton* could only manage ten on a good day with a following wind. There was quite a difference only doing 240 miles a day as opposed to 400. It took us seven weeks to get to Japan with a six hour stop in Singapore for bunkers.

Our first port in Japan was Otaru which was a tiny port on the northern island of Hokkaido. It came as a real surprise how primitive the place was. Most of the buildings were wood and the toilets were really basic with just holes dropping into open sewers. It smelt a bit in September so I dread to think what it was like in the height of summer. We arrived about noon but because of a problem with the paperwork couldn't start discharge until the following morning. The Old Man gave everybody their sub of Japanese yen after lunch and there was a mass exodus to the nearest bars. I decided to complete my voyage report before I ventured ashore and this took me until about four o'clock. I was having a shower when the Chief Steward appeared to say there would be no evening meal as the entire catering staff were in a bar and refusing to return but he offered to make up some sandwiches. He then had to go and tell the Old Man who went ballistic. I had no sympathy for him though as the lads had been seven weeks without beer and they didn't need many before they were completely legless.

I was just contemplating whether to venture ashore when Keith Bosley, the Chief Engineer, appeared and dragged me up into town. Keith was a single bloke in his fifties and he loved Japan and had been there numerous times so he was just the man to show me around. We first stopped off at a tiny restaurant for a meal and it was a real education. Nobody could speak English and the menu was all in Japanese so I had visions of it developing into a real farce but they produced plastic replicas of all the meals for us to choose from. They were amazingly realistic with everything from prawns to hamburgers complete with fried egg and chips. I was going for the hamburger but Keith would have none of it and insisted on Japanese food of noodle soup followed by sushi and rice which I didn't much care for. There were no chairs and we sat cross legged on the floor in front of low tables. The owners seemed really pleased with us eating the local food and they provided free beer.

After the meal we progressed into town. Every bar we went into had at least two members of our crew falling about in a drunken haze and spoiling the atmosphere and we were just about to give up and return to the ship when a Japanese man appeared at the door of a bar in an agitated state and beckoned us over. Inside were a couple of the ABs (able seamen) totally drunk and arguing over the bill and threatening to wreck the place. Keith managed to placate them and extract money for their bill. We then organised a taxi and poured them into it and sent them back to the ship. We paid the taxi driver in advance so there wouldn't be any trouble when he unloaded them. The grateful bar owner then insisted on giving us free beers for our trouble. We'd only been in about half an hour when the door burst open and three of the engineers fell in. They were in a worse state than the ABs. We decided to give up so organised a taxi to return to the ship. Keith felt sorry for the bar owner so we took the engineers back with us. As we passed the next bar we could see the two original ABs falling around inside so they must have come ashore again. We decided not to get involved this time and just headed back to the ship for an early night.

The next morning Keith and I both got a large bunch of flowers delivered to our cabins. They must have come from the bar owner but how he knew who we were we couldn't figure out. Also we got some odd looks from the rest of the crew wondering what we'd been up to. The Old Man had his wife travelling with him so I presented the flowers to her and wormed my way into his good books.

We started discharging at eight in the morning after the labour had spent half an hour exercising on the quay first. They were really efficient and we'd have sailed in a couple of days but the weather was atrocious and delayed everything. I didn't get ashore much as Keith advised me to wait till the bigger ports later on. After a week we sailed to Maizuru which was another tiny port on the main island of Honshu. Keith and I wangled a day off to travel down to the old capital of Kyoto which was about two hours away by train. He'd been there before and we had a tour of a castle and a museum about Samurai warriors and I found it pretty amazing. We then went on a tour of a geisha house. I expected it to be an upmarket brothel but everything was above board and the geishas were fascinating. We had to take tea sitting on the floor while they made polite conversation. It felt really good. As we were coming out we ran into the Old Man and his wife who had also travelled down. He seemed genuinely surprised we were taking an interest in the culture rather than spending all our money on beer. Keith being an opportunist asked the Old Man if it was all right to take another day off and stay in Kyoto for the night as there was a Samurai festival the next day. The Old Man was so impressed with us that he agreed and said he would get the Third Mate to do my cargo watch the next day. As soon we left them Keith flagged a taxi down told the driver to head for the rail station. He then admitted there wasn't a festival at all and he was going to show me the real Japan.

At the rail station we jumped on a train for Kobe which concerned me a bit as our shore passes were only valid for the area around Maizuru but Keith wasn't bothered and off we went. We got to Kobe about four o'clock and as Keith obviously knew where he was going I just tagged along behind. We took a taxi and arrived outside a very impressive building which turned out to be a huge massage parlour. He reckoned we needed refreshing before our night out. I don't really enjoy massages and this was no exception. We started off in a steam box thing which nearly cooked me and no sooner had I staggered out than we had to jump into an ice cold pool. After that I was allowed to relax in a warm pool before we were taken to a huge room full of Japanese blokes all being beaten up by the masseuses. My masseuse was only tiny but she was really strong and managed to twist me into impossible positions. I had to give up when she started to walk up and down my back. I was really glad to get out and back on the street where I was surprised to find it was getting dark and my massage had taken over two hours. We set off walking and wandered through all sorts of markets and duty free shopping malls. I was amazed how cheap everything was. Keith knew exactly where he was going and we arrived at a tiny restaurant in a back alley. We sat down and ordered beers and were joined by a very attractive Japanese woman called Mona. She turned out to be Keith's long time girlfriend who he'd known for about twenty years and who owned a small bar in the centre of Kobe. He must have been in contact with her when I was being pummelled to death in the massage parlour. They both decided I needed company. After a quick phone call we were joined by a stunning girl called Michiko dressed in a fantastic kimono.

I hadn't a clue what to eat so Keith did all the ordering of the meal. I couldn't understand the menu but I could see from the prices that it was well expensive. The restaurant specialised in Kobe beef steaks and they were unbelievable. The steak was served on a sizzling hot metal plate with only a lump of horseradish sauce. It was so tender the girls ate theirs with chopsticks. From the restaurant we progressed to a really swish nightclub and as Mona knew the owners we bypassed the huge queue waiting outside and also got in for free. There was a spectacular show and we had a good table at the front. Sometime after midnight we left and I was delighted to find that Michiko was intending to spend the night with me so we all booked in to a hotel. I discovered that the kimono may look amazing but it's really complicated with numerous layers and a huge belt called an obi. It took her ages to undress – it was like pass the parcel with me getting more and more excited.

Next morning was a bit of a downer, though. Japanese breakfasts must be the worst in the world. Who wants to eat cold sticky rice and gherkins first thing in the morning? And the green tea was rubbish. Also it turned out that Michiko wanted payment for services rendered. I thought it was too good to be true. I also had a feeling I owed Keith quite a bit of money for the meal and drinks.

After booking out of the hotel we went into the centre of town as I wanted to buy my father a camera. Once I'd decided on the model which was the latest Pentax SLR the girls took over and haggled the price down even further. I also got an exposure meter and some film thrown in. The price was unbelievably low. We then did a quick tour of a local castle before saying goodbye to the girls and catching the train back to the ship in Maizuru. We changed trains at Kyoto and got back to the ship about three in the afternoon. Dave Charles, the Third Mate, wasn't too happy having to cover my cargo watch but he owed me a couple for his time in prison in Rosario.

That evening I wandered along to see Keith and find out how

much I owed him and was pleasantly surprised to find that I only owed for the meal and the rail fares which came to about £20. He insisted on paying for my massage because it had given him a lot of amusement. We had another couple of days discharging in Maizuru then we sailed south down to Moji in the entrance to the Inland Sea. Before arriving in Japan I didn't even know it had an Inland Sea. It was a nightmare to navigate and there were hundreds of fishing boats and even more barges and small coasters and nobody seemed to comply with the International Collision Rules. Luckily we employed a pilot who spent most of his time screaming abuse through a megaphone at passing vessels. Moji was a fair bit larger than the previous ports and a lot more commercial. We spent three days there finishing off the discharge. Mona travelled down from Kobe and stayed on board in Keith's cabin much to the Old Man's annoyance. Mona said that Michiko would travel over if I wanted but I was a bit wary of the Old Man and I wasn't sure what it would cost me so I declined.

That afternoon before we finished cargo we found out that our next voyage was to be down to Northern Australia for a load of bulk raw sugar for Japan. I had a hectic evening drawing the courses on the charts and finding out how far it was. I was interested to find a couple of areas we had to avoid south of Japan because of underwater volcanoes. I was certainly getting to know my way around the world. We sailed on the 24th September and again had to brave all the traffic in the Inland Sea.

The Mate was impressed with the way the Japanese had discharged the cargo. He was expecting a huge job cleaning the holds ready for sugar but they were already spotless and it was just a quick wash out and they were ready so the crew were available for painting and cleaning the ship.

It took two weeks to get down to Australia. We passed one or two islands on the way and went quite close to Bougainville Island. It was amazing as the Bougainvillea shrubs were in flower and there were huge swathes of pink and purple running down to lovely sandy beaches. A couple of days later we arrived at the Great Barrier Reef and picked up a pilot to guide us through. We nearly ended up aground while waiting for the pilot as we were all watching a huge shark circling us and failed to notice the tide carrying us onto the reef.

After about six hours wending our way through the islands of the Barrier Reef we arrived at our loading port of Mourilyan Harbour. It was a fantastic little port which was entered though a narrow channel into a small bay. The pilot did some really great shiphandling to turn us inside the bay and put us alongside the loading facility without tugs. He waited outside for an hour until the tidal flow was strong enough then used it to turn us. There was only one pier with a conveyor system for loading the sugar. The sugar was like brown demerara and it was fascinating the way it moved as it piled up in the holds. We loaded about 8,000 tons in three days and then we had to move south to Mackay to finish off as Mourilyan was too shallow for a full load. It was even quicker in Mackay and we loaded the remaining 4,000 tons in less than ten hours so I didn't even set foot ashore. Then it was out through the Barrier Reef and north towards Japan.

The first port was Tokyo where we tied up to buoys in the middle of the harbour. The stevedores fitted grabs to our cargo gear and we discharged into barges. It was surprisingly efficient and we discharged half our cargo in four days. I managed to get ashore for a day and was very impressed with the Ginza which was the centre of town. It was an amazing sight with all the neon signs and hundreds of people scurrying about. Everything was expensive compared with other ports though, so I limited myself to a couple of beers. The second port was Yokkaichi which was a small port in Nagoya Bay and the sort of place I preferred. We'd just finished tying up when there was a knock on my door and Michiko was standing there. She had travelled up from Kobe with Mona. I thought I would be in trouble with the Old Man but he never said anything and she stayed on board for the nine days we were there. My cabin was spotless and all my laundry was washed and beautifully ironed – I could cope with this! She organised all sorts of trips ashore up to Nagoya and the surrounding area. I visited loads of different temples and she could explain all the customs and traditions. I found the gardens amazing. I also tried all sorts of local food but found some of it weird. I think the only one I really liked was tempura where everything was fried in a delicious batter. When we came to sail I had a dilemma as to whether she required payment so I went and asked Keith. He said just to give her something towards the rail fare but I got Mona to buy her a handbag she had admired when we were ashore so everything went swimmingly.

We sailed from Yokkaichi on the 12th November and set off for another load of sugar from Australia. On the way down we passed through some local tropical thunderstorms on my watch one night. I thought it had all gone past so wandered outside onto the bridge wing. There was a strange sensation as the air felt like it was buzzing and there were little sparks coming off the radio aerials. Suddenly there was a whoosh and a bolt of lightning went into the sea off the starboard bow only a couple of hundred feet off. There was a loud hissing and loads of steam and a strong smell of sulphur like when you strike a match. A couple of seconds later came the bang of the thunder. The ship being empty acted like a sounding box. The noise was deafening. I think everyone on board arrived on the bridge, some clutching life jackets, in the next few minutes. The crew thought we'd hit a mine or something. The rest of the trip to Australia was an anticlimax after that.

This time we only loaded in Mackay and they managed to load 12,000 tons of sugar in an impressive twenty two hours. I got ashore for a couple of hours to sample the local beer then it was back to Japan again. Our first port was Hakata on the west coast. It was very industrialised and we were miles from the town so hardly anyone went ashore. After three days we sailed all the way through the Inland Sea to Kobe. The Japanese pilot spent twenty four hours on the bridge conning us through all the other traffic. I was a nervous wreck after a four hour watch so I don't know how he coped. We tied up to buoys in Kobe late in the afternoon and started discharge into barges.

It was my night off so I had a quick shower and was waiting at the gangway for the ferry ashore and when it appeared off stepped Michiko. How she found out where the ship was baffled me. Needless to say I didn't bother going ashore that night. I had to work the next day so Michiko got busy with my laundry. The day after we went ashore and I got myself a new Seiko watch, a really swish short wave radio and some more accessories for my father's camera. Michiko did all the haggling so I got some good deals. In the evening I was dragged to see a Japanese opera where unusually all the singers were female. I wasn't looking forward to it at all as I felt it was way above me. In the end I really enjoyed it and I could understand the plot even though it was in Japanese.

We only had another day in Kobe then we moved across the bay to Osaka. Again we were tied up to buoys in the middle of the harbour and it was a real pain getting ashore and back. On top of that the weather was rubbish and it was cold and wet. We ended up having Christmas there but it was a quiet affair compared to the previous ones. We sailed in ballast on the 29th December to Canada. I was really sad to be leaving Japan and especially Michiko. We wrote letters to each other for a few months.

The trip across to British Columbia was terrible. We took a great circle route because it was shorter and ended up way up north close to the Aleutian Islands in howling gales and freezing fog. I was glad they didn't have icebergs in this bit of the ocean. We were really pleased to arrive in Vancouver after a fortnight even though it was cold and wet. We loaded a full cargo of sawn timber in British Columbia in five different ports. It was a slow load as they stowed every plank individually to get the maximum on board. We also loaded timber on deck about ten feet high which was quite impressive. We took three weeks to load and we were quite sad to leave as the stevedores were a good bunch and we made quite a few friends.

We sailed south towards Panama but after a week at sea all the timber on deck on the starboard side became wet as the prevailing winds were from the south west and we were continually shipping water. As it got wet it became heavier and consequently we took on quite a starboard list which concerned me somewhat but Tom Willey, the Mate, seemed confident so I relaxed a bit. It was a pain eating and drinking, though, because everything kept spilling unless you supported one side of the plate. It also caused us a problem going through the locks in Panama. After Panama we stopped off at Curacao for bunkers and things improved as we put fuel in tanks in the bottom of the ship and it straightened us up a bit.

Our first port of discharge was Brest. It looked a really miserable place with dull grey buildings and huge drab submarine pens from the war. I quite enjoyed my stay there, though, as we found a little bar down by the docks where they made us feel really welcome. Mind you, it required a knife to cut through the cigarette smoke from their Gitanes. A couple of the locals had flown Spitfires in the war and they had an endless supply of stories which kept us amused. The discharge was quite slow as they were loading direct onto lorries and kept running out of them. We eventually sailed on the 28th March up the Channel to Bruges. To get to the berth we had to go stern first up a very narrow canal for about three miles. I thought we were never going to get there. I found Bruges a lovely little port and we were only a short walk from the centre so I got about quite a bit. It wasn't very touristy then and a pleasant place just to amble around. We discharged for three days then back down the canal to the open sea. At least we were pointing in the right direction but we very nearly knocked a bridge down when a gust of wind caught us. Years later I nearly knocked it down again when piloting a dredger up the canal.

Our last port was Rotterdam where I paid off. The Old Man said the ship was going to be there about ten days and wanted to know if I would come back for another trip but after ten months I felt I needed more leave than that and I was also thinking of sitting for my next certificate. We all caught the ferry across to Harwich and then the train home. Looking back the trip seemed a lot longer than the ten months but I'd certainly got to see the world this time.

CHAPTER TWELVE

Studying for my Mate's Ticket

South Shields
6th April 1964 – 3rd July 1964

We had to do a certain amount of time at sea before we were allowed to sit the examinations for our certificates. When I got home off the *Clearton* I found I was six days short for sitting my First Mate's Certificate which was a real bind as I would have to do another trip. I then realised that I had worked on the *Clearton* for six days before signing on so I banged off a letter to the company asking for written proof half expecting them not to reply. A couple of days later a letter arrived with the necessary proof and also asking if I was available to join a ship the next day.

As I now had enough seatime I borrowed Dad's car and nipped over to South Shields College and signed up for the course. I also took my eyesight test and got my seatime checked again in case I'd got it wrong but everything was good. I then looked around for some digs. Both places I previously stayed at were full so I got an address from the college office. It was a house on The Kingsway just behind the college and close to a good pub. It was run by an old couple, Mr and Mrs Hardisty, and they just let out one room and the price was good. I was supposed to get breakfast and an evening meal but the cooking was dire and I tended to top up on fish and chips.

I went home again and as my bank balance was looking good decided to buy a car. I ended up with a little mini van (WHH 920) only six months old and very low mileage. It turned out to be a great little car and certainly gave me good value. I bought the van on a Saturday and moved over to South Shields on the Sunday.

I started the course on the Monday morning and was a bit disappointed that I only knew a couple of people there. I then realised that I was taking the course at the earliest opportunity and as time passed my old acquaintances started appearing. It was really good seeing them again and catching up. I felt part of a gang and it was pleasantly comforting.

Although the digs were nice enough I felt I was intruding even though they said I was welcome to watch television with them. I would retreat to my room and surprised myself with the amount of work I got through. About ten o'clock I used to have a wander down to The Bamburgh pub for a pint but I didn't know anyone there so felt a bit out on a limb. I started off taking the van but Mr Hardisty soon cottoned on and would appear as soon as I emerged from my room looking for a lift to the pub. He was a hypochondriac and had been on the sick for years and I couldn't stand him. He wasn't very popular in the pub either as he used to insist on playing the piano very badly. I think people used to buy him pints just to stop him playing. After a week I stopped taking the van and started walking to the pub much to his disgust.

I used to go back to Carlisle for the weekends mainly to get a decent meal. I didn't do much but one time Adrian Todd got in touch. He was working as an instructor at Eskdale Outward Bound. I nipped down to see him and he came up with the idea that as we all had a week off at half term we should go and lie in the sun somewhere. As a result Adrian and I with one of his instructor mates loaded the van up and set off south. We flew over to France from Southend by Silver City Airways complete with van and then headed south until we reached the Mediterranean. We arrived at a place called Narbonne but it seemed quite expensive and we couldn't find much to do so we nipped over the border into Spain to a little place called Port Bou. Adrian's mate could speak pretty good Spanish and found us a nice place to stay. We spent three days drinking beer and eating paella and lying in the sun and then drove home again albeit bright red with skin peeling off everywhere. We flew back across the Channel to Southend then drove up north to Cumbria. I dropped them off at Eskdale and went home for a few hours then it was back to Shields to study. We must have been mad.

When I got back to the college quite a few of my old classmates had joined the course and they started meeting up in The Bamburgh in the evenings so it was a good social life. It was as well I left the van at the digs as I had trouble walking on more than one occasion. One evening when I got back to the digs all the doors were open and the neighbours were standing outside. When I went in the kitchen was in a real mess with red streaks everywhere. I thought one of the Hardistys had done the other one in as they were always arguing but it turned out Mrs Hardisty had been boiling some beetroot in a

67

pressure cooker and it had exploded. It must have been a hell of a bang as the pan was completely destroyed. The kitchen still had the odd red mark on the walls when I left a month later.

The situation at the college was the same as when I'd studied for my previous certificate in that we had learnt most of the stuff on our Pre-Sea Course so we were merely revising and starting to get bored. Half a dozen of us put our papers in to take the exam before the summer break. We sat it the last week in June and again I passed with flying colours. I was feeling a bit smug. Actually I think everyone passed so the examiners must have been in a benevolent mood.

I passed the orals which were the final part of the exam on a Friday morning in Newcastle. As I was already there I looked in at the Pool to see what jobs were available but they were mostly tankers and nothing caught my eye so I nipped back to South Shields and packed up my stuff. The Hardistys were not pleased and said I hadn't given them written notice that I was leaving and demanded another month's rent. I was starting to get a bit short of money at this stage so this was a bit of a blow. In the end I split the difference and gave them two week's rent but they said they were going to complain to the college.

I went home for the weekend and reviewed my financial situation. It wasn't great but I had decided to go back to a better class of company now I had my mate's ticket and talking to people on the course, I'd come up with a short list of good companies. One was Cable and Wireless who operated cable-laying ships where the work was really interesting and the pay was good too. The other companies were MacAndrews who ran lovely little passenger/cargo ships down to the Mediterranean and back, and Booth Line, which ran from Liverpool across to South America and went all the way up the Amazon. I wrote off letters to apply for jobs but none had any vacancies so it was back to the Newcastle Pool to see what was going. There were loads of jobs for Third and First Mates but there seemed to be a very few for Second Mates unless I was willing to go on to tankers. I was just about to relent and go with Shell Tankers when the clerk put a new board up for a very small vessel trading to the Mediterranean wanting a Second Mate. I jumped at it and after a medical was offered the job of Second Mate on the *Gracechurch*.

CHAPTER THIRTEEN

Mediterranean trading on a small ship

m.v. Gracechurch
3rd July 1964 – 27th August 1964

I joined the *Gracechurch* in the Tyne Dock Engineering Yard. I travelled over by train as I'd been persuaded to leave the minivan with my brother Andy. He promised to look after it for me.

On arrival at the dock gate the watchman told me the *Gracechurch* was on Berth 3 which was at the far end of the yard. When I got there I found the berth occupied by a small tanker so I lugged all my gear back to the dock gate and complained bitterly to the watchman about his misinformation. It turned out the *Gracechurch* was tied up outside the tanker but was so small I hadn't seen it. I eventually got on board via a vertical ladder after lowering my suitcases down on a rope. I was beginning to regret my decision.

After a look around it didn't seem as bad as I'd thought. The ship was clean and everything looked as though it worked. At just over 1000 tons it was by far the smallest ship I'd sailed on. I wondered whether I'd be seasick once we got into the open sea. My cabin was quite spacious and after a very pleasant lunch I reckoned I could cope. We spent the rest of the day taking stores which was a right bind as we had to carry everything over the tanker and lower it down on ropes. I had been hoping to nip up to South Shields that night and see if I could find any of my mates but I was knackered and just went to bed. Next morning there were even more stores but we organised a crane to lift it all on board so it went a lot easier.

We sailed in the afternoon for Rotterdam to start loading. We only had two mates so we had to do watches of six hours on six hours off when we were at sea. I soon got used to it though it didn't leave much time for socialising. If you weren't on watch you were either eating or sleeping. Also she didn't carry a radio officer so we had to listen to the radio as well. I enjoyed the radio work though I'd never done any before. We used to listen to coast radio stations for traffic lists to see if there were any messages for us and I was surprised to hear our name on Scheveningen Radio. As it was two o'clock in the morning I didn't want to wake the Old Man so I decided to get the message myself. I called up and was taken aback when they came straight back and told me to change to working frequencies. After some frantic fiddling and button pressing I managed to tune the transmitter and the receiver to the correct frequencies. The radio operator asked if I was ready for the message and I said yes before realising I didn't have a pencil and paper so there was a mad scrabble to unearth these. The message was to tell us we were berthing in Prinzwilhemshaven/Citex on arrival. I had to ask her to spell the Prinzwilhemshaven/Citex bit and still couldn't get it but I said I had received the message and signed off. I then spent a nervous few hours until the Mate got up in case I'd spelt it wrong and we went to the wrong place but it was all right in the end.

We berthed right in the middle of Rotterdam and started loading straight away. We were loading general cargo mainly for the British Army in Tripoli and Benghazi in Libya. The load was chaotic as no one had a cargo plan and Allan Blake, the Old Man, and Arthur, the Mate, both had their wives and daughters on board for the trip and they just wanted to get ashore and see the sights. I managed to get some semblance of order working with the foreman but we had no idea what cargo was going to appear when we got to London to complete the loading. I even had a cargo plan drawn up although nobody else was interested but it kept me happy. We loaded in eight hours and sailed for London.

We berthed in the East India Docks which was the farthest I'd ever been up the Thames. The docks were getting pretty old and run down but it was easy to imagine the old days with all the sailing ships tied up alongside working cargo. We were assigned a Cargo Superintendent, or Supercargo, to supervise the loading so it should have gone easier but it was a nightmare. He had no idea what cargo was booked so we just piled it on board as best we could. We loaded some coils of lead piping in the bottom of the hold and then put some cases of lorry engines on top of them. I remember thinking it wasn't a good idea and sure enough the lead pipe was flat when we came to discharge it.

The ship had a specially built refrigerated compartment so we could carry frozen food for the NAAFI. The last day was assigned to loading the freezer cargo and it turned out to be chaos. All the cargo arrived in different vans and lorries and at one stage we had over fifty lorries waiting to be unloaded with all the drivers complaining about the delay. Each vehicle would only have a couple of items and some of them weren't refrigerated so lots of stuff seemed to be melting. The variety of food was unbelievable. There were boxes of smoked kippers, about half a ton of ice cream, frozen lamb and mutton, oysters, cases of butter, about ten different types of cheese, loads of bacon and pork products. It was all top quality so they certainly didn't stint themselves in the Army. We actually loaded it pretty quickly and there was hardly any room left in the compartment but I think it was pure luck rather than good judgement.

The final day was spent loading Army lorries on deck and securing them. There was a bit of panic just as we sailed when someone came running down with all the keys for them. It would have been interesting when we came to discharge if we'd forgotten the keys. The Old Man's family left before we sailed but the Mate's wife and fourteen year old daughter stayed on for the trip and we sailed on the 10th July

We had been fitted with a new auto pilot while we were in London and had a hell of a job with it after we left. The instructions seemed to be for a different model but we eventually got it working. We didn't have a gyro compass and it worked on the magnetic compass somehow. I thought it was very ingenious though it emitted a loud beep when it put port helm on and an equally loud burp when starboard helm was applied. It drove us mad for the first few days and we used to keep our watches out on the bridge wing so we didn't have to listen to it. The Old Man gave me permission to disconnect the speakers in the end because he could hear it in his bedroom down below.

The bridge equipment was very basic but I enjoyed the navigation as I had to use old practices and methods. Being a lot smaller and of shallower draft we sailed a lot closer to the coast than I'd ever been before. When we got to the Isle of Ushant (the most westerly tip of France) we actually went between the island and the mainland and through a narrow channel called the Four Roque Channel. The Old Man did the piloting as he'd been through before. The tide was behind us and it was amazing with all the tide rips and swirling water as we went flying through only yards off the rocks. I was quite relieved when we came out of the other end and into calmer water. It saved about forty miles on the passage but I decided that if ever I got the option again I would go round the outside.

The trip down into the Mediterranean went very well and I really enjoyed sailing close in to the Spanish coast. When we turned the corner round St Vincent we were so close we had to crane our necks to look up at the lighthouse because it was so high above us. We could hear the people on the shore as well. In years to come they made traffic lanes and everyone had to keep at least ten miles off so it was nice to have done it.

Our first port in Libya was Tripoli and as Allan, the Old Man, had been there loads of times he decided to take the ship into port by himself. As we approached the entrance there was another ship sailing out down the channel. To make our intentions clear Allan asked me to blow one short blast on the whistle which would mean that we would stay on the starboard side of the channel and we would pass port to port with the other vessel. The only trouble was the whistle was on the funnel and it was connected to the bridge midships by a fifty foot wire lanyard. When I gave the short blast the wire bounced and it produced two short blasts. The other ship promptly answered with two blasts and altered course across our bow. We had to turn sharply to port and very nearly went aground. The Mate's wife appeared on the bridge to see what was going on but left promptly when she heard the language! Allan then decided to confirm our actions with another two short blasts which he insisted on doing himself but this came out as three which meant our engines should be going astern. Allan looked at me, swore, and went and stood on the bridge wing and made apologetic gestures to the other ship as it scraped down our starboard side. It didn't actually touch but it was close and the language from the other ship was choice. You didn't need to speak Arabic to get the gist. After that we moved very slowly down the channel until a pilot came out and took us in.

The discharge in Tripoli was even more chaotic than the load. The stevedores wanted to discharge the army lorries using our derricks but they could only lift five tons and the lorries weighed at least ten. They wanted to avoid hiring a crane as it was very expensive and wanted to try to make ramps and drive them off but that would have been disastrous. Eventually, after half a day arguing, they got the use of a crane and lifted the lorries off. The next day we had to discharge the freezer cargo. The NAAFI sent down open army lorries and we just piled the stuff into them. The temperature must have been in the hundreds and everything was melting. It was criminal really but we never got any complaints back. We had another couple of days there but I didn't venture ashore.

We then sailed along the coast to Benghazi to complete our discharge. We had a bit of bother finding the place as it was blowing a sandstorm and visibility was very poor. We couldn't identify any landmarks on the radar and the radio beacon at the port was off the air. We couldn't decide whether we should go left or right so we flipped a coin and went right and luckily found Benghazi after an hour's steaming. We had to wait at anchor for a day anyhow as our berth was occupied. The Cook announced we would have a barbecue on deck so we cut an old oil drum in half and made a quite presentable barbie. It was a fantastic spread with delicious steaks, venison and even some langoustines. When I thought about it afterwards I had a feeling the NAAFI in Tripoli might be short one or two items. We berthed the next morning and they discharged the rest of our cargo very quickly and efficiently and we sailed late that night.

We had instructions to head in the general direction of Naples as the company didn't have a cargo set up for us. We went up through the Straits of Messina which I found amazing as Allan insisted on keeping close to the shore. When we came out of the top of the Straits we passed some huge whirlpools caused by the tide. I have been through loads of times since and never seen them again. They were so big I think we would have been in bother if we'd entered them.

As there were still no instructions we headed northwards at slow speed. Off the island of Stromboli we passed close to some fishing boats and ended up trading a couple of bottles of whisky for some tuna. It was my first taste of fresh tuna and the cook did a great job grilling the steaks on the barbecue. I was beginning to enjoy life on the little boats. The only problem was the Old Man and the Mate didn't get on and there were constant arguments and always a bad atmosphere on board which was starting to get me down.

We eventually got instructions to proceed to Salerno to load 800 tons of tinned tomatoes. The message came just at the right time as we were sailing past the port when we received the message. We executed a hard right and arrived at the entrance within the hour. Surprisingly they took us straight in and started loading immediately. There was a large warehouse full of cartons of tinned tomatoes. In those days nobody in England used tinned tomatoes so I've a feeling it was for the catering trade. Needless to say the Cook liberated a few tins and we seemed to have tomatoes as an accompaniment to every meal on the way home. Salerno is a lovely little port and it was really pleasant just to wander around. There were a couple of good bars in the square and it was great sitting outside in the evenings knocking back the Peroni beer. I had my first proper pizza there though it was ages before we could get them in UK.

On the last evening there was an earthquake about eleven at night. All the lights went out and it felt weird with the ground shaking. There was quite a lot of noise with tiles and things falling off the roofs and then it went completely quiet. The locals produced candles but we were most put out when they closed the bars. The only lights left on were the ships in the harbour so we could see where we were going when we headed back on board. The only trouble was we'd forgotten about the fountain in the middle of the square and most of us fell in though it wasn't too deep. It amused the locals at least.

We had a couple of hours work loading the next morning then we sailed about noon. Half the cargo was for Hull and half for Rotterdam. It was an uneventful passage back and as the tide was against us at Ushant I was pleased that we didn't go through the Four Roque Channel again. We arrived in Hull on the 15th August and berthed in the Albert Dock. The discharge was nice and easy using shore cranes so there wasn't much to do. The ship was again inundated with people's relatives. The Old Man's wife, daughter and his sister arrived and then the Mate's son and his girlfriend turned up. The Second Engineer's 'wife' also appeared though I've a feeling he found her in a local bar on the first night. You couldn't move in the accommodation and mealtimes were ridiculous. The Mate's son ended up sleeping on my settee which I wasn't too impressed with.

The next day they all decided to go up the road at lunch time for a couple of pints and a bar meal but I volunteered to be duty officer just for some peace and quiet. I made a sandwich for my lunch and had just sat down with a bottle of beer when there was a knock on the door and it was the Mate's son's girlfriend, Julie. She was only eighteen and very pretty. She said she didn't feel like going to the pub and had stayed on board. She accepted my offer of a beer and climbed up onto my bunk with it. She was wearing a very short mini skirt which left nothing to the imagination and suddenly my day seemed a lot brighter. After another beer she announced that she had to take her stockings off as she only had one pair with her. She was just taking the first one off when the head stevedore shouted down the alleyway that I needed to open the hatch so they could start work.

The word 'bollocks' came to mind. I shot out and opened that hatch which took about ten minutes but I ended up with my hands covered in grease from the hatch wires. Back in the cabin it took ages to wash my hands but I was pleased to see she had waited for my return before removing the other stocking. I sat on the bunk with her and we'd just started to snog when the stevedore shouted that it was raining heavily and I needed to close the hatch. I couldn't believe it. I shot out on deck but of course everything went wrong with the wire jamming in a pulley but eventually I got it closed and beetled back to the cabin. Again I had to spend ages cleaning my hands of the grease. I vowed to invest in some working gloves at the earliest opportunity. I climbed back onto the bunk and resumed where we'd left off. Two minutes later and the bloody stevedore shouted that the rain had stopped and would I open the hatch again. I was getting seriously pissed off at this stage not to mention highly aroused and I had to arrange my trousers before I ventured on deck. I also managed to find a pair of working gloves so I would keep my hands clean. The hatch opened like a dream in record time and the rain clouds had disappeared. I'd cracked it! I shot off back to my cabin but as I entered the accommodation I glanced at the quay and they were all coming back from the pub and just about to climb on board. I just had time to nip back to my cabin and warn Julie that they were back so she was sitting demurely on my settee when they entered. The Mate's wife noticed I hadn't eaten my sandwich and commented that I must have been busy. Little did she know.

That night we were all invited to a party on shore. It was in the home of the previous Second Mate and everyone was welcome as long as we brought some drink. One thing about the *Gracechurch* was that there was never a shortage of booze. I think it had one of the best stocked bond lockers I've seen, despite its size. We loaded a taxi up and all went ashore to the house which was only a short walk away. It was a terrific party though I bet the neighbours weren't impressed. I had a couple of smoochy dances with Julie and she ended up sitting on my knee. Her boyfriend was not at all amused and kept dragging her off. A bit later on when I was replenishing my beer in the kitchen Julie appeared and dragged me into the garden. We found a quiet spot behind the garden shed but no sooner had we started than the kitchen door opened and it was her boyfriend in tears shouting her name. That put the mockers on it and we quietly went back to the party. It wasn't my day.

The following day Julie and boyfriend left the ship. She asked me to write but she said her father was very particular about who she went out with so I had to write through her friend. I could see all sorts of problems so I never did.

We had another couple of days discharging then sailed for Rotterdam. We were cruising along happily off the north Norfolk coast early the next morning and the Second Engineer, who should have been in the engineroom, was having a cup of tea with me on the bridge when there was a load bang and the engine stopped. He shot off down below then phoned up a couple of minutes later to say the gearbox was seized solid and we were a tow job. The company organised a tug to tow us into Great Yarmouth for repairs. I don't know where they found the tug, but it was the oldest and scruffiest I've ever seen. It was a coal fired steam tug called the *Richard Lee Barber* and it broke down about three times before it got to us. They eventually got us safely into Yarmouth and tied up at a repair yard. The tug tied up astern of us and I think that was the last trip it ever did. I thought we'd be in port for ages but somewhere they unearthed a spare gear box and fitted it and we sailed two days later.

We got to Rotterdam on the 25th August and again the cargo operations were a nightmare. We were discharging the tinned tomatoes and trying to load at the same time. I got really fed up with it and the Mate and the Old Man were getting worse with their bickering so I decided to hand my notice in and get off when we got to London. It only took them a day to unload the tomatoes and throw the other cargo on and we sailed the next night. We berthed in the East India Docks and I paid off and made my way home. I heard later that the Old Man and Mate both got sacked for drinking when they got back so maybe it was just as well I got off.

CHAPTER FOURTEEN

Back to the Far East again

m.v.Thistledhu
14th September 1964 – 21st February 1965

Having arrived home from the *Gracechurch* I intended to get another job as soon as possible but the weather was fantastic and I still had the minivan so I took advantage and had a couple of weeks just chilling out. On Friday 11th September I went over to the Pool in Newcastle to see what was on offer. This time there were loads of jobs going and I was spoilt for choice. In the end I opted for the *Thistledhu* of the Albyn Line which operated upmarket tramps. She was chartered to the Far East and I rather fancied another trip to Japan. The only down side was that, again, there was the possibility I could be away for over a year. I had to go for the usual medical and when I got back to the Pool I had been accepted and they had put me on pay straight away even though I didn't need to join until Monday two days later.

My brother, Andy, was home from University so we decided to have a night out on the Saturday and just as we were going out he got a phone call from a couple of girls wanting him to help move them out of a flat because they knew he had access to the minivan. We decided we could postpone the boozing so we nipped up to the flat in London Road and loaded the van with the two girls and all their bits and pieces.

As the back of the van was completely full, one of the girls, called Diane, had to sit on my knee for the journey and I remember thinking she was rather nice. Little did I know we'd be getting married five years later. We dropped them off at their respective homes and then progressed to the Jazz Club at the Pheasant. I can't for the life of me think why we didn't invite them out but maybe the beer was calling.

I spent Sunday getting over the hangover and packing and on Monday Andy took me over to North Shields to join the *Thistledhu* in dry dock. I was impressed with the ship as it was well built with good accommodation and proper wooden decks. The navigation equipment was really good too. The company insisted on uniforms so I felt I was getting back to Port Line standards.

After a two days we sailed in ballast for Casablanca. As we were early for our charter we just ambled down at half speed and took fifteen days to get there. We loaded a full cargo of 11,000 tons of bulk phosphate. It took three days but I only went ashore for a look around the local market once. We were really glad to sail because the phosphate dust seemed to get everywhere. I think everybody turned out to help wash the ship down when we sailed. The cargo was destined for Shanghai so we set off through the Mediterranean to the Suez Canal. After the canal we had one stop at Aden for bunkers and we arrived in Shanghai a month after leaving Casablanca.

Shanghai was an amazing place. It was the height of Mao Tse Tung's rule and we had to sit through a lecture on communism once the ship was tied up. At the end we all were presented with little red books of Chairman Mao's Thoughts. I took mine home at the end of the trip but it got lost somewhere over the years.

They discharged the phosphate using canvas slings which they emptied into lorries and rail trucks. I could see us being there weeks but they were actually very quick.

It was interesting going ashore as there were hardly any cars and we got about in rickshaws. We were 'encouraged' to only visit certain places: namely the International Seaman's Club and the Friendship Store. The Friendship Store had all sorts of artefacts and jewellery for sale. We could only buy using foreign currency which was a bind. There were some fantastic carvings of wood and ivory going for a song but we only had Chinese money. I vowed to make sure I had English pounds the next time I visited. The Seaman's Club had the longest bar in the world and would have been a really opulent place before communism. It was still very impressive. We had a slap up meal of king prawns washed down with loads of Tsingtao Beer and I think it came to less than two quid. On the way back we swopped places with the rickshaw drivers and pedalled ourselves with the drivers shouting directions from the back. It was great fun but really hard work as they had no gears. It certainly sweated the beer out.

They managed to discharge us in under four days and at the end the holds were spotlessly clean and they had swept up every last bit. The Mate was really pleased as he didn't have to do any cleaning for the next cargo.

We sailed late at night on the 29th October but we had a major problem as we were going down the Yellow River. We phoned down the engine room to tell them we had finished with steam on deck for the winches but the engineer closed the wrong valve and shut off steam to the steering gear. Consequently when we came to alter course at a bend in the river nothing happened and we ploughed straight on. The Pilot went mad screaming "The plawns. The plawns." We had no idea what he was on about but eventually we got things working again and manoeuvred back into the channel where we were promptly ordered to anchor by a gunboat. It seemed we had gone through an area where they reared prawns and we had destroyed the nets allowing the prawns to escape. We were boarded by some high ranking naval officers and the ship was placed under arrest. We were stuck there for over a day until the company managed to deposit a large sum of money as a bond. I was quite glad when they let us go but not half as pleased as the Old Man.

Our next orders were to proceed to Singapore for bunkers but nothing after that. It was turning into a mystery tour. The day before Singapore we got instructions to go to Fremantle to load pig iron for Japan. I had a mad morning checking through our charts because we didn't appear to have the charts to go through the Kepulauan Islands south of Singapore or the charts for the Sumatran coast. The Old Man sent a telegram to the agent in Singapore and the charts were waiting for us when we got in, thank goodness. We got to Singapore about five in the evening and I had to spend all my off watch time drawing the courses down through the islands. We sailed at eleven at night and I found myself on watch for the first part of the passage through the islands. Ernie Smith, the Old Man, was dead nervous and once we got going I could see why. The radar didn't pick up the coastline as it was mangrove swamp so nothing was recognisable and the lights were out on half the buoys. It was pretty hair-raising but we emerged into open water just as I came off watch. Ernie gave me half a dozen cans of cold beer as a thank you which was really appreciated. Even though I was dead tired it was lovely sitting on deck in the warm air with the dawn approaching clutching an ice cold can of lager.

Our course took us south along the east coast of Sumatra and down through the Sunda Strait. We passed loads of plantations each with their manager's house and own little jetty. I think they were coffee but I imagined it would be a nice life trading along this coast dropping in at the jetties for the bags of coffee and unloading supplies. The Dutch East India Company seemed to have it all sewn up, though, so it was not to be. As we went through the Sunda Strait we passed Krakatoa which had been split in half by a volcanic eruption years ago. It must have been a hell of a bang because it was clearly heard in Singapore 300 miles away. I have a feeling it was still active because there seemed to be wisps of smoke coming off the top. I was quite happy when we were safely past.

We berthed in Fremantle on the 13th November and started loading the billets of pig iron. It was very slow as they brought the iron down in lorries and tipped it into skips which were swung on board then emptied into the hold. We were in a really good berth close to the centre of town and the weather was good and the beer even better so they could take forever to load as far as we were concerned. The Old Man had some relatives living there so he disappeared and left us to our own devices. They were supposed to load threequarters of the iron in the bottom of the ship and the remaining quarter up in the tween decks to balance it. It was very expensive securing the iron in the tween decks as it was necessary to use loads of timber to stop it moving about. The Mate and the Head Stevedore decided that as the weather forecast was good they would just load all the cargo in the lower holds and split the money for the timber between themselves. I thought it a bit odd putting all the cargo down below but figured they knew what they were doing.

We sailed after loading for fifteen days and headed north towards Japan. This time we didn't use the Sunda Strait but went through the Lombok Strait at the eastern end of Indonesia. We then steamed up the Makassar Sea between Borneo and Celebes. I was fascinated by this sea. It was a light greeny blue with hundreds of sea snakes and dolphins swimming around. The depth stayed a constant forty feet for a day's steaming (about 300 miles). I kept checking it even when I was off watch but it never varied.

We had a good passage until we were a day south of Japan when we encountered the tail end of a typhoon. There wasn't much wind but the swell was huge and seemed to be coming from two different directions. We started to roll violently and it made no difference which way we headed. It got really serious with things breaking adrift and flying about. The magnetic compass broke off its base on top of the bridge and started smashing around and no one could get close to secure it because it was too dangerous. The cooks had to vacate the galley as the pots and pans were tipping over, throwing boiling liquid everywhere. It was fortunate that no one was injured and it was quite frightening. Luckily it died away after a couple of hours and we steadied up and continued on our way. The Old Man couldn't understand why we rolled so much until he found out that all the cargo was in the bottom of the holds with nothing in the tween decks. He gave the Mate a real roasting and tried to get him sacked immediately but the company couldn't get a relief out so we had to keep him.

We spent the rest of the day trying to repair things but we had to get carpenters and repair workers in when we got to Japan. Most of the cabin furniture had been smashed so we all got new chairs and coffee tables and things. I got a really suave swivel chair so came out on the plus side.

Our first port was Chiba at the top of Tokyo Bay and Ernie, the Old Man, decided to save the company some money and do the pilotage in Tokyo Bay himself. We anchored outside Chiba about two in the morning to wait to berth. Ernie was quite pleased with himself until dawn broke and we found we had anchored in an area where the port was being extended. We were surrounded by drilling rigs and piles sticking out of the water. How we got in there without hitting any of them was a miracle. It took a bit of manoeuvring to extricate ourselves before the harbour pilot came to take us in.

We tied up and started discharging into barges using large canvas bags. It was really quick and they discharged threequarters of the cargo in three days. We then moved round the Bay to Yokohama to finish off. Here we discharged using huge magnets on shore cranes. It was really dangerous as the billets of iron kept falling off as the cranes were swinging around. We all kept off the decks but the Japanese kept running about picking them up and throwing them ashore. I managed to get ashore for some shopping and bought myself the latest Pentax camera and a slide projector. It must have been half the price of buying it in the UK.

It only took a day to complete discharge and we sailed on the afternoon of the 18th December back to Australia but this time it was Sydney. As it was daylight Ernie decided to dispense with the Bay Pilot and this time we got out without incident. I was getting to be quite an expert on the trip between Japan and Australia and we took the same route as I'd done on the *Clearton*. We had Christmas at sea as we passed the island of Guam. We picked up the American radio station on the island and it seemed odd hearing the latest pop records way out in the Pacific. We went close to Bougainville Island again but it wasn't as colourful as the previous times.

We arrived in Sydney on New Year's Day but our cargo wasn't ready so we anchored just by the Harbour Bridge. We had to wait eleven days which was a bit of bind as we couldn't get ashore and worse, we ran out of beer. We persuaded the Old Man to let us take the lifeboat away for a trip. We quickly found an off licence and clubbed together and bought about thirty cases of beer. The owner took it down to the lifeboat in a pickup for us and we loaded up and headed back. The Old Man was in his cabin but he came out as we were retrieving the lifeboat as the hoisting winch was making some odd noises. He wasn't best pleased when he found it was lifting a boat full of beer.

We berthed at Piermont on the 12th January and they loaded us with 11,000 tons of wheat in less than twenty four hours. We had to really run around getting the ballast water out and hatches open and closed that we didn't have time to go ashore. It was a bit different from Port Line. By coincidence, my first ship, the *Port Phillip*, was tied up on the other side of the dock and I tried to get over to see if I knew anyone but they sailed before I got a chance. I was really disappointed because I felt I was bound to know a couple of people and catch up on old times.

We sailed the next afternoon and headed off towards the UK/Continent. Everyone was hoping that it was the UK as we would get a chance to pay off as we'd have got five months in by then. The *Thistledhu* ticked on at a respectable thirteen knots and we had a very pleasant passage across the Indian Ocean to Suez stopping off at Aden for bunkers. Usually there were all sorts of delays and hassle going through the Suez Canal but for some reason we went straight through without stopping. We arrived at four in the morning just in time to tag on to the end of the northbound convoy. I think it was the easiest transit I've ever done. Once we cleared Port Said at the north end of the canal we got instructions to proceed to Belfast to discharge. This meant we could pay off but it was a bit of a pain to get home.

We docked at a silo in Belfast on the morning of the 21st February and I paid off. We got a bus up to Dun Laogaire and caught the ferry over to Stranraer. I had somehow contacted Dad and he came and picked me up at Stranraer when the ferry docked at ten o'clock at night. It was really good of him to come because it was a miserable journey with heavy rain all the way and we eventually arrived home at two in the morning.

CHAPTER FIFTEEN

A brand new ship

m.v. Melbrook
10th May 1965 – 16th December 1965

When I got home from the *Thistledhu* I found I'd amassed quite a healthy bank balance as we hadn't been able to get ashore much. I had the minivan to get about in so I decided to take a long leave. One day I noticed an advert in the Cumberland News about learning to fly at Carlisle Airport with a cheap introductory flight. I decided to give it a go. I got taken up in a tiny Auster Aiglet and thoroughly enjoyed it. The instructor, Ernie White, explained that there was a subsidised scheme paid for by the government to encourage people to learn to fly so there would a reserve of trained pilots in case of war. They paid for the fuel used and also contributed to the instruction. I think it worked out about £5 an hour which seemed too good to miss so I signed up. I went up at least twice a week and was getting close to going solo when I started to run out of money and had to return to sea. I have to admit that my landings weren't up to much but although Ernie was a great bloke he didn't explain that it was necessary to more or less stall the aircraft as you landed and I always ended up landing halfway down the runway. Adrian Todd was still around so we managed to get out climbing most weekends but I had a hard time keeping up with him as he was so fit. My leave seemed to be passing very pleasantly. I went to the Jazz Club at The Pheasant whenever I could and it was there that my brother Peter re-introduced me to Diane. I took her home and after a very nice smooch arranged to meet again. We went out together quite a lot and I began to think that life on shore could be very pleasant but what with the flying lessons and Diane's booze the money started to run out.

After seven weeks at home I had to find another job. I mentioned to Ernie that I had to go across to Newcastle to the Pool and he suggested we fly over and count it as cross country experience. It actually worked out cheaper than going by train. We flew over early one morning and landed at Newcastle airport. I left Ernie with some old mates in the Flying Club and caught the bus in to the centre. At the Pool one ship stood out from the rest. It was the *Melbrook* which was a brand new ship just back from its maiden voyage and lying in Glasgow waiting for orders. I found out that the ship was an 'everything aft' design which meant all the accommodation was at the back and a really modern design. I asked to be put forward and had to go for the usual medical. I casually mentioned that I'd flown in and was in a bit of a hurry. It was magic – I was rushed through my medical and sent to the company offices on the Quayside. They were also impressed with my mode of transport and after ten minutes I had the job and a rail voucher to Glasgow. I caught the bus back to the airport and Ernie and I flew home landing back just after lunch. That was the way to do things.

I had a few days at home and on the 10th May took the train north to Glasgow. The ship was tied up at Meadowside Quay waiting for orders with only a skeleton crew aboard. When I joined the crew reduced to a minimum. There was only me and a Third Engineer left on board. We had a seaman who came at night to be a watchman and a cook who turned up to cook the meals. It was odd being on a ship with no one else around. They put a television on board for us so we were well looked after. I also used to get a 'night on board' allowance of £2 a night as I wasn't supposed to leave the ship. I spent my time leisurely doing the chart corrections and checking the safety gear. A Skipper called Jake Tully turned up after a couple of days and gave us some spending money, had a quick look around, and left saying he'd be back in a week. It was quite nice being left in charge. We had about a month of this when Jake arrived and said we had orders to go over to the St Lawrence for grain back to the UK. Two days later the rest of the crew appeared and started preparing the ship for sea. It was odd having all these people on 'my' ship. We put the ship into dry dock for two days just to get the bottom painted.

I rang home one night and Andy answered the phone and said there was a great party going the following night and if I could get off he would come up and pick me up. We must have been mad. He drove up in Dad's car and picked me up at about seven in the evening and we set off back to Carlisle. Diane was going to be at the party so I was really looking forward to it. We were delayed by an accident on the A74 and didn't get to the party until after ten o'clock. Diane had gone home with someone else and the party was winding down with very little booze left, so we gave up and went home. We had to get up early the next morning to get me back to the ship so it was something of a waste of time.

The ship sailed on the 16th May and set off across the Atlantic to Canada. We had to load at Three Rivers but our cargo wasn't ready so we had to lie at anchor in the middle of the St Lawrence for five days. We obviously weren't anchored in a very good place as we were nearly hit three or four times by ships coming down the river. We had quite a quick load when we did eventually get alongside. We picked up 15,000 tons of wheat and maize in a day and a half. There was nothing much ashore and the locals wouldn't talk unless we spoke French. I bought the latest Beachboys record as a present for Diane and some rather nice carved wooden bowls made by the local Indians.

The *Melbrook* was fitted with the latest MacGregor steel hatches which were a huge improvement on the wooden hatch boards and canvas covers I'd been used to. It surprised me how quickly we were ready for sea after we'd finished loading. We sailed on the 5th June for Avonmouth. We had to anchor for a week when we got there as our berth was occupied. On the third night I went up to the bridge for my watch at midnight and after a cup of coffee with the Third Mate wandered out onto the bridge wing. The ship was making a funny bouncing movement and I suddenly noticed that the land was moving past us. We were dragging anchor in the strong ebb tide. There was half an hour of mad panic while we got the engines ready and people out of their beds. We re-anchored the ship and when I checked we had only been 100 feet off a sand bank with the tide going out fast. There would have been some awkward questions if we had run aground but we got away with it. The Old Man seemed impressed that I'd been on the ball but I had a feeling I should have noticed it much earlier.

We berthed in Avonmouth at the Spillers Wharf. They made dog biscuits mainly and we had to walk through the factory to get ashore and it was interesting to see all the 'Shape' biscuits moving along conveyors. They actually smelt really good and I was almost tempted to eat some. They took a week to discharge us mainly because all the silos were full and there was no room for our cargo. I decided to post the record to Diane but had a major problem wrapping it. In the end I went into a record shop and they gave me a special box for posting records. I think it cost more to post than did to buy it.

As the ship had returned to the UK we had to change articles which meant we could sign off. The company said the ship was going to do the same run again so most of us re-signed as it would only be another month at the most. We sailed on the 28th June and no sooner had we sailed than we got a change of orders to go to Vera Cruz in Mexico. I didn't mind as I'd never been to Mexico but there was a lot of grumbling that the company had not been entirely truthful and we'd be away for a long time. It took a fortnight to get to Vera Cruz. It was a lovely old port and the water was so clear it was easy to see the bottom when we looked over the side. We were loading a full cargo of maize which seemed odd to me as Mexico usually imported maize. The grain arrived in rail wagons and it was shovelled out into canvas bags and loaded on board. It went quite quickly considering the fact that they stopped for three hours for a siesta in the middle of each day.

I loved the town itself. It was built round a huge square which came to life every night. All the cafés and bars had seating outside and there was a continual stream of entertainers and musicians passing by. I knocked about with Pete Tate, the Radio Officer, and we'd wander up to the square most nights. It occurred to us that we hardly saw any of the crew when we were there so after a few enquiries we found they all when to a place called El Ranchito. The next night we decided to give it a try so we jumped in a taxi. The driver shot off and soon we were travelling down dirt tracks through the jungle. We thought we were going to be turned over but we suddenly arrived in a clearing with a huge tin shed in the middle. The place was jumping and there were hundreds of people dancing outside. The music was playing at full volume and they played *Wooly Bully* by Sam the Sham over and over but no one seemed to mind. The noise was unbelievable as they had a huge generator going full blast providing power and everyone was shouting at the tops of their voices. There was a ramshackle bar at one end serving ice cold beer and Coke and a sort of barbecue doing steaks and hamburgers. We got a couple of beers and a steak sandwich and just stood there soaking up the atmosphere. We figured the Mexicans certainly knew how to enjoy themselves. It was a complete contrast to the sedate proceedings in the square. I don't know what time it closed as we headed back to the ship about three in the morning and it seemed to be getting busier and noisier. After that we alternated between the square and El Ranchito when we went ashore.

The night before we sailed the Mate gave me a couple of

complimentary tickets to a nightclub that he'd been given. Pete and I decided to give it go and as we couldn't find it we grabbed a taxi. Again we set off into the jungle but this time we arrived at this large house set in lovely grounds. We were definitely underdressed and we had to borrow a couple of ties before they would let us in. It turned out to be a really high class brothel but the beer was cheap and the girls were gorgeous so what the heck!

It was an amazing place. On one side of the courtyard was a huge vivarium with iguanas and snakes and things and the other side was an aviary with loads of multicoloured parrots and birds of paradise. There was also a large room with a stage and some pretty good cabaret acts. All the girls were wandering about in bikinis looking really sexy and in the end we both succumbed and ended up staying the night. We got back to the ship just in time for breakfast looking rather sheepish. When we came to check our wallets we found we'd only spent about twenty quid each so it had been quite a cheap night.

Louis, the Third Mate, had bought a tame iguana from someone ashore. God knows what he was going to do with it or how he was going to get it home. It was all right when it was calm but if it got upset it could puff up to twice its size, turn red and hiss alarmingly. We presented him with an ultimatum that it went or he would so he returned it to the bloke before we sailed which was a relief as I'd have hated to meet it wandering about in the middle of the night.

We sailed on the 25th July and headed back towards the UK. We stopped off at Freeport in the Bahamas for bunkers but we had to anchor off and they sent the fuel out in a barge so we couldn't get ashore. Two days before we got to the Western Approaches we got orders to discharge in Germany. The cargo was for Hamburg but we docked in Nordenham for a day first to lighten the ship as the berth in Hamburg was too shallow for us. We then moved up to Hamburg and spent five days discharging tied up to buoys in the middle of a dock using floating grain elevators which loaded into barges. It was awkward getting ashore because we had to use a ferry boat which dropped us in a little village to catch a bus into the city centre. We had some of really pleasant evenings ashore in the village as they had a couple of good bars. One of them was part of a restaurant which specialised in German sausages and they kept bringing us samples to try. There must have been hundreds of different types and most of them were really tasty.

As we neared the end of discharge the company said that we

would be doing the same trip again so we all blithely re-signed the articles and we sailed on the 16th August. We sailed out into some of the thickest fog I've ever been in. We doubled up on the watches with me being on watch with the Old Man and the Mate and Third Mate on together. It was really stressful as there were lots of fishing boats going every which way on top of all the cargo ships. It lasted until we passed Dover and it was a great relief to see the Dungeness Lighthouse as we went past.

Halfway across the Atlantic we got a change of orders to proceed to Houston to load grain. It was a bit of a disappointment as we were all looking forward to going back to Vera Cruz. As we headed up the Gulf of Mexico towards Houston I couldn't believe the number of oil rigs and platforms. They were supposed to leave shipping lanes clear but they were right up to the edge of the lanes and it made navigation very difficult especially with all the supply boats nipping around. We picked up a pilot at Galveston and sailed about thirty miles up the Houston Ship Channel to get to our berth. When we tied up we found that we were now going to load food aid for India. There was just about a mutiny on board as this meant it would be at least three months before we'd get back home when we'd all reckoned on a couple of weeks.

The loading went very slowly as I think the shippers were cleaning out all the elevators ready for the next year's harvest. The grain was rubbish really and was already infested with weevils and things. We thought they would be pleased to get rid of it and look good in the process. When we finished loading they came and sealed the hatches and fumigated the cargo to try to kill the weevils. We all had a day ashore with meals provided so it worked out all right. The Old Man organised a trip to the Houston Space Centre so quite a few of us went along. It was pretty impressive as they had one of the space capsules on show.

We sailed the next day and wended our way out through all the oil rigs again. We stopped off at Gibraltar for bunkers and I was very impressed with the place. I'd been past loads of times but never actually entered the port. It was like a lump of England transplanted into a nice climate. There were some problems with the payment for the fuel oil so we were alongside for almost a day and I got a chance for a leisurely wander about. It seemed more English than England if that was possible and it was odd to see the shop names from back home. I spoilt myself and bought an Omega Seamaster watch from a duty free shop at a really good price. There was also quite a lot of mail waiting there for us as for some reason we hadn't received any in Houston. I got a letter from home saying that my brother Andy had sailed on a liner called the *Windsor Castle* on his way to Mombasa to take up a job in Uganda and we would both be travelling through the Mediterranean about the same time. We eventually got our fuel oil and sailed from Gibraltar on the 21st September.

There had been very low morale on the trip from Houston as several of the engineers and some of the catering staff didn't want to go to India so the Old Man had arranged for them to be paid off in Gibraltar but they would have to pay their own fare home. They had made life miserable for everyone else on board and it was a real relief when they went. The Old Man had managed to buy some English beer at a really good price so life was generally pretty good. We got to Suez five days later and transited the canal that night. I came on watch at midnight and was amazed to find that the ship ahead of us in the convoy was the *Windsor Castle*. It was quite frustrating as we unable to communicate with them and Andy would be oblivious to the fact that I was a couple of hundred yards behind him. When we cleared the canal the *Windsor Castle* stopped and anchored to await passengers so we overtook them. I think they must have passed us during the following night as I never saw them again because we stopped off in Djibouti for more bunkers.

We had a nice passage across the Indian Ocean as the southwest monsoon had finished and although it was pretty hot it wasn't too humid and the sea was like a mirror. Our first port in India was Madras. Nobody seemed very interested in our free cargo of grain and it was just discharged in a large heap on the quay. The rats and birds had a heyday. It took about five days to discharge about a third of it. I had the odd wander ashore but didn't take to the place. It was very dirty and dusty and there was a constant crowd of kids following and begging so it wasn't a pleasant experience. I was quite pleased when we sailed off up the Bay of Bengal to Calcutta. When we got to the entrance to the Hoogly River we picked up a pilot from a cutter anchored off the entrance and I was surprised to find he was British. It was like going back in time. He boarded in an immaculate white uniform followed by two Indian bearers carrying his bags. They made sure he was well looked after and carried all his meals and drinks up to the bridge for him. The pilot was a really nice bloke and been to South Shields the course ahead of me. He reckoned he now had quite a good life but he had to put up with power cuts, unreliable water supply, a poor telephone system and rubbish food. His wife came out for a few months in the cool season. I thought I might like to give it a try when I got my Master's Certificate but by that time they had sacked all the British and employed locals.

Initially we tied up to some berths on the side of the river called Garden Reach. It was a real pain as a tidal bore was expected so we had to tie up using our anchor chains. We had to disconnect the chain from one anchor and lower a length of it onto a barge which was taken to the stern to tie up to huge shackles on the quay. We then had to secure the bow with more chain. We had a gang of Indians to help and they were fantastic. They were half the size of us yet they manoeuvred the huge chain links as though they weighed nothing. It still took over three hours to secure the ship though.

The bore was supposed to come at eleven o'clock at night so we all stood by. There were rumours that it could be ten feet high so it would be pretty impressive. We were somewhat pissed off when we were stood down at midnight as it hadn't materialised. We then had to get up at five in the morning to retrieve the anchor chains and move into Calcutta Docks. I really hated Calcutta before I'd even set foot on shore. Actually once we'd settled down and started discharge and I wandered up into town I found it pretty interesting. It was way upmarket after Madras and the buildings were quite impressive. There was a Merchant Navy Officers' Club just outside the main dock gates which was quite palatial and had a pretty good restaurant and a huge swimming pool. We spent most of our time ashore there though a couple of us went down with food poisoning which we suspected was from the restaurant.

One night when we came out of the club we found the water level had risen so much that we had to wade through knee deep water to get back to the ship. The ships looked really odd tied up in the middle of this expanse of water. We then realised that we had no idea where the quay edge was so it became rather dodgy. Someone then hit on the idea of employing a local to walk ahead of us. We got back safely in the end. For some unknown reason I bought a little green parakeet which was really cute. I regretted it once we got to sea, though, as it used to keep waking me up when I was trying to sleep. It was extremely tame and would sit on my shoulder whenever I was in the cabin.

It took nine days to discharge the remainder of the cargo and we got orders to proceed to Mauritius to load a cargo of sugar back to the UK. The day we sailed some of the crew went down with some sort of illness which gradually spread to most of us. It turned out to be Dengue Fever. I wasn't too bad and managed to do my bridge watch but also had to cover for the Mate who was really ill. We had two days at sea before we got to Colombo in Ceylon where we stopped for bunkers. It was quite a performance tying up as most of the crew were still laid up in their bunks but we managed in the end. The Old Man arranged for a doctor to come on board and prescribe some medicine and after we had refuelled we lay alongside for a day to let people recover a bit.

We sailed in the evening of the 1st November and headed off south towards Mauritius. The weather was completely different from our outward trip as it was humid and overcast all the time. We had quite a problem navigating as we didn't see the sun or stars for three days. There was supposed to be a radio beacon on Mauritius but it wasn't working and then our radar packed in. When we found the island we were on the eastern side and we should have been on the west side so we arrived about eight hours later than we intended.

We tied up to buoys in the middle of Port Louis harbour and as it was the season for tropical storms we had to put all sorts of extra moorings out. The cargo of sugar was brought out in bags on barges. The bags were then slung on board and the labour cut them open and emptied them into the hatches and the empty bags were sent ashore for refilling. As we had 14,000 tons to load I could see us being here for ages but they turned out to be surprisingly efficient. At six in the morning the barges and labour were brought out to the ship. Each gang had a quota of 400 tons to load and then they could knock off. Consequently they worked really hard and would be all done by one o'clock in the afternoon. We would close the hatches and wash the ship down and then we had the rest of the day free to go ashore.

Mauritius really impressed me as it seemed to have everything from golden beaches with coral reefs to high rugged mountains with areas of wild jungle and huge swathes of cultivated land on the eastern side where they grew the sugar and everything else. The people were a real mishmash as well: African, Indian, Chinese, Arabs and a sprinkling of Europeans. They all seemed to rub along well together. On the main street in Port Louis every restaurant was from a different culture and the smells of cooking were unbelievable. We wandered about all over the place and I found it fascinating. I came across a bloke in a back street carving tobacco pipes out of a rock called meerschaum. His carving was amazing. I decided to buy one for Dad but the prices were way out of my league and I ended up with just a plain one with a smooth bowl which I still felt was expensive. Dad was made up with it when I got it home though.

There was a British Seaman's Mission there, with a nice swimming pool, which sold cold draft lager so we spent quite a bit of time there. The couple had an aviary with all sorts of exotic parrots and things. I offered them my parakeet as it was beginning to drive me mad cleaning up after it. We couldn't find any regulations about importing birds but just to be on the safe side they arranged for one of the harbour pilots to bring it ashore on the quiet. The pilot put it in an old sock and stuck it in his trousers and took it ashore. We heard later that it managed to escape from the sock and started crawling around in his underpants. I gather he got some odd looks from people as he walked to the Mission. It was nice to see it flying about in the aviary that evening and it even flew over to see me which quite pleased me.

They loaded the 14,000 tons in seven days though we lost one day because of a tropical storm and we sailed for home early on the 15th November. I had drawn all the courses on the charts to go back through the Suez Canal and we set off happily in a north westerly direction. When the Old Man came up at noon to check our position he suddenly realised that we were going the wrong way. He had been told to go round the Cape of Good Hope as Suez, although a lot shorter, was too expensive. We did a sharp left hand turn and headed off south west. We ended up going quite close to Madagascar which looked a fairly wild place with very little civilisation to be seen.

It was an uneventful trip home but it got a bit exciting when we stopped off at Dakar in Senegal for bunkers. There was some sort of revolution going on with jeeps loaded with soldiers everywhere shooting in the air. We were only in for six hours and were extremely glad to sail as it was starting to look pretty serious.

Just after we left we got our orders to unload the cargo at Tate and Lyles Berth in Liverpool which was good news as we'd be home for Christmas. When we got to the Mersey we had to anchor for a week waiting for the berth. We were all worried they would send us somewhere else and end up missing Christmas but in the end we went alongside on the 16th December and paid off on arrival.

.

CHAPTER SIXTEEN

A proper steamship

s.s. Tynemouth
15th January 1966 – 1st May 1966

I still had the minivan when I got home from the *Melbrook* so it was nice to be mobile. I went out most nights with Diane to various pubs. Adrian Todd was home at the same time so I got a bit of climbing in as well. It was good to have Christmas at home and this was only my second since I'd gone to sea.

A couple of weeks into January I decided I'd better earn some money again so went over to the Pool in Newcastle. There were quite a few jobs on offer but one caught my eye. It was the *Tynemouth* belonging to the Burnett Shipping Company. It normally traded over in Canada in the Great Lakes but as the lakes were frozen it came back to the UK for dry docking and maybe do one or two trips before the lakes reopened. There was plenty of money to be made in the Great Lakes as there were big bonuses and lots of overtime when going up and down the Seaway. I was given the Second Mate's job and joined in dry dock in South Shields on the 15th January. It was a bit miserable as there were only a couple of officers on board with a full crew of Somalis. As there was no Mate I had to supervise the crew which I didn't really enjoy because they were a bolshie lot and had an aversion to work. Just before we sailed they were relieved and replaced with a full crew from Djibouti. I couldn't believe the difference. The new crowd were really keen and happy and a pleasure to work with.

After ten days everybody else joined and we sailed to Antwerp. Apart from the Chief Steward and me all the officers had been on board for the previous voyage and had taken their leave while the ship dry docked. The *Tynemouth* was powered by a steam reciprocating engine and I was amazed how smooth and quiet it was. All my previous ships had been diesel powered.

After a brief stop in Flushing at the entrance to the River Schelte for bunkers we berthed in Antwerp to load a full cargo of 5,500 tons of zircon sand which is used in making ceramics and glass. The shippers took one look down our holds and refused to load anything as it was so rusty. We had to spend a week with all sorts of shore labour cleaning and painting the holds. It must have cost a fortune. Mind you the holds looked really good when they were finished. Once they got started we loaded the sand in twelve hours and sailed early in the morning on the 8th February. We had a really miserable trip down the Channel and across the Bay of Biscay. We seemed to be constantly fighting gale force winds and huge swells. The steam main engine was really quiet itself but it was fitted with a turbine on the shaft which made it a lot more efficient. The trouble was that the ship was pitching and the propeller kept coming out of the water. The turbine used to make a noise like a wounded buffalo when the propeller went back into the water and it was impossible to sleep through. We used up quite a bit more fuel than was expected so had to drop in to Gibraltar to top up.

We took the sand to Genoa and they worked round the clock to discharge us so I didn't get ashore much. I wasn't very impressed with what I saw. The American Fleet was in on a courtesy visit so there were American seamen everywhere and there seemed to be fights breaking out all over the place. It took four days to discharge the sand and then we sailed for Casablanca arriving there five days later.

We loaded a full cargo of phosphate which I wasn't looking forward to but we were at a new berth and there was hardly any dust blowing around this time. It took quite a long time to load as the plant was brand new and kept breaking down. Again I didn't go ashore much as the place didn't feel very safe.

We sailed after four days and thankfully the weather was really good as we headed up the Iberian Peninsula and across the Bay of Biscay. We got orders to take the cargo to Rieme in Belgium. We had quite a job figuring out how we were going to get there as it seemed miles inland but we were saved when we got a message from the Antwerp Pilot asking for our ETA. When the Pilot came on board he told us we had to go twenty miles up the River Schelte to a place called Terneuzen then another thirty miles up the Ghent Canal. We started up the canal about six o'clck and it was a lovely spring morning with pockets of mist here and there. I was off watch so I just sat on deck with a mug of tea and a bacon sandwich and watched the scenery go by. It was really relaxing.

Rieme was quite industrial with nothing much to look at but one day I got a bus into Ghent for a look around. It was a very pleasant place but it was a cold day and nothing much was open. I could see it would be lovely to walk around in summertime with all the outdoor cafés and bars. They only took three days to unload the phosphate but the ship was covered in the phosphate dust when we sailed and it was hard to wash off the decks and hatches. We went back to Antwerp again to load another cargo of sand and they failed us again because of all the phosphate. We had five days alongside cleaning the holds before they would load. The company must have got good freight for the sand as it cost them a fortune to clean the holds each time. We sailed again from Antwerp on the 18th March with orders to discharge half the cargo in Barcelona and the rest in Salerno.

We had a decent passage this time, the only problem being thick fog in the Dover Strait where we nearly sank a French trawler. After that we had a nice clear run to Barcelona where we berthed right at the bottom of the Ramblas, which is the main street. They used shore cranes to discharge so we had a leisurely four days there. I liked Barcelona a lot and it was really lively in the evenings. We had a couple of good nights ashore before we sailed for Salerno. Again, this was a great port though a lot smaller than Barcelona. We berthed right beside the main square where there were some very friendly little bars along one side.

The sand was going to a factory which made tiles and the owner took us up for a tour. It was an old fashioned place but the tiles they produced were amazing. They made some bespoke tiles and we couldn't believe how expensive they were. It took five days to complete the discharge and then we sailed for Savonna in the Gulf of Genoa to load some sort of iron ore. The loading was very slow as the ore was brought in by lorries from some distance away. The locals were friendly, though, and offered to take us up into the mountains to ski at the weekend. Only the Third Engineer went as he could ski and he had a tremendous time though he reckoned they were mad because some of the slopes were just about vertical.

We sailed on the 18th April with instructions to unload in Hartlepool. After the ship discharged she was going to the Great Lakes for the season. Although I really fancied working in Canada there were quite few people on board I couldn't get on with and the thought of being stuck with them for the next nine months rather put me off so I asked to be relieved when we got to Hartlepool. We arrived on the 29th April and I paid off the next day. I stopped off in Newcastle on my way home and popped into the Pool to see what the job situation was like and found there were loads of interesting ships and I was offered a job there and then but I felt I needed a bit of leave.

CHAPTER SEVENTEEN

A decent Company for once

m.v. Baxtergate
18th May 1966 – 29th September 1966

I decided that I enjoyed working in the Mediterranean so as soon as I was home I applied for jobs with the MacAndrew Line and Prince Line and some others that traded there. They all replied surprisingly quickly but none had jobs available. They all said they would keep my name on the books and be in contact, so things looked optimistic. I didn't have a very good leave though because I fell out with Diane for some stupid reason and after a week I decided to return to sea. I went over to the Pool and again there were loads of jobs to choose from. One that caught my eye was with Turnbull Scott. The company had a really good reputation and usually kept all their own staff but they wanted a Second Mate for a four month voyage to the Far East so I applied and they came straight back and offered me the job. The ship was the *Baxtergate* and she was arriving in Bordeaux in a couple of days but they put me on pay straight away.

I travelled back to Carlisle feeling I'd rather shot myself in the foot as I'd made things up with Diane and didn't really want to go back to sea so soon. The next day I got a letter from Prince Line offering me a job but I was already on pay with Turnbull Scott so I had to turn it down. I got my joining instructions and I had to travel down to London and then fly to Bordeaux. This was the first time I'd ever flown to join a ship so I was quite excited. I had to change in Paris for a local flight to Bordeaux and somehow lost my baggage. I didn't realise it was booked straight through and I had an anxious hour or so running about looking for it until things were explained. I arrived at Bordeaux airport and was met by the ship's agent who loaded me and my bags into a little Citreon 2CV and set off at a tremendous speed down narrow roads to the port. I was beginning to think we wouldn't make it because his driving left a lot to be desired. I remember we drove through vineyards and lovely countryside though I couldn't really appreciate it as I had to hang on tight as we hurtled round the corners.

The *Baxtergate* had arrived the day before and was cleaning holds and building shifting boards ready for loading a cargo of wheat. The shifting boards were vertical walls of timber that went longitudinally along the middle of the holds to stop the grain from moving around and were a real pain to put up. The cargo wasn't ready for another ten days so there was no mad rush. The weather was perfect so it was quite pleasant. I found out the previous Second Mate had walked off after an argument with the Old Man and I soon found out why. The Old Man was a really unpleasant character who did a lot of shouting and bullied everyone. I ended up having a stand up row with him when he accused me of coming back drunk one night and waking everyone up and I hadn't even been ashore. He eventually found out it wasn't me but never apologised. A couple of days later he overheard me telling the Mate I was fed up and going to walk off if he carried on like this. He then became really nice and friendly as the company would have started asking questions if two Second Mates had walked off.

Life improved a lot. The Mate was a real character – he was Polish but had taken all his certificates in the UK. One afternoon he took me up the road and we went wine tasting with the Agent. I think he was really knowledgeable about the wines and could speak prefect French so I felt a bit out of things but they took time to explain to me about good and bad wine. We were somewhat under the weather when we got back on board. I'd bought one or two bottles on his recommendation and I think he'd bought several cases. He told me I had to take them home but I only kept them a couple of months before trying them.

While we were in Bordeaux they were refurbishing the quay and we used to watch this small gang of Frenchmen renewing the surface with stone setts. There was one huge bloke with two labourers. They would start at seven in the morning and the big bloke would start laying setts with the other two ensuring he had a steady supply. He had an enormous belly which almost touched the ground when he bent over. It looked most peculiar with his legs straight and his back parallel to the ground. He would work for at least two hours without straightening up and laid an unbelievable area. They would knock off for two hours for lunch. They sat in the shade of some trees with a couple of bottles of wine. The corks were attached to the bottles by string which seemed strange to me. They had enormous bread rolls filled with salami and cheese. Somehow they managed to get back to work again for another few hours. It was amazing to watch and they finished the whole quay before we left. I couldn't have worked bent over like that for more than five minutes never mind two hours.

Eventually the cargo was ready and we moved up to the silo. When we came to start loading nobody could find the Mate and we didn't know which hatches to start. The Old Man went mad and started ranting and raving. I went into the Mate's cabin to see if there was any paperwork lying around that would tell me. I found a loading plan and we started loading. I then took the plan back to the Mate's cabin and as I was leaving I heard a funny noise from his wardrobe. When I opened it the Mate was inside, totally paralytic, having drunk quite a few bottles of his wine. I was just trying to figure out how to hide him when the Old Man came in and saw him. There would have been another huge stand up row but the Mate wasn't capable of standing up. In the end the Old Man sacked him. He left next day and the following day a new Mate joined. It was a pity because the old one had been a real character and I got on well with him but the new Mate turned out to be a cracking bloke as well.

We finished loading on the 4th June and sailed in the evening. If you loaded grain in the States or Canada you had to produce reams of paperwork to prove the ship was stable and it all had to be inspected and checked before the ship was allowed to sail. In France they work on the principle that it was us who had to sail on the ship therefore we would make sure it was stable before we sailed so there were no regulations which I thought was a cool way to look at it.

We sailed out via the Suez Canal and stopped off in Singapore for bunkers on our way to Shanghai. The main engine of the *Baxtergate* was a new design of Doxford called a 'P' type. It seemed to have a recurring fault in the top pistons in that the bolts holding them together kept shearing and we had to keep stopping every other day to renew them. We had picked up a supply of spare bolts in Suez but when we got to Singapore the Chief Engineer ordered high tensile bolts which seemed to do the job. We got to Shanghai without further problems and berthed on the 6th July. It was two years since I'd been and now the Cultural Revolution was in full swing. We all had to attend a lecture on Mao's ideas and again were given the little red book containing his thoughts. The discharge went pretty slowly as they unloaded the grain in canvas slings and then bagged it on the quay before loading it onto dilapidated lorries.

We had a bit of a problem one evening. One of our derricks needed lowering a bit and as I was doing this with a seaman the wire jumped off the winch and the derrick came crashing down. Luckily no one was hurt but the derrick damaged some wires connecting loudspeakers on the quay. The loudspeakers used to broadcast propaganda and terrible Chinese martial type music day and night. It was lovely when it all went quiet. Then all hell broke loose. A lorry load of Red Guards arrived and arrested me and the seaman and took us to a local police station. There was a lot of shouting in Chinese and it appeared they thought we had done it deliberately. We were put in a cell with some dodgy looking Chinese and it had the makings of a very long night. A couple of hours later they hauled us outside to find they had arrested the Old Man as well. He had just gone to bed so wasn't the happiest of people. He had no idea what was going on until I told him. We were made to write grovelling letters of apology to the Chinese people for insulting their industrious nation and the Old Man had to promise that our electrician would repair the wiring as soon as we got back to the ship. We were released and taken back at about three in the morning and I was expecting to be carpeted the next morning but surprisingly nothing more was said. It was quite unnerving, though, and I was very careful lowering derricks after that.

It took eight days to discharge and then we had a day removing the shifting boards and cleaning the holds before we moved up to Hsinkiang to start loading general cargo.

Hsinkiang was the port for Beijing and it was surprisingly modern after Shanghai. They took security very seriously and confiscated all our cameras and binoculars before we entered the port as there were all sorts of naval bases along the river. We started loading general cargo the next morning and it was good to be loading interesting commodities instead of the bulk cargoes I had been stuck with latterly. We were loading for five UK/Continental ports so we had to be on the ball with our cargo plans. The loading was overseen by a Chinese Supercargo who was really good and never seemed to sleep in the five days we were there. I was amazed by the diversity of the cargo. There was a lot of porcelain and chinaware all beautifully packed in crates with straw. Also there were drums of chemicals which took a lot of loading as they had to be kept separate in case they reacted with each other. We loaded five or six brand new grand pianos one of which was destined for Reykjavik in Iceland. I often wondered why someone in Iceland would order a piano from China. In one of the holds they built a secure locker which was loaded with bales of animal furs. They looked absolutely fabulous being mostly white and grey. I think they were artic fox or something like that and worth a fortune. They were unloaded in London. We then moved over to Dairen on the Korean Peninsula. There we loaded mainly machinery and plant for another eight days. The loading was slow because it rained just about continuously and we couldn't open the hatches in case we damaged the cargo already on board.

After that we sailed down to Hong Kong where we tied up to a buoy in the middle of the harbour and the cargo was brought out in huge junks. Their shiphandling was amazing as they manoeuvred alongside us just using the wind and tide. In Hong Kong we mainly loaded cartons of clothes and plastic toys. It surprised me that they had been made in mainland China and the Chinese used the port as another outlet. I always thought that they didn't like Hong Kong and the British being there but I suppose business is business. We were there six days by which time the ship was almost full.

We sailed on the 12th August down to Singapore to finish off. We loaded at anchor and they brought our cargo out in barges which weren't half as impressive as the junks. Here we loaded drums of lubricating oil and chemicals most of which were secured on deck. I swapped watches with the Third Mate and went ashore for a look around. It was a fantastic place with some amazing old buildings. By chance I met up with a colleague from South Shields who was sailing as Second Mate with a Hong Kong Company. Needless to say we overdid the beer and I was well under the weather when I got back on board at midnight. We sailed shortly afterwards and I was on watch. I don't know how the Old Man didn't notice how inebriated I was but he left me in charge once we cleared the harbour. How I managed to navigate up the Malaccan Strait without sinking any fishing boats or running aground was a miracle. The Quartermaster spent most of the time making strong black coffee for me and reminding me it was time to check the ship's position. By the time the Mate came up at four o'clock to relieve me I'd just about sobered up and was feeling terrible. I got off the bridge as soon as I could and dived into bed. When I got up just before lunch I put my shore going clothes away and was surprised to find a pair of girl's panties in my pocket. I also seemed to have more money in my wallet that I'd gone ashore with. I can't remember ever meeting any girls ashore and I am intrigued to know where the money came from but they will be forever one of life's mysteries!

It was an uneventful passage home with only the odd engine breakdown and we arrived in Liverpool on the 11th September. Just as we entered the locks there was a bang and the main engine seized solid. We had to get a couple of extra tugs to help us into the same berth in Husskisson Dock where I'd joined the *Port Phillip* when I first went to sea. The company asked me to stay on round the coast for the discharge so I agreed. I was hoping they would offer me a permanent job because the pay was above average and I would be on pay when I went up for my Master's Ticket. Unfortunately it didn't work out because just before we left Liverpool I was told that three of their permanent staff had just passed their certificates and were returning to sea so they were overstaffed. The company paid me off when the ship got to London three days later but they said they would be in touch if there were any vacancies because I'd got a glowing report from the Old Man. I thought he hated me.

I left the ship as she started to discharge in London and as I left I noticed they were unloading the grand piano for Iceland. It still had a few miles to go.

CHAPTER EIGHTEEN

Nearly did for me!

m.v. Findon
3rd November 1966 – 16th March 1967

When I left to join the *Baxtergate* I'd sold my little minivan to my brother, Peter, so as soon as I got home my first priority was to buy a car. My intention was to buy a Saab 96. They were winning all the rallies so I had to be part of that! I wandered down to Mike Telford's garage in Shaddongate only to find there was nothing in stock. He persuaded me to buy a nice Triumph Herald which he'd just got in. I still don't know why I bought it as it wasn't very sporty but it was certainly a smart little car and I got to really like it.

After my previous miserable leave I was determined to enjoy myself a bit more and get a job with a decent company. I had a couple of weeks doing nothing much and then wrote off again to several shipping companies which had good reputations to see if there were any jobs going. I needed about three months seatime before I could sit my Master's ticket and if I could get with a decent company I should be on pay while I studied for the exam. I got the usual replies in that they didn't need anyone at the moment but they would be in touch. After two weeks at home with nothing forthcoming I had to go over to Newcastle and see what the Pool had to offer. Most of the jobs were with tramps going away for over a year or tankers. There was one job that caught my eye with the north east company, Stephenson Clarke, which was second mate on the *Findon*. She was a 4,500 ton collier which had been trading between the north east and Brighton supplying the power station with coal but the contract had come to an end. She was now chartered to carry several cargoes of urea to Norfolk in the States and bring timber back to the Netherlands. I figured I would get my seatime in nicely so applied and got the job.

Joining was a complete contrast to the luxury of flying to Bordeaux. I had to join the ship in Antwerp so I was told to catch a train to Harwich and take the night ferry to the Hook of Holland and then a train to Antwerp. They sent me a rail warrant that actually covered the whole journey. I thought it would be a nightmare but it went surprisingly smoothly. When I got off the ferry in the Hook I got straight onto a train direct to Antwerp. I was on board for noon and we shifted into the loading berth the next morning. The loading was quite slow and took three days. The urea was to be used as fertiliser and was odourless as long as it was dry but when it got wet was a different matter. When we washed the decks after loading we smelt like a urinal but I don't know whether we got used to the smell or it died away because we didn't notice it after a while.

The *Findon* was quite a nice little ship with comfortable accommodation but she was just the wrong size for Atlantic crossings. She was too small to go straight through the waves and too big to go over them so we bounced and crashed our way over to the States and I was relieved to arrive in Norfolk on the 25th November. Our berth was way up the Elizabeth River miles from anywhere. There was one diner/bar within walking distance and it cost a fortune by taxi into Norfolk so we mostly stayed on board for the week it took to discharge. We had to wash the holds out after discharge so again we smelt really awful.

Our next destination was Nova Scotia to load pulp wood. This consisted of four foot lengths of tree trunks destined to be made into paper. Our first port was Baddeck on Cape Breton Island, which was an amazing place, approached from the north down a long inlet and absolutely beautiful. We didn't have the proper charts and it was arranged that a local fisherman would pilot us in. It was a very tenuous sort of arrangement but just as we approached the entrance a fishing boat appeared from behind a headland and our 'pilot' boarded. He was a real character and his first priority was to swop some lovely fresh cod they had just caught for some bottles of whisky. He admitted that we didn't really need a pilot as it was a deep inlet with no submerged hazards but he did a cracking job of berthing us on a small wooden jetty.

Alexander Graham Bell had made his home in Baddeck and he reckoned it was the loveliest place on earth and I could see where he was coming from. There was a museum dedicated to him with a lot of his artefacts just close to our berth. Not only did he invent the telephone but he was involved in all sorts of things including a hydrofoil that used to get up to speeds of over 70 mph which was pretty good for the 1920s.

It was a tiny place with only a couple of small stores, a post office and a bar. We got all secured about ten in the morning and got the hatches open and the ship ready to load. There was no sign of any timber or any labour so we reckoned on a long stay in port but we couldn't have been more wrong. Just after noon a load of pickups full of men drove in from every direction and they were followed by huge trucks loaded with timber. The timber was coming straight out of the forest and the smell of the sawn pine was unbelievable. As each truck arrived its load was measured by two blokes with measuring sticks who noted how many cords of timber there were. The truck then drove onto the wharf and the slings of timber were picked off without the truck really stopping. It had to be hand stowed in the hold but they were so expert that very few of the logs had to be moved each time they landed a sling.

They loaded 2,500 tons in two and a half days. We sailed on the evening of the 10th December and Ernie, the Old Man, decided not to take a pilot. I think he regretted it because once we'd set off the inlet seemed a lot narrower than when we came in and there were no lights or buoys, but we managed in the end.

Our next port was Mulgrave on Nova Scotia itself in the Strait of Canso which separates Nova Scotia from Cape Breton Island. The weather had been really pleasant up to then but as we arrived in Mulgrave the wind started to blow from the north and it turned bitterly cold. We had all sorts of problems on board as the ship wasn't built for extremely cold weather. All our fresh water systems froze and we had to keep the steam winches turning over all the time to prevent the steam pipes from freezing.

The stevedores turned up next morning and we started loading the rest of the timber. The locals didn't seem bothered by the cold although they were well covered up. It took them four more days to finish loading and we ended up with a big deck load. It took quite a long time to secure as everything was frozen solid. When we came to let go it took us over an hour to get the ropes undone as they were frozen stiff. We couldn't stow them below deck as we couldn't bend them to get them down the hatch so we had to tie them to the deck and hope we didn't take any big seas on board.

We sailed on the 16th December and were anticipating a really miserable trip across the Atlantic. To have a wash we had to go out on deck and down aft to the engine room and go down below and fill a bucket and then take it back to the cabin. If you were lucky you ended up with half a bucket of icy water. Needless to say we didn't smell very good.

We had only been on our way for a day when we found ourselves in the Gulf Stream and the temperature shot up and everything melted fairly quickly. We spent a few days repairing all the pipes that had broken but at least we could have a shower. It was a reasonable trip over the Atlantic with no major bad weather. We had Christmas somewhere in the middle and the cook put on a really good spread considering.

We arrived in Velsen in the Netherlands to discharge on the 28th December and when we were told that the next voyage would be the same again quite a lot of the crew paid off but I needed the seatime and another trip would be just right. I figured it couldn't be as bad as the previous trip – little did I know. The discharge went quite quickly. We were in a small dock off the main Amsterdam Canal and the stevedores just unloaded the timber over the side into the water and shore cranes with grabs picked it up and piled it up on shore. It was a pain getting ashore though, as the ship usually ended up ten foot off the quay and we had to walk over the floating logs to get ashore. I'm sure Health and Safety would say something now, but it was just accepted in those days. It was all right sober but we had a couple of mishaps returning to the ship after a few beers and I have to admit being one of the ones that fell in. The water was bloody freezing.

We were in Velsen about a week as it was over the New Year and the plant closed down for the holidays. It was very pleasant as it was just a small village with only two bars and they made us very welcome. One night four of us fell out of a bar about two in the morning and jumped into a waiting taxi and told the driver to take us back to the ship which he did. When we got there and asked the fare the driver said he wasn't a taxi at all and he thought he'd been hijacked. He had been waiting for his wife who worked in the bar. When we asked why he hadn't said anything he said he'd been terrified and we could see his point. He could see the funny side and we gave him some money for petrol. He gave us a lift for free a couple of times after that.

We sailed from Velsen on the 4th January down to Antwerp to load another cargo of urea and again it was a slow process, taking five days to load the 4,500 tons. The trip to Norfolk was a lot more pleasant than the previous one as we managed to avoid any major storms. We actually took a day less to make the crossing. We berthed

106

in the same place and it took them five days to discharge us. We sailed on the 2nd February and had the usual two days smelling horrible until we'd cleaned and washed the ship down.

Our first port of loading this time was Digby in the Bay of Fundy. It was another tiny port with only two jetties and it had the unenviable record of being the port with the greatest tidal range in the world. I don't know how it worked but I seem to remember it was about twelve metres. It was a real pain as we had to stay on watches all the time to keep adjusting the mooring ropes as we went up and down. We had to stop loading when the tide was low as our derricks weren't high enough to lift the timber off the lorries on the quay but it went pretty smoothly considering and they managed to load the majority of our cargo in five days and then we had to move to Mulgrave again to pick up the last 500 tons.

It should have only taken us a day to get to Mulgrave but as we approached the Strait of Canso we were hit by a real belter of a storm. The temperature plummeted and then we were hit by a blizzard. The only good thing was that we were close to the land so the seas were relatively calm. The radar wasn't much help as it couldn't penetrate the snow and in the end it was so cold that the oil in the gear box froze and it seized up. The Old Man decided the only option was to anchor until the storm had passed so three of us were sent up to the bow to let the anchor go. When we got on the focstle we found everything was frozen solid under a layer of ice. To free things up we piled rags all around the anchor cable and windlass and poured diesel over them and set them on fire. It was pretty spectacular but it took nearly an hour and three fires before we eventually managed to drop the anchor. We discovered afterwards that we had nearly set fire to all the paint and stores in a locker under the windlass. Now that would have been even more spectacular!

When we got back to the bridge and thawed out we found that the Old Man and the Mate had managed to get some radio bearings and find out roughly where we were but to ensure that we weren't dragging the anchor the Old Man decided that someone would have to go up into the bow every two hours and listen to the anchor chain to check that it wasn't dragging on the bottom. Needless to say there weren't any volunteers. The wind seemed to get worse and the snow was driving horizontally and piling up all over the ship. With the cold wind came all the problems of the previous trip with the heating not working properly and all the fresh water pipes freezing. With the snow on deck it was a major expedition to go down aft to the engine room for water and inevitably half of it was spilt on the way back. We stayed at anchor for nearly three days, though on the last day the wind veered and the snow stopped and we could see where we were. The temperature rose again and we managed to get most things working. We picked up the anchor without having to set fire to the focstle and berthed in Mulgrave four days later than expected.

The remainder of the timber was loaded, mostly on deck, in a day and we sailed in the evening. We still had problems with getting fresh water but the engineers managed to get the heating working properly so things didn't seem too bad.

The first few days out were pretty good weather-wise though the swell was huge after the storm. Then the wind started to pick up again from astern and we were blowing along quite nicely surfing down the swells. Then late in the afternoon we took a huge wave over the stern that flooded the galley and sent a lot of water into the engine room. We all agreed that we had to turn around and heave to pointing into the wind.

Everything was lashed down or chocked off and the Old Man ordered the wheel hard a'starboard. I don't how far we rolled over as we turned but it was easier walking on the walls than on the deck at times. I was sure we were going over but she came around surprisingly quickly and we slowed the engine to a minimum and pointed into the wind and waves.

It was actually quite comfortable once we settled down as we just went up and down on the waves though we had to be on the ball and speed the engine up at times when we slid backwards down the waves. We stayed hove-to overnight and at least it was reasonably comfortable and not rolling too much. At four in the morning Geordie Ramm, the Mate, came up to relieve me. He took over watching our speed while I made us a brew of tea. Just as I was pouring the tea I glanced up and Geordie had speeded up instead of slowing down as we careered down a wave. I shouted a warning but it was too late and instead of climbing the next wave we went straight through it. I honestly thought we'd had it. The noise was unbelievable as half the timber deck cargo came adrift off the foredeck and flew in all directions. A baulk of timber smashed one of the wheelhouse windows and the wheelhouse filled with freezing water. The water got into the electric connection boxes and there were sparks and flashes everywhere. Every conceivable alarm seemed to be going off while everything else electrical had packed in. As all the wheelhouse doors were shut the water couldn't escape so it was awash in three feet of sea water with a howling gale blowing in through the broken window but at least we were still afloat.

The helmsman was sufficiently on the ball to keep the ship heading into wind as the gyro compass had packed in and Geordie recovered enough to control the speed again. I tried to open a door to let the water out when suddenly there was a bang and it all disappeared. The Old Man had come rushing up to the bridge and when he opened the chartroom door a couple of tons of icy water greeted him and washed him back down the stairs. He was lucky not to have been seriously hurt. He thought we were underwater and was very relieved to find the water flow abating and could hear Geordie and me cursing volubly on the bridge.

It took us a quite a while to organise some plywood and fix it into place over the broken window and once that was done we started trying to sort things out. The wind was dropping off quite quickly but the seas were still pretty high. We dug out the spare magnetic compass and fixed a light over it so the helmsman could steer a course. I was amazed to find the radar still working but the majority of electrical equipment was beyond repair.

Geordie and I nipped below for some dry clothes and the cook appeared on the bridge with some large mugs of hot soup and rolls he'd miraculously rustled up and suddenly things took on a rosier hue. It was starting to get light so we had a look around to assess the damage. Nearly all the timber deck cargo from the fore deck had gone. Some of the wood was found on the top of the wheelhouse later. About half the cargo on the after deck had gone and the chains and wire lashings that had secured it were hanging over the side and we were worried it would foul the propeller. When we looked astern the sea was covered with baulks of timber as far as we could see. It looked really weird.

As the weather was easing all the time we decided to try to get the lashings back on board so we all got our oilskins on and ventured on deck to retrieve them. It was hard work and it was a good hour before everything was stowed safely. The wind had really dropped off by then so we turned around and set off in the right direction at last.

I managed to have a hot shower and then polished off a huge breakfast before I crawled into my bed for a well earned sleep. When

I got up at noon for my watch I found that the Sparks had managed to get the gyro compass working again so we could use the auto-pilot. The sun had come out so I managed to get a sight and work out our latitude. I got another sight about four o'clock and got a decent position and was surprised to find we hadn't lost all that much time.

The trip after that was pretty good weather-wise but it was a bit of a bind because a lot of equipment wouldn't work. The Second Cook had hurt his hand quite badly when a door slammed on it so Ernie, the Old Man, diverted into Falmouth to have it checked out. We also took the opportunity to fill up with fresh water and take on some stores as most of the fresh food had been destroyed by the sea water. It was then a couple of days and we were back in Velsen discharging. We fed quite well while we were there as the galley stove had been damaged so it was organised that we could eat in the workers' canteen. The cooks did a great job and put out loads of delicious food every day. We also got a couple of cans of beer with each meal which went down very well.

A company superintendent had travelled over to sort out the storm damage as they wanted the ship to do another trip but when he saw the state of everything it was decided to send us straight to dry dock in the Tyne after discharge. We arrived there on the 10th March and my intention was to stand by the ship in dry dock and then leave after Easter and start studying for my Master's Certificate. I soon realised that it hadn't been the best idea in the world. Everybody else left and I was the only one on board at night. One or two engineers turned up during the day but I had to provide all my own meals. There was a dockyard canteen which knocked out some pretty good meals at a reasonable price so apart from breakfast I managed all right.

As I was the only deck officer on board I was constantly chased around showing the dockworkers where things were and checking that jobs were being done properly. We had to have a full safety equipment survey which meant collecting all the fire fighting and life saving equipment, cleaning it and having it ready for inspection by a surveyor. I thought I did a pretty good job and had everything neatly laid out in the wheelhouse. The surveyor turned up and was duly impressed. While he was checking everything he asked me to fire off the spare cartridge for the rocket gun which was used to fire lines across to other vessels in distress. It consisted of a large gun into which the rocket was inserted and then the cartridge was fitted into the breech and hey presto when the trigger was pulled the rocket shot off followed by miles of light line. It was usual practice to fire off a spare cartridge at the surveys to ensure the cartridges were still in good condition.

I fitted the cartridge but as it was absolutely teeming down with rain I decided just to poke gun out of the wheelhouse door to avoid getting wet. When I pulled the trigger there was a huge explosion and the wheelhouse filled with smoke. The surveyor had forgotten about giving me the job so nearly had a heart attack when it went off. It even gave me a shock and I was expecting it. His assistant was checking an oil lantern which he dropped and smashed on the deck. The surveyor called me all the names he could think of and couldn't believe I fired the gun off in the wheelhouse. My excuse that I didn't want to get wet seemed a bit weak. Anyhow, he passed everything and went ashore muttering, stopping off at the pub by the dock gate for a whisky to steady his nerves.

After we'd been in a few days the company announced that we would be reduced to coastal pay rates and also have to pay for our own food even though I was doing them a favour. I told them where to stick the job and paid off.

There were still three weeks to go before the Easter break so I decided to go straight to South Shields College and at least I would be doing something useful. The previous trip I'd met up with Warren Wilson and his wife Doreen who had been on the *Thistledhu* with me and they had invited me to stay with them in their pub, The Locomotive in South Shields, so I went home, dropped my seagoing gear off, picked up my books and travelled back to Shields to start studying.

CHAPTER NINETEEN

A little holiday in Sweden

m.v. Kingsnorth Fisher
28th March 1967 – 11th April 1967

I only had a week at college before they broke up for Easter but at least I could do some studying over the holidays. I set off back for Carlisle on the day before Good Friday and on impulse I stopped in at the Pool in Newcastle to see if there were any relief jobs going for a couple of weeks. I never really expected anything and when I went in they were already closing down for Easter. I glanced at the boards and there was nothing so I turned around to leave and bumped into Sandy, the manager. We exchanged greetings and he asked what I was looking for. His face lit up as he'd just got a request for a Second Mate to join a brand new design of ship to take it to Gothenburg for five days to demonstrate it at a trade fair. I said I'd take it and we completed the paperwork in record time and I left with instructions to join the *Kingsnorth Fisher* in North Shields the day after Easter Monday. I ambled across to Carlisle and had a very pleasant Easter before travelling back to join.

The *Kingsnorth Fisher* was brand new and had been specifically designed to carry heavy electrical transformers round the coast to power stations. It had a huge ramp up which the transformers would be transported on low loaders. They could then either be lowered into a huge hold or secured on deck. I'd never seen anything like it before and it seemed extremely complicated but really interesting at the same time. The designers wanted to show her off so it had been arranged that we would pick up an empty transformer casing on a low loader and take it over to Gothenburg and show it off at a big trade fair that was going on there.

We loaded the transformer on the 31st March and sailed the next day. We had also taken on loads of booze and all sorts of food to treat any visitors. We also had an extra cook/steward to help out with the catering. The ship berthed right in the centre of Gothenburg close to where the exhibition was being held. All the crew were issued with matching boiler suits and hard hats and we actually looked quite professional. We gave the ship a good clean and John Pritchard, the Mate, decided we should have a practice demonstration just to make sure we knew what we were doing. It was a total disaster – hydraulic pipes burst, electric motors blew fuses, the communication system packed in and the low loader's engine wouldn't start. It was after midnight before we got some semblance of order and the hydraulic oil spills cleaned up. It didn't bode well.

It was organised that we would do demonstrations at eleven in the morning and three in the afternoon. We had another practice at ten and although not perfect we didn't blow anything up. We all cleaned ourselves up and combed our hair ready for the first demo. Unfortunately nobody turned up so we stood about like tins of milk until noon. The cook had laid on a lovely buffet with smoked salmon and prawn vol-au-vents and everything and rather than let it go to waste we set to and consumed most of it. There was also a table set up as a bar with cold beer and spirits so we sampled some of that as well. We were in fine form by three o'clock and we actually got about a dozen people down for the demo. It went like clockwork and everyone left very impressed. The cook had made another buffet with scones and cream and nice cake but the visitors had hardly touched it so the cook was quite happy for us to polish this off as well. As they had very strict drink drive laws in Sweden none of the booze had been sampled by the visitors so the Old Man issued us all with half a dozen cans of beer each as it seemed a pity to waste it. We had the ship all secure by half past four so we sat around drinking beer and yarning until bedtime. I was beginning to enjoy this.

We stayed there for another four days doing a couple of hours work a day, eating lovely food and consuming quite a lot of beer. I must have put on about a stone in weight. The demonstrations went very well and I have to admit we got pretty good at it. Not too many people showed up but we gave them their money's worth. On the last day some of the directors of the company appeared with some important executives from the Central Electricity Generating Board who had chartered the ship for five years. They were very impressed and one of the directors told the Old Man to give the crew a case of beer each. Little did he know!

We sailed back to North Shields and docked in Albert Edward Dock about noon. We unloaded the transformer and low loader straight away and the ship got orders to sail the following day up to

Granton, in the Firth of Forth, to pick up a fifty ton electric motor. I cleaned my cabin and packed my gear and then wandered up to see the Old Man to pay off. He had completely forgotten I was leaving and hadn't asked the company for a relief. As the college was still on holiday I volunteered to stay on to Granton as it was only one more day. I then had the brilliant idea that if I picked up my car and took it on the ship I would be able to drive back. The Old Man was happy with that so I shot over to Carlisle, said a quick hello to my bemused parents and drove back to North Shields. I drove up the ramp and parked the car outside my cabin door. We sailed straight away and berthed the following evening in Granton. The Old Man paid me off and I gave him and the Mate a lift up the road to the pub and drove home.

I had a few days at home until the college opened again and I could resume my studies for my Master's Certificate.

CHAPTER TWENTY

Studying for my Master's Ticket

South Shields College
12th April 1967 – 20th July 1967

I travelled over to South Shields on the morning of Monday the 17th April and went straight to the college. I couldn't believe the number of blokes in the class. Normally there would be twenty or less but I think there about thirty five. For the people who were on contracts with their companies life at the college was very easy as they were still on full pay so most stayed there for as long as possible and had a sort of extended leave. For blokes like me who weren't on contract we had to sign on the dole and collect our unemployment benefit once a week and live on the money we'd saved up at sea. Our priority was to get our ticket as soon as possible and get back to sea and earning money again. I think about two thirds of our class were on contracts so were just swanning around and enjoying life. Luckily I met up with Alan Clish and a couple of others from my Pre-Sea Course and all of us wanted to study so we studied together during lunch breaks and the odd evening.

The only fly in the ointment was my choice of digs. In hindsight staying in a seamen's pub whilst trying to study seriously was not the best thought out plan. It actually worked out quite well initially as Warren, the manager, hated opening up at six o'clock and liked to relax and watch the news on TV so I volunteered to open up for him each evening. It was usually pretty quiet anyhow so I wandered around doing a bit of restocking and pulled the odd pint for the early birds. Warren would appear at about seven and I retired to my room to study for three hours. I would then wander down for a couple of pints with the intention of going to bed about eleven. Unfortunately this rarely happened as Warren would have a 'lock in' which carried on until two or three in the morning. About one o'clock I was usually dispatched to an Indian restaurant on Ocean Road called the Star of India. They would fill up a large pan with the curry of the day and another with rice and to complete the meal there was a big box of assorted naan breads and poppodums. This was then taken back to The Locomotive where Doreen would produce the plates and cutlery. It was usually about four in the morning when I fell into bed. I would get up about half past eight and have a cup of coffee before setting off for the college. For lunch I used to have two Cornish pasties in the college canteen washed down with a large mug of coffee. For some reason I used to have terrible indigestion and heartburn.

I found studying for my Master's ticket a lot harder than the previous ones. There were several subjects completely new to me and I had to work pretty hard. It took me ages to get my head around magnetism – I just couldn't get it at all. There was a piece of apparatus called a deviascope which was just a model of a ship fitted with a magnetic compass and we had to remove any errors in the compass by playing about with little magnets and bits of soft iron. Nothing made sense at all but one evening Alan Clish spent some time explaining it all to me and suddenly the light dawned and after that it was a doddle. The other subject that kept me busy was Ship Master's Business. It covered everything from accounts, working out crew wages and tax to legal matters relating to charters and the carriage of cargoes. I felt if I was going to fail on anything it would be this.

I stayed over at Shields during the week but travelled home each Friday afternoon and back again first thing Monday morning. I still did a bit of studying at home but went out most nights with Diane. She used to test me on buoyage and navigation lights and the Rules of the Road. We'd sit in a corner of the pub with Diane showing me diagrams of lights and buoys. I actually think she was better at them than me in the end. It certainly helped me with my knowledge.

After about three and a half months at the college I had attended most of the lectures and started to spend my time working through old examination papers. After a week of this I became bored as it was very repetitive and I didn't seem to be learning much. The summer holidays were looming and I thought I might have a go at the exam before we broke up as I had a pretty good chance of passing some subjects and could re-sit any I'd failed after the summer break. I discussed this with Alan Clish and a couple of others and we all thought it was worth a try. Four of us went up to Newcastle the following day, paid our fees and put our papers in to sit the last examination of the term. When we got back to the college and the others in the class heard what we were doing they all decided to have a go. Normally there were only four or five candidates sitting for each exam but it ended up with over thirty putting their papers in. The examiners were somewhat overwhelmed and a message came back to the college that if any of us were 'just having a go' and failed, the examiners would give us seatime which meant we had to go to sea for six months before we could resit. They said we could retract our applications without any penalties. After a bit of soul searching we decided that we may as well have a go as we'd probably have to go to sea to earn some money. As it turned out not many deferred the exam.

The examination usually lasted a week with written papers on the first four days with a test in signalling one morning. We then had an hour demonstrating our prowess on the deviascope and a four hour oral examination on anything and everything nautical. There were so many of us, though, that the orals were scheduled for the two weeks after the writtens.

The written exams went pretty well and I felt reasonably confident until I talked to some of the older hands. It turned out they had been revising the exact same test paper the previous week so they knew all the answers and they were all confident of passing. It didn't help that I had quite a few different answers so I was resigned to going back to sea. My oral exam was scheduled for the following Friday morning at eleven o'clock so I went back to Carlisle to swot up on things. I was intending to stay home all week but Diane was working so on the Tuesday I went back to Shields to practice with some of the others. When I got there I found I'd passed all my written papers and also the signals and the dreaded deviascope. I was over the moon. By coincidence Alan Clish was also there and he'd also passed everything so the pair of us adjourned to The Locomotive and got pissed. Next morning I went up to the college feeling really ill and met up with Alan who was worse than me. We both agreed we weren't learning anything so we both went home again.

I spent the next few days sitting at home trying to revise and on Friday morning travelled over to Newcastle to the exam centre. I got there early and checked in with the clerk and went to the waiting room. I'd only been in a few minutes when Ginger, one of my classmates, came in with a long face. He'd failed everything except the signals but at least he hadn't been given seatime. I asked what the exam was like and he said the examiner was in a foul mood and was asking a lot of questions about Rules 7 and 9 of the Collision

Regulations. I went into total panic as these were about the lights on small vessels and fishing vessels and I hadn't done much revising on this. I quickly got my books out and started reading up on them as I had an hour before I was due to go in. I'd only been revising ten minutes when the clerk stuck his head around the door and said I could go in so I wandered down to the exam room. When I entered it went from bad to worse. The examiner was the same bloke who had surveyed the safety equipment on the *Findon* when I'd fired the rocket gun off in the wheelhouse. He looked at me and asked where we'd met before. I professed ignorance but he was sure he knew me from somewhere. He gave up trying to remember and started the exam. His first question was what did I know about lights for small vessels. I started to recite Rule 7 and had only said a couple of lines when he stopped me and asked about something else. I only knew one more line so if he hadn't stopped me I would have stuttered to a halt and probably failed miserably. He then went on to ask about buoyage which I was pretty good at so things started to improve. I struggled a bit with some of the questions about business but did all right on the seamanship. After fifty minutes he said that was enough. Normally the exam took two hours so I was sure he'd got fed up and failed me but he produced the pink PASS chit from under his papers and congratulated me on a good exam. As I was standing up to leave he told me he'd remembered where he'd met me and I was the silly twat who fired the rocket gun off in the wheelhouse. He said that once he'd recovered from the shock he thought it was very funny and it was one of his favourite anecdotes.

I wandered back to the waiting room to pick up my belongings and bumped into Alan Clish who had also just passed with another examiner. We had a celebratory pint in the bar at Newcastle station before going our separate ways. I decided to nip back to South Shields and collect all my gear from The Locomotive and tell them I'd passed. I got there about one o'clock and loaded the car up. When I went into the bar to say goodbye to everyone they all insisted on buying me a drink. I was totally legless by three o'clock and went to bed to sleep it off.

I woke up at seven feeling decidedly poorly but set off for Carlisle anyhow. I must have been still well over the limit but really wanted to get home to tell Diane and Mum and Dad the good news. I was going to tell Diane first so took the main A69 into Carlisle. Just before Corby Hill I lost it completely and went sideways into a ditch. I had to phone Dad to come and pull me out. He wasn't too impressed with my sobriety or lack of it but we got the car back on the road and drove home. I think I went straight to bed as soon as I got in the house so Diane didn't hear the good news until the following morning. It cost me a bit to sort the damage to the car so that quietened me down for a bit. I decided to have some time relaxing at home before looking for another job as I still had a bit of money in the bank.

CHAPTER TWENTY ONE

Up to Chief Officer

m.v. Kingsnorth Fisher
19th August 1967 – 24th November 1967

I had a very pleasant leave doing very little. I gave Dad a hand painting the outside of the house helped by Andy. It took ages as we had to prime the rough-cast first and the actual painting took forever but the weather was really good and there was a plentiful supply of cold beer. My bank account was getting well down and I was just thinking I would have to go back to sea when I got a phone call from the personnel manager of James Fisher in Barrow. Somehow he knew that I'd passed my Master's ticket and was offering me a job back on the *Kingsnorth Fisher*. I'd really enjoyed all the hands-on technical stuff on there and the ship would be going to unusual ports around the coast so I accepted. I had another four days at home before I had to join. John Bannister was keen to see on board a ship so he gave me a lift over to Wallsend and had a look around. The ship was lying idle waiting to load her cargo the next day. I sought out the Second Mate and told him I was his relief. He wasn't expecting to be relieved and as the Old Man had told him off for drinking a couple of days earlier he thought he was being sacked. Just then John Pritchard, the Mate, appeared and told me he'd just finished packing and I could move in to the cabin. I was signing on as First Mate! He spent half an hour showing me the paperwork and explaining what jobs were ongoing. He said I would have no problem with working the ship as I'd seen it all before and with that he disappeared ashore to catch a train. The Old Man lived locally and had gone home for the night so I unpacked and sat down somewhat bemused and contemplated the situation.

The First Mate's duties were far more demanding than the Second Mate's. The Second Mate was in charge of the navigation and had to keep all the charts and nautical publications up to date. On general cargo ships he also had to produce the cargo plan and that was about it, so it was quite a cushy number. The First Mate, on the other hand, was in charge of the day to day running of the vessel which involved making sure it was well maintained and painted. As such he had to detail the crew to carry out the various jobs. He also was in charge of the loading and the stability of the vessel. This was on top of doing his bridge watch of at least eight hours a day. It was a big jump but I decided I might as well give it a go.

The Old Man arrived early next morning and we shifted along the quay and loaded a 150 ton transformer using Swan Hunter's big crane. It all went pretty well and we spent a few hours securing the transformer. Being my first job I think I may have overdone the lashings but at least I knew it wouldn't fall overboard though the crew were muttering a bit at the end. We sailed in the afternoon down to Tilbury where we jacked the transformer up onto a low loader and discharged it down the ramp on the stern.

No sooner had we unloaded than we got orders to proceed to Birkenhead to load a large generator for Lerwick in the Shetland Isles. When we arrived in Birkenhead we found that it was a complete power station that we were loading consisting of the generator, the building to house it, a large fuel tank in sections, a control room and loads of pipes and cables on pallets. We also had to take the low loader with us that had to deliver it all to the site. We first berthed stern on and drove the low loader on board up the ramp and then moved along the quay and loaded everything else with a shore crane. It was quite a problem stowing it all as I had to make sure we could unload it at the other end. It went very quickly in the end and we sailed in the evening of the 25th August. We had to sail to catch the tide so we spent the first few hours at sea lashing everything down. I then had to do a six hour bridge watch so I was really knackered and beginning to wonder whether the First Mate's job was worth the extra money.

We had a beautiful trip up the Irish Sea and up the coast of Scotland. The last time I'd been up through the Minches was on the *Craigallian* in 1962 and I'd forgotten how lovely it was. We were carrying the drivers for the low loader with us and I think they spent all their time on the bridge admiring the scenery. We arrived in Lerwick early in the morning expecting to be unloaded and away by noon but all sorts of things went wrong. We had to wait for the top of the tide before we could drive the low loader and the generator off and then we only just managed it as the quay wall was so high. The lorry then disappeared off to the site. It took him four hours to return so we were hanging about waiting for ages. It took ten minutes to load him up again and then another four hour wait. At least we got a chance to look around Lerwick. It was a picturesque little place and I bought a couple of Fair Isle sweaters at a good price. In the end it took us two days to discharge. We were supposed to bring the low loader and its drivers back with us but this meant waiting eight hours for the tide to come in and it was decided to leave them to find their own way back. The drivers were most put out as they would have to drive down the full length of Scotland instead of cruising sedately down its coast.

We arrived back in Eccles in the Manchester Ship Canal and laid up for a week as our next cargo had been delayed so we could have waited for the tide in Lerwick and brought the low loader back in the end. After five days we moved up to Pomona Dock in Manchester and loaded a huge transformer for the new power station being built in Kingsnorth in the River Medway.

This was loaded as it should be by driving it up the stern ramp so it went pretty smoothly. We took a couple of hours securing it as we were becoming quite expert by now. The company also decided that we should have a payment of £10 for every cargo we lashed so I had no shortage of helpers. We had quite a rough passage across the Bristol Channel and we rolled around a lot. I was concerned in case my lashings on the transformer weren't strong enough but it never moved.

I was enjoying working on the coast and getting to small and out of the way ports. The Old Man, John Cairns, had just come from deepsea as well but he was very nervous and didn't enjoy the shiphandling side of it at all. We were small enough to get into quite a few ports without taking a pilot but he always insisted on taking one. I was itching to have a go at manoeuvring the ship but never got the chance. The *Kingsnorth Fisher* was really easy to handle as she had twin screws and a bow thruster. We ended up having to take three pilots on our way up to Kingsnorth. One took us from Margate to the River Medway and then another took over for the ten miles up the Medway. We used a 'mud pilot' called Albert Turner to put us alongside the berth at the power station. Mind you, Albert was worth having around as he would turn up with the newspapers and fresh milk and let us borrow his pickup for trips up to the nearest town.

We discharged the transformer without problems and set off north to North Shields to pick up a huge electric motor from Parsons. We berthed on the evening of the 11th September and as we weren't loading until next morning the Old Man nipped off home. Two of us decided to venture ashore and ended up in an infamous pub called 'The Jungle'. It must have been the early hours when we got back decidedly the worse for wear. I wasn't too happy to be woken at six o'clock to be told the motor was ready to be loaded. The Old Man was still ashore so I had to move the ship back into the loading berth myself. The loading went very smoothly and when the Old Man turned up at eight o'clock we had the motor lashed down and were ready for sea. I thought he'd be pleased but he gave me a real dressing down for moving the ship without him. I thought I'd done him a favour. He would have been even less impressed if he'd known we were still half pissed from the night before. We sailed at nine o'clock and it turned out he'd arranged for some friends to have a look around the ship and they arrived on the quay to see us sailing out of the lock. I kept out of his way for the rest of the day.

We had a terrible trip to Manchester with a howling gale and huge seas for the most part. I was glad to get into the shelter of Liverpool Bay. We went straight up the Ship Canal to Pomona Dock again and discharged the motor on arrival. We loaded another transformer right away and sailed immediately as it was needed in Barry to replace one that had blown up. We had to do the lashing on the way down the canal. We never seemed to stop and everyone was getting tired and irritable.

After Barry it was back to Manchester again to load a large fuel tank for Folkestone then Manchester again to pick up a failed transformer for Granton. We had hardly any time in port and I was beginning to wish for a long trip deepsea to settle down. The passage from Manchester to Granton gave us a bit of time. I reckoned it was shorter going round the north of Scotland, and more scenic, but the Old Man didn't like the passage through the Minches and we went south and round the bottom. It took a couple of days and it was nice to get into a routine of bridge watches.

We only expected to be in Granton for a short while but the tractor unit broke a half shaft as he started to pull the trailer off. The driver reckoned it was our fault for not releasing the restraining wire quick enough. He ended up in a real shouting match with the Old Man while I kept my head down because I knew it was our fault. They managed to renew the shaft in six hours and we discharged the transformer without further problems.

We then got orders to go to Ardrossan to pick up some plant for the Kingsnorth power station. This time we had to go round the top of Scotland and through the Minches so it turned out all right in the end. Again it was a lovely trip and we had a fantastic passage through the Pentland Firth. The tide was in our favour and we shot through in double quick time. The wildlife was unbelievable. I think there must have been some large shoals of fish about as we saw seals, dolphins and even whales and the air was full of diving gannets.

We arrived in Ardrossan early in the morning of the 3rd October and had the cargo loaded and lashed quickly. It was some prefabricated sections of chimneys which would have been a real pain to take by road. We had just finished securing everything and were standing on deck drinking coffee and watching the ferry to Arran sail. There was quite a gale blowing and as the ferry left the berth the wind took hold of it and he nearly crashed into the breakwater. John Cairns took one look and announced that we would be staying put until the wind died down a bit. As a result we stayed tied up for another two days which was quite pleasant though we couldn't do much work outside as it rained continuously. The Bosun and some of the crew wandered up to the local pub for a pint at lunch time and I was annoyed to find that they hadn't returned to work in the afternoon. I gave them half an hour's grace and when they still hadn't returned I decided to go and drag them out of the pub. I was just setting off when they appeared around the corner of a large shed. They were slightly the worse for wear but were all dressed in identical bright yellow suits of oilskins. They had met up with some girls who worked in a factory making waterproof clothing and the girls had run them up some made-to-measure waterproofs at very reasonable prices. Needless to say we all had to go and get ourselves kitted out so when we came to sail the next day everybody turned out looking very smart in their bright yellow gear. The storm hadn't abated much, in fact when we cleared the breakwaters it seemed worse than the previous day. We had a terrible passage southwards with huge seas and head winds. It only got better when we turned round the Lizard and set off up the Channel. As we passed the Scilly Isles we could see the wreck of the tanker *Torrey Canyon* and there were still traces of oil in the sea.

When we got to Kingsnorth we had to wait for the transport to come and remove the chimney sections. The mud pilot, Albert Turner, had left us his pickup so we had a some really pleasant evenings in the local pub at Hooe. It's a good job there were no police around for our drive home as there were about ten of us packed into the pickup for the three mile trip back to the ship and the driver was chosen from anyone who could still stand.

Once we'd unloaded we had to scoot back to Manchester to pick up yet another transformer for Tilbury and then it was off again to Granton to load a large piece of plant for the Tyne. On the way up to Granton we heard that we would be dry docking in Jarrow so that brightened us up a lot. We unloaded the plant in North Shields and entered the dry dock at Tyne Dock on the 24th October. The whole dry docking was a bit of a disaster. As First Mate I should have made a list of all the defects that had occurred and any modifications that needed doing but I wasn't told so the superintendent assumed everything was running smoothly and we would just need the usual overhauls of gyros and radar and a paint job. He got somewhat annoyed when I kept appearing with lists of equipment that wasn't working properly and things that needed modified. Eventually it all got sorted out but I seemed to spend all my time arguing with people about how things should be done. At least it was only a short walk to The Locomotive in South Shields every night. By the end of the drydocking I had more or less decided to pack it in and go deepsea again. I didn't get on very well with the Old Man either which didn't help.

We sailed from Jarrow on the 7th November with orders to go to Faslane in the Gairloch. It appeared that the new boilers for the Kingsnorth power station were miles behind schedule and they needed something to commission the new turbines so someone came up with the idea of using an old boiler from the *Queen of Bermuda,* an old passenger liner which was being scrapped in Faslane. It sounded really interesting and we had yet another passage round the top of Scotland so life brightened up. When we got to Faslane there was no berth available so we had to tie up alongside the cruiser *HMS Sheffield* which was there being scrapped. It was really interesting even though they had taken most of the superstructure off already. I couldn't believe the size of the guns and how little space there was in the turrets. The noise must have been terrific when they were firing.

On our first day in we assembled a frame for the boiler to sit on and the next day a floating crane came from Glasgow and lifted the complete boiler off the *Queen of Bermuda* and loaded it onto our frame. It all went very smoothly and once we'd secured it off we went to Kingsnorth.

125

We discharged fairly quickly and then got a message that our next cargo of a transformer had been delayed as it had failed a test so we went to Tilbury to lay up for a few days. When we had been in dry dock the superintendent had pointed out that all the blocks and pulleys of our cargo equipment needed a good overhauling so I decided this was the ideal opportunity. We got everything out on deck and started dismantling and greasing everything. It was going really well when the Old Man appeared and announced that he wanted the outside of the accommodation painted. I thought he was joking but he had decided that the ship was looking scruffy. It was the final straw for me so I went after him and told him to ask the company to relieve me. We had a bit of a shouting match with him saying I was overreacting and taking a 'hissy fit'. We stowed all the cargo gear away again and started cleaning and painting. I was dying for it to start raining and stop things but the bloody weather stayed fine. My relief turned up after a couple of days and I stayed on for another week showing him how things worked. The last week was very pleasant as the new Mate was easy to get on with and we spent most evenings up the pub. We got all the accommodation painted and the cargo gear overhauled so everyone was happy and I paid off when the ship got orders to sail on the 24th November.

CHAPTER TWENTY TWO

Coals from Newcastle

m.v. Thomas Livesey
15th December 1967 – 8th January 1968

When I got home I had a good long think about the job of First Mate. It was a huge step up from Second Mate and if the truth was known I hadn't really enjoyed it. I felt I wasn't quite up to it and was worried in case I got things wrong resulting in an accident. After a week I convinced myself to revert back to Second Mate for while and learn the First Mate's job properly. It was quite a drop in money but I had to admit that I really enjoyed being Second Mate. I travelled over to the Newcastle Pool the first week in December to see what jobs were around. I was pretty disappointed as normally there were loads of good jobs going just before Christmas as no one wanted to ship out at that time. The only job of interest was with Manchester Liners but they traded across the North Atlantic and that was the last place to be in winter. I left my details with Sandy, the manager, and he said he would let me know if any decent jobs came in. A few days later he rang to say there was a Christmas relief wanted on one of the colliers taking coal from the north east down to the power stations on the Thames. I'd never been right up the Thames and it rather took my fancy especially as it was only for three weeks. He then told me it was the First Mate's job and managed to persuade me that it would be a doddle as the ship would run itself. He also told me that I had to have my full uniform complete with cap as the company insisted that everyone dressed correctly. It seemed a bit odd for a little ship carrying coal but I packed it anyway.

I joined in Seaham Harbour on the 15th December where she was halfway through loading the cargo of coal. The Mate was waiting for me, all dressed up his going home suit with his bag packed. He took all of ten minutes to show me around the ship and hand over the paperwork and he was gone. I was on a ship that I knew nothing about with coal pouring down chutes into the holds. This was worse than joining the Kingsnorth Fisher as at least I'd known how that ship worked. I went back to the cabin and started to change into some working gear when a steward appeared in full white uniform with a tray of tea complete with sandwiches and chocolate biscuits. He told me most of the crew were home until the ship sailed and there was only a seaman and an engineer on board. He said that the previous Mate had forgotten to send the recall telegrams to get everybody back for sailing and volunteered to organise that for me so I agreed. It also meant he could get a couple of pints in while he was ashore but I didn't mind.

I wandered around the ship and found the duty seaman and the engineer sitting on the afterdeck drinking tea. They reckoned everything was going fine and the cargo would finish by nine o'clock and we had to wait until midnight for the tide. I asked about the ballast water and was assured it was all out and anyway the engineers looked after that side of things. I then had to worry about exactly how much cargo we had to load and where to load it to keep the ship on an even keel. I was desperately trying to remember the formula to calculate how to trim the ship when a shore foreman appeared looking for a cup of tea. When I asked how much cargo we had to load and where were we going to put it he shook his head and said we didn't bother with calculations but just poured it into the holds until it looked right and assured me it always worked. We were supposed to sail one foot deeper at the stern than the bow so when we used fuel from the back on the trip we would be on an even keel going up the Thames.

As everyone seemed so laid back I began to relax and wandered up to the bridge to check the equipment out. It was like going back fifty years. There was no auto-pilot and the helmsman had to steer by the points of the compass on an old magnetic compass in the middle of the wheel house. The only way to take bearings was to use an instrument called a pelorus on the bridge wing combined with the ship's magnetic course. This was really going back to basics. At least there was radar which seemed a pretty good model. I was still looking around when the steward appeared to say the evening meal was ready. I was the only one and I ambled into the saloon in my shirt sleeves. The steward, kitted out in a white jacket, served a delicious meal by silver service. I felt distinctly underdressed. When I asked he said that everyone wore full uniform at meals and when on duty. It seemed way over the top for a ship carrying coal but I thought I would go along with it.

After the meal I dug out the ship's stability information ready to calculate where to put the final part of the cargo so we would be correctly trimmed. I was just going out on deck when the foreman appeared and said there was about 200 tons to go and if we put 170 into the back of number three hold and the remainder into the centre of number one it would be spot on. I told him I'd like to check myself and he didn't seem to mind so I ran around like a headless chicken for quarter of an hour taking drafts and doing endless calculations and came to the conclusion that if we put 170 tons into the back of number three and the rest into number one it would be about right. It took an hour to load the final cargo and it turned out exactly right. We finished loading about nine o'clock so then I had to get the ship ready for sea. I was going to help the seaman close and batten the hatches but he insisted that the other crew would do that when they came back. By eleven I was getting quite nervous and none of the crew or the officers had appeared but nobody else seemed bothered. At about quarter past eleven a couple of taxis arrived and disgorged six or seven people who promptly disappeared below to reappear in working gear and start closing hatches and battening the ship down for sea. It was all done in twenty minutes by which time the Old Man had come on board with the remaining officers. I introduced myself and the Old Man signed me on the articles and five minutes later we sailed.

As there were only two mates we had to work six hours on/six hours off and as soon as we cleared the breakwaters I found myself alone on watch trying to figure out where we were and in which direction to head. As I was putting the position on the chart the helmsman stuck his head in the chartroom and asked, "Will east-south-east a quarter east be all right?" I said it should be about right and frantically tried to convert my course in degrees into points of the compass. Needless to say the helmsman was exactly right! I began to feel slightly redundant.

On all my previous ships the bridge was at least fifty feet above the water which meant the horizon was about twelve miles away. Here we were only fifteen feet above the water so we were lucky to see six miles from the top of a big wave. It felt really odd when we passed close to buoys as we looked up at them and they seemed huge.

It was really peaceful and quiet on the bridge, though, as the engines were aft and the only noise was from the radar. At three o'clock the relief helmsman appeared complete with a tray of sandwiches and a pot of tea. This was very civilised.

The rest of the watch went quickly with the helmsmen entertaining me with tales of other colliers and various disasters. The Second Mate, Jimmy Day, appeared at six o'clock to relieve me so after a quick chat I went down below to turn in. I slept like a log until eleven o'clock when the steward woke me with a bacon sandwich and a cup of tea. I suddenly realised that I hadn't given the crew any jobs for the day so quickly showered and dressed and went off in search of the Bosun. I found him and the duty seaman overhauling the wheels on one of the hatches. He said they had to splice a couple of new mooring wires before we got to London and as he obviously knew more about the jobs than I did I left him to it.

The accommodation was split into two with the Old Man, two mates and the radio officer living midships under the bridge and everyone else living aft. The galley was aft but the eating saloon was midships which meant all the food had to be carried along the deck. This was not the best idea in bad weather with waves breaking over the deck but we always seemed to get delicious hot food regardless. I wandered back to my cabin and put my uniform on and went into the saloon for an early lunch. After the meal I went up to the bridge to take over the watch. Jimmy had both wheelhouse doors wide open and there was a gale blowing through. He explained that unless both doors were kept open at meal times the windows steamed up because of the hot air coming up from the pantry. I thought he was joking but sure enough when I tried to close the doors within a couple of minutes we couldn't see out. He said it was all right in summer!

After lunch the Old Man came up to see how we were getting along. He was a real character and like nearly everyone else on board had spent all his life on colliers. I asked why we still used compass points instead of degrees and he said they had always used compass points and why change something if it worked. I had no answer to that one. He went on to explain my duties which were very few. The main one was to keep the coal fired boiler in the accommodation supplied with fuel because it was a bugger to light if it ever went out. He also told me I got five shillings every time we went up the Thames for 'flattening out' everything so we could get under the bridges and we also got £2 a month uniform allowance so we had to wear our uniforms to prove the money was well spent. After he left I went to check the ship's position and found the helmsman had altered course in the right place without being told and was already on the correct new course. It seemed everything was automatic!

I spent the rest of my afternoon watch trying to negotiate my way through a huge fleet of herring drifters which had nets extending out to nearly a mile. Life certainly wasn't boring on these little ships.

The next morning I was on watch as we wended our way up the Thames Estuary and the Old Man let me do the piloting up to Tilbury where the river starts to narrow. There was a reporting station at Tilbury for the colliers and as we passed we got our orders as to which power station to go to and any other relevant information. Our instructions were, "Nine Lemons for two and no juice," which translated into Nine Elms Power Station for two tides and we weren't fueling this time. I stayed up on the bridge for the trip up the river. We picked up a mud pilot at Gravesend to take us up through the bridges. Without any instructions the crew appeared on deck and began lowering the masts and opening the hatches and removing any object that projected higher than the bridge top. It was all done in half an hour and I'd earned my first five bob without raising a finger!

In those days there was no Port Control with the VHF radio blaring out information and instructions every five minutes. Everybody abided by the Rule of the Road and it seemed to me to work really smoothly. We went up the river on a rising tide so we seemed to scoot along. The trip had to be timed to perfection as we would go aground if we were too early and worse if we were late we would stick under a bridge. There were also the variations in the tide to consider and if it had been raining a lot the river could be higher than predicted. The Old Man and the mud pilot were checking the tidal height on boards as we progressed up the river and constantly adjusted our speed. I was way out of my depth so I left them to it.

It seemed no time before we were into the centre of London and passing under Tower Bridge which didn't need to open for us. As we passed through the Pool of London we started to meet the empty colliers coming down after discharging and we had some interesting moments avoiding a tug and string of barges trying to turn around in the middle of the river. There were eleven bridges to navigate going up to Nine Elms and as we went under the last bridge I could touch the underside of the arch as we shot through.

As soon as we berthed they started discharge with grabs on shore cranes and in six hours they had discharged us. By this time the tide had gone out and we were left sitting on the mud. We waited another three hours until the tide lifted us off the bottom and then we sailed just before midnight back down the river. It was even more impressive going down in the dark with all the shore lights. I was warned to stay inside the wheelhouse as we passed under bridges as late night revellers thought it good fun to drop empty bottles on us as we went through. There were always a couple of broken bottles to sweep up next day. About two in the morning we cleared the last bridge and the crew appeared to raise the masts and batten the ship down and I had the job of raising the radar scanner and making sure the radio aerials were hoisted correctly. An hour later we dropped the mud pilot at Gravesend and the Old Man left me on my own to take the ship out of the river and to sea. I really enjoyed it though I had a hard time working out the courses in points and quarter points but the helmsman kept me right. Jimmy, the Second Mate, appeared at six to relieve me so I had a shower and a bacon buttie and went to bed.

It was quite an odd life on the colliers as they never found out which ports they were going to until the last minute. When I got up at lunch time everyone was wandering about with long faces as the instruction had come through to do a quick load in Sunderland and sail on the next tide. Everybody hoped for at least two days loading so they could get home for a while. The only bright side seemed to be that most of the crew lived in or near Sunderland. It was my turn to be off but there was no way I could get home to Carlisle and back in the time so I told Jimmy Day I would start the loading for him if he wanted to nip home. We arrived in Sunderland just in time to catch the tide and berthed at eleven o'clock at night. I couldn't believe how quickly the off duty crew got off the boat. Five minutes after we tied up I was left having a mug of tea with the night watchman and the duty engineer and the ship all shut down for the night. A shore foreman wandered over and shouted that we wouldn't start cargo until the morning so I went to bed not forgetting to bank up the central heating boiler.

I was woken up next morning by a loud crashing and banging as they started loading the coal. I was amazed as they locked the full railway wagons onto a sort of cradle and then just turned it upside down and the coal poured down a chute into the hold. They started off at a great rate and I could see us finishing before lunch time but there were long delays while they moved the empty wagons into sidings and brought in full ones.

132

Jimmy appeared with the morning papers just after nine and as I didn't know Sunderland very well I told him he could go home again and to come back for the end of loading about five. I didn't need to tell him twice. He came back again about two in the afternoon and suggested I could go ashore for a drink before the pubs closed. He recommended a pub just outside the dock gates and said he'd paid for a couple of pints for me so if I mentioned his name I'd drink for free. I found the pub all right but was a really scruffy place that I would normally have avoided. It felt really menacing and unfriendly but it was Vaux's beer which I liked so I ordered a pint. The barmaid plonked it down in front of me and requested payment. I told her Jimmy Day had put a couple of pints in for me and it was like I'd flicked a switch. The whole atmosphere changed and everyone started laughing and joking again. The barmaid said they thought I was a off duty policeman as I was still wearing black uniform trousers and a white shirt under my coat. I had a really good hour in the pub and was more than slightly merry when I got back on board.

We sailed about nine in the evening of the 21st December and set off south again. It turned out to be the same as the previous run up to the Nine Elms Power Station except we were instructed to discharge quickly and sail on the next tide. It was getting close to Christmas and the sole topic of conversation going up the Thames was about whether we would have to do another run before Christmas. The general consensus was that we'd get a few days off so that looked promising but not too good for me as it was my duty and I'd be stuck on board by myself and probably have to cook my own dinner.

As we progressed up the Thames we started flattening out the masts and things. The Second Mate's job was to lower the radar into a recess but due to some oversight he tried to lower it with the scanner still turning which resulted in a graunching noise followed by a bang as the gear box seized. When we got tied up we had a look at it and the gear box was definitely knackered so we called up Decca and asked them to send a technician with a new gear box. He arrived soon but without the new box. There wasn't time to get one but the technician said his office was right beside Westminster Bridge and he would lower a new box to us when we sailed out. It seemed a great idea. We sailed an hour later and when we came around the corner there was this box hanging on a rope in the middle of the centre arch. The Bosun and I ran up to the focstle to collect it. The bloke on the bridge had gathered quite an audience, all waving and calling advice to us. The technician shouted that he needed his rope back so the Bosun and I were frantically trying to undo the knots as we went under the bridge. There was no way we were going to get the rope off so in the end the Bosun and I just hung on to the box and pulled the rope out of his hands. I think it must have hurt him quite a bit judging by the screams from the bridge. When we came out the other side we looked back and he was brandishing his fists and possibly swearing though we couldn't hear. We fitted the box in half an hour and had a working radar by the time we cleared Tower Bridge.

It turned out that it was my watch for the river passage so I was left to take us down the river from Gravesend again. As we cleared the Thames Estuary we got a message that the ship was to lay up in Sunderland on arrival and start loading at noon on the 29th December. This meant six days lying around which I wasn't looking forward to until the Old Man explained that the ship would shut down completely and I could go home for Christmas and come back to load the ship on the 29th. Life suddenly seemed good again as not only would I be at home for Christmas but on full pay. I made a R/T call home and arranged for Dad to come over and pick me up when we arrived in Sunderland. We arrived there about five o'clock in the evening. It took about an hour to secure the ship and lock everything up. Dad arrived spot on time with Diane, which was a nice surprise. I don't think he was all that impressed with the ship, though, and he felt I should be on something bigger and better but it suited me at the time.

I had a lovely Christmas though it was a bit of a panic buying presents as I hadn't even thought about that side of things. I got the train back to Sunderland early on the morning of the 29th and was back on board by about ten o'clock. I had a bit of a run around opening the hatches ready to start loading and then we had to shift the ship 300 yards along the dock to the loading berth. I thought it would be impossible with just two of us but some dockers moved our wires along and it went really smoothly. So far so good. Now all I had to do was light the bloody boiler. It was really cold in the accommodation without heating and I was getting really fed up as the boiler kept going out. I was seriously thinking of using diesel or petrol to get it going when Jimmy Day appeared. He'd been in his local having a pint and thought he'd see how I was doing. He explained the intricacies of the vents and doors and we had it roaring away in ten minutes. The cook hadn't turned up so there was nothing for lunch so I nipped up the road with Jimmy and got a huge meal of fish and chips and sat in the pub to consume it washed down with a couple of pints of Vaux's best bitter.

Life wasn't too bad at all! Jimmy organised sending the recall telegrams to everyone as I still couldn't figure that side of things. We sailed at nine in the evening slightly overloaded as I hadn't figured on the coal being wet after standing in the wagons for a week and it weighed considerably more than I expected. The Old Man didn't seem too bothered, though, because he reckoned there wouldn't be any inspectors or surveyors out at this time of year.

We had a terrible passage down to London with really strong head winds and big seas. It was like being on a submarine with the decks awash most of the time. The cook and steward did sterling work to bring our meals along the deck from the galley down aft. I don't think they ever lost anything but it was close a couple of times. We got orders to discharge in Fulham which was an extra five miles up river and two more bridges. We arrived just after lunch on 31st December and they started to discharge us before we'd actually tied up. The crane drivers wanted an early finish and they unloaded us in double quick time but we still had to wait for the next tide before we could sail.

We left at ten o'clock and it was an amazing trip down the river as hundreds of people were out celebrating the New Year. All the bridges seemed crowded with revellers and it got bloody dangerous with all the stuff being dropped onto us as we passed through the bridges. It took us ages to sweep up the broken bottles and things the next morning. We got orders to load the next cargo in Hartlepool and we got there in the early hours of the 2nd January. It was my turn to be off again and I wasn't looking forward to wandering around Hartlepool for a couple of days but there was no cargo available and they didn't intend to load until the 5th so I shot off home first thing in the morning as soon as the trains started running. I managed to get three days at home but I wasn't entirely at ease feeling I might be late back to the ship when they called but the telegram arrived early on the morning of the 5th and I rejoined with time to spare and we sailed late in the afternoon.

The weather this passage was a complete contrast with no wind and lovely blue skies though it was very cold. It was back to Nine Elms again though we took ages to unload as they only seemed to have one crane driver so we missed the tide and had to wait alongside for another twelve hours. Then it was back to Seaham again and the Old Man got a message that the regular Mate was returning so I would be paying off.

We arrived in Seaham at noon and my relief was waiting on the dock so I got straight off and caught the train home.

It had been an interesting three weeks and it was an experience I wouldn't have missed for the world. There were some real characters sailing on these boats. Ten years later the coal industry started to wind down and the collier trade got less and less and eventually stopped altogether.

CHAPTER TWENTY THREE

Tomatoes for Marks and Spencer

m.v. Golden Comet
18th January 1968 – 25th April 1968

After I'd been home a few days I came to the conclusion that Carlisle in January isn't the best place to be. I had sold my Triumph Herald to my brother and was having to rely on borrowing Dad's car which was a pain so I ended up buying a second hand mini traveller to get about. I'd also got my head around the First Mate's job and was feeling quite confident. I went over to Newcastle to see if there was anything decent on offer on the Pool but it was very quiet although there were always lots of jobs on tankers. I left my details with the clerk and then drove on to South Shields and wandered around my old haunts to see if I knew anyone. I ended up in The Locomotive and somewhat over imbibed so had to stay the night. When I got home the following day there had been a phone call from a company called Ropners offering me a job. I rang them up (reverse charge) the next morning and they were looking for a relief mate on a little refrigerated cargo boat that went down to the Canary Islands and loaded tomatoes back to Dover. They invited me over to the Head Office in Darlington for an interview and a medical. I travelled over the next day and it seemed a really nice family run company. I got the job and was put on pay even though I wasn't due to join for another ten days. I had a really good leave after that as I felt secure being on pay and my bank balance was looking pretty healthy even after buying the car.

I travelled down to Dover and joined the *Golden Comet* in Granville Dock where she was discharging boxes of tomatoes onto waiting lorries. I was very impressed as although it was only 2,000 tons and smaller than the *Thomas Livesey* she had a huge crew for her size. There were three mates which meant the work load was considerably lighter and an extra steward for the officers to clean our cabins. The ship was nice and clean too as she mainly carried foodstuffs. The Mate spent the afternoon showing me around and ran through all the paperwork. Everything seemed really well run. His wife appeared in a car and he left me to it at about five o'clock. They stopped discharging at seven in the evening and we all went ashore for a few drinks. I went back early as I was knackered after travelling down but it must have been five in the morning when most of them rolled back on board. I thought I would have trouble getting the crew to work but they all appeared on time to start work.

We finished unloading just after lunch and had to wait two hours for the tide which gave us loads of time to batten the ship down as there was quite a strong south-westerly wind blowing up the Channel. I had been warned that the ship rolled quite a lot but was totally unprepared for the movement when we cleared the breakwaters.

I thought the bloody ship was going over. She steadied up once we turned into the wind but it was really frightening for a time. Nobody else seemed bothered as they'd seen it all before so I figured if it hadn't turned over before why would it now. We bounced all the way down the Channel heading into a gale which wasn't very pleasant but when we turned the corner and headed down the Bay of Biscay that's when the boat really rolled. By the time we reached the Spanish coast I was seriously thinking of packing my hand in and getting off when we got back to Dover. The weather took a turn for the better as we cleared the Bay and the remainder of the trip down was in flat calm with lovely cloudless skies so I decided to do at least one more trip. It was a really happy ship with a nice bunch of officers and crew. The Old Man used to organise card games every night though I had to give up on these as they went on into the early hours and I wouldn't have got any sleep.

Our first port was Santa Cruz in Tenerife where we arrived at eleven o'clock in the morning on the 24th January. We had a quick survey to ensure our holds were clean and at the right temperature and started loading the crates of tomatoes straight away. The load went very quickly and by six in the evening we had loaded all the available cargo and we sailed over to Puerto de la Luz on Las Palmas to complete loading.

We berthed at about nine o'clock and there was a mad rush to get ashore. Everybody seemed to have their own favourite night club or bar so I tagged along with the Old Man and we went to a night club called the Bowler Hat which was owned and run by a couple from Bradford. It was a cracking little club with a good cabaret and decent beer and we were treated like locals so the prices were pretty good. I don't think it ever closed and by three in the morning I gave up and went back to the ship to sleep.

As in Dover most of them rolled back after five but again they were all there when we had to open the hatches to resume loading. We had a visit mid morning by the Harbour Master and some of the tomato growers. They were really interesting to listen to as they explained about the best tomatoes coming from an area on the west coast and these tomatoes always went to Marks and Spencers. They gave us a couple of crates for ourselves and they were amazingly sweet and tasty. They then all adjourned to the Captain's cabin for drinks. The loading finished about two in the afternoon but it took us until four to get the Harbour Master and his cronies off the boat. The Old Man was decidedly under the weather so I suddenly found myself unberthing the ship and taking it to sea. I managed a reasonable job without damaging anything and I really enjoyed the ship handling.

The ship was a lot better when she was loaded and the weather was still pretty good. We hit another storm in the Bay of Biscay and although we didn't roll very much I was horribly seasick. I ended up with diarrhoea as well so when we arrived at Dover I was knackered. The Old Man insisted I went to see a doctor as I was pretty much out of it. The Doctor diagnosed gastric enteritis and insisted I paid off and had some recovery time at home. Alan, the Old Man, paid me off straight away and got on to the company to organise a relief. He insisted I left all my gear on board because he wanted me back again but I felt very uneasy in case the company (Ropners) didn't want me back. Anyhow I packed my stuff up and left it on board and took the train home with a travelling bag and a large crate of Canary tomatoes.

I got home feeling slightly the worse for wear but after a couple of days I was back to normal. I was fed up of eating tomatoes, though, as Mum was determined not to waste them. Ropners phoned up after I'd been home a week and confirmed that they wanted me to rejoin and also that I was still on pay. (Not a bad life at all.) I had another week at home and I decided that as I would be based in Dover I would take my little mini traveller down with me. It was an interesting trip down as I got a bit lost and ended up travelling through the centre of London in the rush hour. I had hoped to get to Dover in one go but the London excursion added a couple of hours to the time so I stopped off in a hotel in Chatham for the night. I was very surprised in the morning when I opened the curtains and found I was looking at the Kingsnorth Power Station with the *Kingsnorth Fisher* tied up on the pier. I was half tempted to go and say hello.

I got down to Dover Docks about ten in the morning to find the ship had missed the tide and wasn't berthing until noon. I got talking to one of the dock police about where I could leave the car when we sailed and he suggested I could leave it on his drive. This worked out very well because I just left the car in the docks when we sailed and he took it home. I said he could use it so he was over the moon. The car was always waiting on the dockside when we arrived all nicely polished and full of petrol.

The *Golden Comet* berthed just after noon and the Mate who had relieved me was over the moon to see me. He was used to large tankers and had hated every minute of the trip and they had been winding him up saying I wasn't better and he'd have to do another trip. It took ten minutes for him to hand over and I gave him a lift up to the station and he was gone. He was in such a hurry that he forgot the crate of tomatoes he'd been given. Rather than waste it I went up to the station later and sent it home. Mum was going to be really sick of tomatoes.

Alan, the Old Man, was really pleased when he found I'd got a car and that evening after cargo had finished we piled into it and drove to St Margaret's Bay just outside Dover and had a fantastic meal in a restaurant on the beach. It must have been really expensive but I have no idea who paid or if we did actually pay because by the time we left we were all somewhat under the weather.

We sailed the following afternoon and this time the sea was reasonably calm and we had a decent run. We went to Las Palmas first this time, arriving in the evening of the 21st February. There was the usual mad rush to get up the road to the bars. We got talking to the owners of the Bowler Hat and they were complaining about how they couldn't get certain things locally like kippers, Marmite, Cheddar cheese, bacon, Corn Flakes and salad cream. Johnnie Baulk, the Chief Engineer, said if they made a list we would get it and bring it back with us and they thought this was brilliant. We ended up with a huge list but we said we would try. They insisted the drinks were on the house so again it was early morning before I got to bed. I was beginning to wonder whether my liver would cope.

The loading went very smoothly and we were all finished by tea time but we weren't required in Santa Cruz until eight the following morning and the passage was only three hours. Alan decided we would stay in Las Palmas for the night and sail at five in the morning so there was a mad rush up to the bars again. It was getting a bit too much for me so I had a quiet walk around the port with Johnnie, the Chief Engineer and had a couple of beers and turned in early. Surprisingly everyone was back for five in the morning and again I got the chance to unberth and take the ship to sea. It was really good experience. We had six hours in Santa Cruz finishing off loading and then it was back to Dover again.

It was a bit of a rough trip back but I was getting used to it. When we arrived in Dover we very nearly ran into a café that they were building on the end of one of the piers. We all said it was a daft place to put a café and sure enough when we returned a fortnight later it had been demolished. It appeared our sister ship, the *Silver Comet*, had run straight into it when she was entering. I don't think they tried to rebuild it.

When we were in Dover I was told that I was only doing one more trip as the permanent mate was ready to come back but they would like me to relieve the mate on the *Silver Comet* for a couple of months. This sounded good to me. I'd also met up with a few of the lads on the cross channel ferries and was thinking of giving them a go after I finished on the *Comets*. Alan, the Old Man, paid off to take some leave and a new Skipper called Alex Dekonski joined. He was a huge bully of a man and I didn't get on with him at all. Previously we had played either solo or pontoon in the evenings but he insisted on bridge. I'm not the best of players so there were always inquests into the hands afterwards. In the end we stopped playing cards and the atmosphere changed on board. At least I was getting a decent night's sleep though.

The next trip we only loaded in Las Palmas so we had two days there. The night club owners were delighted with all the food stuff we'd managed to bring them and gave us an even bigger list for the next trip. We could see this getting out of hand but at least we ate and drank for free in the Bowler Hat!

On the way back to Dover we got a telegram saying that I would be staying on board and not transferring to the *Silver Comet*. This meant I had another trip with Dekonski but at least I didn't have the hassle of packing and moving.

When we got to Dover on the 13th March we were visited by some buyers from Marks and Spencers. They were very happy with the condition of the tomatoes and were going to start shipping cucumbers as an experiment. They asked us to make sure we looked after them and report on any problems. The Chief Engineer and I checked our manuals and found out that the temperature range was a bit more critical than tomatoes and they had to have a certain humidity which we didn't think would be a problem. We said it should be OK. While we were in Dover I met up with quite a few of the officers off the cross channel ferries and really liked the sound of the way things were run so I put out some feelers and arranged to have an interview with Townsend Thoresen when we next returned. We sailed about noon on the 15th March and headed off down the Channel again. For once the weather was good and it really was a pleasant little ship to sail when we weren't being bounced around. On the way down we got a message that we had a passenger for the trip back so we had to clean and paint out the hospital cabin in preparation.

It was another full load in Las Palmas which went very easily. We picked up the consignment of about five tons of cucumbers and made sure they were well stowed. We had the usual night ashore with free booze and food at the Bowler Hat. The list of requirements was getting quite big now and they needed a van to pick everything up from the ship. It was getting out of hand as I'd feared and I'm sure it should have been declared to Customs or something. We only had a couple of hours loading the next morning and were ready to sail by noon. Our passenger turned out to be a nun from some charity who had got herself a free trip. It certainly put a curb on all the bad language on board!

Once we'd sailed we found we had a problem keeping the humidity around the cucumbers high enough and Johnnie, the Chief Engineer, came up with the idea of spraying water into the ventilators a few times a day. It seemed to work though it caused great amusement among the crew who reckoned we were trying to grow them bigger. It was good weather up to Finnisterre and then we hit a real towser of a storm. It was good that we were fully loaded because we didn't roll around as much but it was still very uncomfortable. About two in the morning we were woken up by a tremendous crashing up on the boat deck. When we got up there we found one of the lifeboats had broken adrift and was smashing itself to bits. We got some rope and wires and set to securing it. Just as we finished we turned around and found the nun standing behind us dressed only in her nightie and clutching her lifejacket. She thought we were abandoning ship and had forgotten her! She must have heard some language that nuns shouldn't hear. I went across to reassure her that everything was all right as she was naturally pretty upset. My only problem was that her nightie was soaked through and completely transparent so I had great difficulty looking her in the eye. Once she realised that things were OK she toddled off to bed quite happily totally unaware of the impression she had left on the crew. She had a remarkably good figure and I don't think any of them ever looked at a nun in the same way again.

We arrived back in Dover on the evening of the 27th March and started discharge the following morning. The buyers from Marks and Sparks appeared first thing to see how their cucumbers had fared and we told them how diligent we had been keeping the humidity correct. They gave us a funny look and one of them went ashore and returned with a cucumber. It was shrink wrapped in plastic and totally unaffected by the humidity. Bugger. Still, the buyers were impressed by our dedication.

I nipped off in the afternoon and had an interview with Townsend Thoresen which went very well and they said I could have a job whenever I liked. Things were looking good. On the way back to the ship I also looked at a fantastic flat on the sea front which had great views over the harbour. The rent was pretty reasonable too. The only problem was the landlady wanted a deposit to hold it for me and I didn't feel up to committing myself so I left hoping it would still be available when I got off the *Comet*.

When I got back I found that the Company had decided to work overtime discharging and sail us at midnight as we were a bit behind schedule. We finished at about ten o'clock and were already to sail when the Chief Engineer announced that a lube oil pump on the engine had blown up and we couldn't sail until the next day. This resulted in a mad rush ashore to the pubs by all hands.

The pump was repaired the next morning and we sailed at noon now three days behind our schedule. Alan Joel had rejoined as Skipper so the atmosphere on board improved though we had taken on a new cook who left a lot to be desired. Everything was either raw or burnt to a crisp and the Chief Steward had to go and help out otherwise there would have been a mutiny. It was a good trip down to the Canaries and we did a quick load in Las Palmas and made up a bit of time. On the way back I thought I was going mad. I bumped into the galley boy on deck and noticed he'd had a really severe hair cut which I commented on but he carried on without speaking. The next day I saw him again and this time his hair was long again which baffled me. As we were arriving in Dover I walked out on deck and was met by two galley boys – one with long hair and the other short. It turned out that the short haired one was a student who had run out of money in the Canaries and the crew had felt sorry for him and stowed him away. It appeared I was about the only person on board who didn't know. Anyhow he disappeared ashore as soon as we berthed so nobody was any the wiser.

We had another quick discharge in Dover and we sailed again ten hours later. This was to be our last trip as the tomato season was coming to an end. The load in the Canaries went really slowly as I think they were having trouble finding enough tomatoes to fill us. We took two days in both Las Palmas and Tenerife and then set off back. On the way back we got the orders for the next voyage which was to be loading frozen tuna fish in the Canaries to take to Japan. I rather liked the sound of that but they had a company mate rejoining in Dover so I had to pay off. They also got a new cook which brightened everyone up.

We berthed in Dover on the 25th April and my relief turned up mid-morning. He had been on board before so it was an easy hand over. I nipped over to the Townsend office to see what sort of jobs they had going and was told that they had just recruited some new mates and wouldn't be requiring any more for a while. I was gutted. It was just as well I hadn't put the deposit down on the flat. I went back to the *Comet* and threw my gear into the car along with yet another box of tomatoes for Mum and headed home.

CHAPTER TWENTY FOUR

Second Mate again

m.v. Kingsnorth Fisher
13th May 1968 – 28th May 1968

After my trip on the *Golden Comet* I felt I was getting the hang of the Mate's job so I decided to carry on and find another job as Mate. I also wanted to get with a decent company so after I'd been home a week I started bashing off letters to some of the better companies. I got a few replies offering me Second Mate's jobs but I decided to wait for a Mate's job. I travelled over to Newcastle to see if there was anything worth having on the Pool but nothing caught my eye. In fact there were very few jobs at all for some reason.

I spent another week at home waiting to see if anything came up. I had also decided that I needed to be on the property ladder and have my own place so I spent a lot of time looking for a house but without much success. It also became obvious that to buy a house I needed money and without a job there was a decided lack of the same so I nipped over to the Pool again to see if there was anything of interest. It was worse than before with even fewer vacancies. While I was there I noticed that they needed a Second Mate on the *Kingsnorth Fisher* but didn't give it much thought. When I was home again I got to thinking that if I went back on the *Kingsnorth Fisher* as Second Mate I would soon be promoted to Mate again so I rang them up and they said if I could be in Glasgow the next day the job was mine.

I had a mad panic packing my things and saying a quick goodbye to Diane and caught the train up to Glasgow next morning. The ship was berthed at Plantation Quay and getting ready to load a huge transformer for the Kingsnorth Power Station. The Old Man was Tom Tyson who had relieved me as Mate so he'd been promoted very quickly. Most of the other crew and engineers were the same so it was nice to be back.

The loading went slowly as the transformer was so big we only just got it on board. It took us ages to get it securely lashed and we sailed in the early hours. It was odd being Second Mate again as I seemed to have nothing to do and no responsibilities. The trip down to the Medway went well with good weather all the way. We were supposed to discharge on arrival at the Kingsnorth Power Station but we were a bit late and in the hurry to get the load off before the tide went out we had all sorts of problems. One of the towing lorries broke a half shaft and then the load loader had a puncture and in the end we had to get off the berth quickly before we got stuck on the mud. We then had to tie up at another berth to await the next tide. We got it off all right the next time and sailed straight away for North Shields. We dropped the pilot at the entrance to the River Medway and I took the ship out of the Thames Estuary. I felt I was getting to be an expert by now and by coincidence we met the *Thomas Livesey* in the Barrow Deep Channel. It looked really low in the water compared to us and I could see Jimmy Day, the Second Mate, on the bridge.

We berthed on arrival in North Shields in the Albert Edward Dock and loaded a large turbine from Parsons. It was for Pembroke Dock beside Milford Haven and it was required urgently so we sailed again as soon as there was enough water to leave. The weather was fantastic with blue skies and light winds. I really enjoyed navigating round the English coast when the weather was like that. Pembroke Dock was a pain as we had to put all sorts of extra wires out to hold the ship in position. Luckily Dave, the Mate, had been there before so he knew how things went. It took longer tying the ship up than it did to unload the turbine and we were soon on our way back to North Shields. Again the weather was good and we had a lovely run back arriving at noon on Sunday the 26th May. A few of us nipped up to the local for a couple of pints and on the way back I decided I'd phone home just to see how things were.

Dad said that a company called Headlams had been ringing offering me a Mate's job on one of their ships but they wanted me immediately. I went back on board and the Old Man said he'd pay me off the next day if I wanted as there were no orders for the ship. So first thing Monday morning I phoned up Headlams to see if the job was still going and luckily it was. They gave me the job over the phone there and then. It appeared that they worked closely with Ropners and they had recommended me.

I went back on board and Tom got straight onto Fishers to organise my relief. When he came back he said that Fishers had been going to promote me back to Mate again in the next fortnight but I had already accepted the Headlams job. Actually I really wanted to go deep sea again so I paid off the following morning and headed home stopping off in Newcastle to buy some uniform. I had two days at home to pack all my gear and say goodbye to Diane. I managed to sell my car to my brother, Peter; it seemed to be getting to be a habit. I also invested in a top of the range short wave radio to take away with me. It was second hand and I'd seen it in the White Elephant Shop in Carlisle on my previous leave but they wanted far too much for it. When I went in to look at it again the proprietor offered me it at half price just to get rid of it. I couldn't resist especially as I'd got a bit of money in the bank. The shopkeeper then produced a purpose made carrying box with several manuals listing radio stations, and a huge dipole aerial with yards of wire which was all part of the deal. I was over the moon though I did have some problems later when it came to join and leave ships as it was so big and awkward to carry.

CHAPTER TWENTY FIVE

A year tramping the oceans!

m.v. Egton
30th May 1968 – 12th July 1969

I joined the *Egton* as Mate in Greenwell Dry Dock in Sunderland where she was undergoing a refit. There was only the Old Man, Willie Watson, and two engineers on board as the rest were due to join a week later. Willie was a great character who had been a Skipper in Palm Line for a number of years but had been made redundant when the company fell on hard times. He had the worst pair of legs I've ever seen on anyone. They were very short and all hairy and lumpy with varicose veins everywhere. He insisted on wearing shorts whenever possible so they always seemed to be on show. I found out later that he'd been known as 'Table Legs Watson' in Palm which I thought very funny.

As there were no catering staff we had all our meals in the Dock Manager's canteen and lived the high life for a while. We would wander over for breakfast about nine o'clock and sit down to a huge English breakfast with all the trimmings. Lunch was another lovely table with at least three courses and we got a bottle of beer or glass of wine with the evening meal. Needless to say we didn't get much work done and were somewhat miffed when our crew joined and we had to eat on board again. Actually the ship's cook was pretty good as it turned out but it was still a bit of a come down. The deck crew were all Somalis and I was a little concerned as to how I would get on with them but they turned out to be a happy-go-lucky bunch though when we finally paid off over a year later the work rate had slowed drastically which was to be expected. We undocked on the 10th June and lay alongside for engine trials and to take on stores. There were all sorts of rumours about where we would be trading but by the amount of stores that we took on board it looked as though we would be away for quite a while. Eventually we were told that we were sailing to Antwerp the following day and we would find out there what was happening. It was worse than the Secret Service! We got to

Antwerp the following day and found we had been chartered to a Belgian Company for a trip down to West Africa and back. It turned out that the company had originally chartered one of their other ships (*Runswick*) but she had collided with a lock somewhere and done some serious damage so we were first reserve.

Willie, the Old Man, having been with Palm Line for years, knew West Africa like the back of his hand so it was nice for me to have an expert on board when there were problems. It was fantastic to be loading general cargo again – supervising the stowage and keeping cargo plans. We had a liaison officer assigned to us to help with any other problems. He was a Belgian Second Mate called Dirk with an unpronounceable second name who turned out to be a cracking bloke. He took us to some terrific bars in the back streets of Antwerp. I often went looking for them when I went back there but never found them. He took a couple of us to his home for a meal one evening. He lived right out in the country in a fantastic old farmhouse where he kept poultry and pigs. I don't think he wanted to go to sea but the farm wasn't big enough to support his family. As it got dark he insisted we all stood outside with our drinks and we were treated to this amazing sight of all his hens flying vertically twenty feet up into a pine tree to roost for the night. He said they always did it and they were hilarious when they jumped down in the morning when he took their feed out.

The loading went very well and we were complimented on our professionalism by the Belgians which boosted my ego a bit. The cargo consisted of crates of machinery and plant and tons of tinned food and baby milk which seemed a bit odd to me. We also took quite a few John Deere tractors and about ten new cars. One of them was a Fiat 850 Sport Coupe which I got a chance to drive along the quay. I thought it was a fantastic little car and came to the conclusion that I'd buy one if ever I got the chance. We completed loading in eight days and sailed on the 20th June. We had quite a pleasant trip down. I spent a couple of days erecting the aerial for my new radio and was amazed by the quality of the reception when I switched it on. I could now get the BBC World Service anywhere in the world.

Our first port was Boma which was about fifty miles up the River Congo. We only had a few hours here to unload some food and baby milk which was urgently needed. We finished the cargo operations late in the evening but we had to wait until daylight to sail as we were going another forty miles up the Congo to a port called Matadi

149

and most of the navigational aids on the river were unoperational. The Belgians had recently given the Congo its independence and the Congolese had stopped maintaining the lights and buoys so it was interesting to say the least. The local pilot was amazing and did a terrific job taking us up the river without touching the bottom once. The Old Man had promised him a couple of bottles of whisky as a bonus but he wouldn't give him them until we had tied up in case he started drinking there and then. As soon as he got the whisky he did just that and didn't stop until he finished both bottles after which he lay down and went to sleep in a corner of the saloon.

The unloading went really quickly as it was mainly large crates that went straight onto railway wagons and the rest, mainly tinned food, went into large warehouses where it was guarded by the army. When we went ashore we found a queue of locals behind the sheds waiting to buy the tins of food from the soldiers!

We finished the discharge in four days and then started to load. We started off loading ingots of copper which would be made into copper wire. They were pretty big and it took two people to move one. I found out later that each ingot was worth over £200. In the charter it said that the officers from the ship had to count and check the number of ingots in each railway wagon before they were loaded. It was a right pain as the ingots were just thrown in and there were about eighty in each wagon. We got really fed up and I'm sure the Second Mate used to climb into the wagon and smoke a fag and pretend to count. We found quite a few wagons with fewer ingots than stated on the tally much to the annoyance of the shippers who always argued the point. Once we'd loaded all the ingots they brought in huge bales of rubber to fill up the rest of the space. The bales were made up of sheets of rubber squashed into a cube about five foot square and secured with metal bands. They must have weighed over a ton each. The stevedores were supposed to put a rope sling around each bale to load it but they preferred the easier way of putting a hook under the metal band. This was all right unless the band parted which they often did resulting in the bale bouncing off the ship and the quay destroying everything it hit. It was quite spectacular but extremely dangerous. We all kept well out of the way when the bales were in the air. The loading of the copper and rubber took about ten days and we sailed off down the River Congo to Boma again.

We discharged a bit more cargo here and loaded crates of wood veneers. While we were loading we were taken up into town for a meal and a tour of the mill that produced the veneers. The machinery was amazing. They put huge logs of mahogany and other exotic woods into the machine which took a thin slice of the wood off as the log was rolled – a bit like a giant pencil-sharpener. The veneer was then cut into six foot squares and packed in crates. The grain on the wood looked fantastic and the smell of it being cut was unbelievable. I really enjoyed the tour apart from nearly standing on a giant centipede which I understood could give a nasty bite! We were then taken to a scruffy looking café for lunch which was 'palm oil chop'. Willie, the Old Man, used to rave about this dish so he was over the moon to be offered it. The 'chop' is really a chicken stew cooked in palm oil with yams and mangoes and some pretty hot spices. It has to be eaten with copious amounts of cold beer or gin and tonics. They just about had to carry us back on board as we were so full and the alcohol didn't help.

We sailed on the 22nd July down to Lobito in Angola. Life was completely different here as Angola was run by the Portuguese. The port operated extremely efficiently and the infrastructure seemed to work really well. We could walk about ashore without feeling threatened. We discharged the last of the cargo from Belgium including the lovely little Fiat coupe which I managed to drive around the dock to the car park.

We then moved across the dock and loaded 2000 tons of bulk zinc ore. Willie was really nervous about carrying this as it contained a lot of moisture and as the ship vibrated on the passage the liquid would come to the surface and form slurry. This could make the ship very unstable in bad weather. In the end it had quite a low moisture content and it settled down nicely. Once the ore was loaded we moved back across the dock and loaded the rest of the cargo. This time it was bags of peanuts, drums of palm oil, bales of coconut fibres and packages of exotic hard woods. Willie reckoned overall the cargo was worth millions of pounds.

We had quite a few trips up into town as there were some really good bars and restaurants. My favourite meal was piri piri prawns accompanied by a cold bottle of Portuguese white wine called Lagosta. It only cost a couple of pounds and then we'd walk back to the ship along the seafront stopping off for one or two more cold beers on the way. It was a hard life! We met up with a Scotsman there who was trying to set up a distillery to make whisky. He was producing 100 bottles a week and I gather it was pretty good whisky. The only problem was it was still clear like gin as he was waiting for some old port wine casks to mature it in and would give it the brown colour. None of our lot cared what colour it was.

We eventually sailed from Lobito on the 31st July and headed back to Antwerp arriving there on the 15th August. The unloading went really smoothly and the charterers were over the moon with the condition of the cargo. They were amazed that we had the right number of copper ingots. Ships usually arrived with at least a couple of hundred short which at over £200 a go started to add up. Some of their superintendents came on board to find out how we'd managed it and when we said we had counted all the ingots in the wagons they couldn't believe it. They reckoned none of the other ships had bothered so we got brownie points for that. We'd also spent time ensuring the crates of veneers were stowed properly so they were all in good condition. We were taken out for a slap up meal just before we sailed and I was given a bonus of £500 so Willie must have done all right as well. They said they were trying to recharter us but in the end the company had already organised the next charter and couldn't get out of it. It was a pity because I'd really enjoyed working general cargo again instead of carrying bulk grain etc. We had Dirk again as liaison officer and he took us into Antwerp a couple of times to his favourite bars so in all we had a magic time there. The news came through that our next cargo was to be grain so I had a mad panic about getting the hatches clean enough but it turned out that the Belgians had to redeliver the ship in clean condition so the last day was spent with shore labour swarming all over us cleaning the holds until they were spotless.

Our next orders were to load wheat in France for Japan so I was certainly going to see the world this trip. We sailed on the 22nd August to La Pallice which was a little port beside La Rochelle on the Bay of Biscay. On the way we had to rig up shifting boards in a couple of the holds. These were portable walls that stopped the grain moving around when we rolled. I had all sorts of problems as half the bits were missing and we had to bodge it up. I was sure the surveyor in France would fail it. In the end they just started loading without even checking to see if the holds were clean. The loading went really slowly. They started work at seven in the morning and loaded until one o'clock then had two hours for lunch and came back for another hour and then went home. We also had the weekends off so we led rather a relaxed life. The local agent reckoned that the wheat was all that was left of last year's harvest and they were emptying all the silos around about ready for this season's harvest. La Pallice was about three miles from La Rochelle so we used to wander up into town of an evening and have a few beers beside the marina and watch the world go by. We noticed one little bar where everyone sat outside and it was always full so we decided to see why it was so popular. It turned out that it was on a really bad road junction and there was at least one crash every night and the entertainment was to watch the French drivers shouting at each other. I must admit it was quite entertaining and they were usually only minor dents.

After ten days we had just about finished loading when the Chief Engineer announced he was having a problem with the main engine. They had decided to overhaul one of the cylinders and couldn't get the large nut on top of the piston undone. It turned out that it was a lefthand thread and they had spent two days hammering it the wrong way until they noticed. It was completely solid and he daren't leave it like that in case we had to undo it at sea sometime. We had to call in some shore workers from the local shipyard and in the end they had to burn the nut off so we had to get a new one sent from the UK. The result was that we had to sit in harbour for another four days after we'd finished loading. I don't think the company was all that impressed.

We eventually sailed on the 11th September and headed off round the Cape of Good Hope to Japan. They obviously weren't in a hurry for the grain as it would have taken twenty days less if we'd gone via Suez but in the end it took over six weeks with a twelve hour stop at Durban for fuel and fresh stores. We got instructions to discharge to whole cargo at Hakata which is a tiny port on the west coast of the island of Kyushu. It was mainly a fishing port and it was like going back in time twenty years. Most of the buildings were wooden and the sanitation left a lot to be desired.

The discharge went very slowly as they unloaded using canvas slings directly into lorries. We didn't have much of a time there as there was very little entertainment and most of the bars had 'Japanese Only' signs on the doors and we were only tolerated in the others. A couple of the lads went for a tour of Nagasaki, which was close by, and came back quite depressed at all the devastation the atomic bomb had created. We eventually sailed after twelve days and the only good things I remember were: I'd spent very little money, we'd taken on some very palatable local beer and the Japanese had left the ship spotless so I didn't have to organise any hatch cleaning. The company didn't have another charter for us so we were told to head down to Singapore to await instructions. It really was a mystery tour.

When we got to Singapore we spent a day loading fresh stores and taking on fuel. We also caught up on all our mail from home which brightened us up a bit. We then had to anchor outside the port to avoid harbour dues so we didn't get a chance to go ashore as we'd hoped because Singapore was a really lively place for a night out. The following morning a little boat came alongside with a parcel for the Old Man. It contained our next charter and some charts of East Africa and the port of Lourenco Marques. It appeared we were going there to load a full cargo of coal for Japan. I didn't even know they had coal mines in Mozambique. We heaved up the anchor and set off. I remember we were all fed up as we'd spent the evening answering our letters from home and we sailed off and didn't get a chance to post them and it was another ten days or so to LM.

It actually took a few days longer as we had all sorts of problems with the main engine. It was the same Doxford engine that was fitted in the *Baxtergate* and we were forever breaking down. Luckily the weather was really good across the Indian Ocean and the Somali crew were keen fishermen and were straight out with their lines as soon as we stopped. They caught quite a lot of good eating fish which brightened up the menu on more than one occasion. My radio came into its own on this passage as Willie was an avid cricket fan and there was a test match between Australia and England he was desperate to hear. The BBC used to open up new frequencies and broadcast the commentaries live but they were notoriously difficult to receive. My radio picked them up brilliantly so I ended up with Willie camped in my dayroom for most of the day. I didn't mind as he had an endless supply of cold beer which kept me happy

We eventually berthed in LM on the 29th November and started loading coal using grabs on shore cranes. The loading was pretty slow as, although they worked round the clock, there were big delays waiting for the trains bringing the coal to arrive. I quite enjoyed my time there as it was a very pleasant place to go ashore and it felt safe as it was still run by the Portuguese. I found a great little restaurant attached to a San Miguel brewery. I would wander up of an evening and have a large plate of piri piri prawns washed down with a jug of ice cold beer. Very civilised.

I think the coal was pretty high quality as there was very little dust and it was really hard and shiny. They finished loading after eleven days and we sailed early in the morning of the 11th December. Just as we cleared the port I was walking around the deck checking to see everything was secure when I noticed a lot of fumes coming from the funnel. I glanced down the engine room skylight and was amazed to see the top of the engine engulfed in flames. I ran up to the bridge to tell Willie and we phoned the engine room to find out what was going on and the Fourth Engineer was making coffee on the bottom plates totally unaware that the whole top of the engine room was ablaze. Once he'd stopped the engine we managed to put it out quite quickly as it was starved of fuel but it had done a lot of damage. Luckily we were just outside the port and we dropped the anchor to sort things out. It took nearly three days before we got everything repaired and were able to set off across the Indian Ocean again. We staggered our way along and I was sure we would end up being towed but we managed to get to Singapore somehow. Here we were able to get the proper spare parts and the company sent out a gang of local engineers and they spent three days repairing and overhauling the engine. Again we were anchored off the port and couldn't get ashore which was a real pity as we were there for New Year's Day.

We sailed again on the 3rd January and it was good to be charging along at full speed without clouds of black smoke coming from the funnel. We discharged the coal in four different ports: Kinuura, Yokosuka, Yokohama and Kawasaki in Japan so we didn't get ashore much as we only had a couple of days in each. They were on the main island of Honshu so were much more modern than our previous ports and had duty free shops and really swish, but very expensive, nightclubs. We got a really good rate of exchange so I went mad and bought a top of the range camera with two extra lenses. I also got myself new zoom binoculars, a digital clock, two tea sets and a cassette player so in the end I think I only got to one nightclub which was a rip off though I remember the hostesses were very pretty.

We sailed from Japan on the 25th January and headed off for the west coast of Canada. For some reason Willie decided to steer a great circle instead of the direct route. He reckoned it would be quicker and the weather would be a lot better. We ended up close to the Aleutian Islands and Alaska in some of the worst weather ever. It was freezing cold with a howling gale and even thick fog. The water was forming ice all over the deck so we couldn't work outside. I remember passing

155

some little boats fishing for crabs miles from anywhere and thinking they certainly earned their money.

It was a great relief to berth in Vancouver only to find that the surveyor failed all the hatches because of coal dust. We spent the first few days washing all the holds out again until the surveyor was happy. We then moved across the dock and loaded bulk sulphur in two of the hatches. It must be the worst cargo in the world as the dust gets in your eyes and stings like hell. The stevedores gave us milk to wash our eyes as water just made it worse. Once the sulphur was levelled off in the holds it was covered with plastic sheets and we started loading packaged timber on top. Life got a lot more pleasant once we'd washed all the sulphur dust off but in the back of our minds was the fact we had to discharge it again. All the cargo was destined for East Africa so it would probably take ages to unload.

After a week in Vancouver we loaded in several small ports in British Columbia. It was all package timber with the exception of 1000 tons of saltpetre in bulk which we loaded in Chemainus on Vancouver Island. I was a bit worried as somewhere in my mind I remembered that you made explosives by mixing saltpetre and sulphur. We had about 4,000 tons on board so if I was right it would have made a pretty good bang. No one else seemed worried so maybe it was just me.

It took us nearly a month to load finishing up with sheets of plywood in Longview in the States. The authorities wouldn't allow us ashore in Longview as Willie had forgotten to apply for visas. It was a bit of a pain but the Padre from the Seaman's Mission did a shopping run for us so we had enough toothpaste and razor blades for the month long trip. We got away from Longview on the 1st March and this time Willie, having learnt his lesson, headed well south as soon as we cleared the coast and we had a really pleasant run across the Pacific. We had a quick stop for fuel in Singapore and then off across the Indian Ocean.

The engine was starting to play up again and we were broken down for over twenty four hours right in the middle. For something to do I lowered the lifeboat and went for a cruise around the ship with the Electrician. The bloody engine packed in about half a mile from the ship and I thought the two of us were going to have to row back but we got it going again. While the ship was still broken down the Radio Officer announced that he'd been in contact with the company's only other ship, the *Runswick*, and she was also broken

156

down about twenty miles away. I bet there was some muttering in head office that day.

Our first port was Mombasa where we spent a day discharging the plywood before heading south down the coast. We were intercepted by a British warship which was blockading Rhodesia to prevent any cargo being landed for them. When they saw we were British they gave us a wave and went on their way. Our next port was Beira in Mozambique and we unloaded the timber directly onto lorries. We later found out the lorries were going straight to Rhodesia. After that it was on to Lourenco Marques again for six days so I managed to have some more meals of prawns. I also got given a case of Mateus Rose wine which I fully intended to take home but once I tasted a bottle....

We discharged the last of the timber in Lourenco Marques so all we had left was the sulphur and the saltpetre which we had to discharge in Durban. We had a miserable ten days there while they unloaded the sulphur. I found out that some of it was going to a gunpowder factory which didn't brighten my mood. Willie had some relatives in Durban so he disappeared on arrival and turned up again when we were cleaning the ship. The charterers employed shore labour so at least there wasn't sulphur dust blowing everywhere when we sailed.

We sailed on the 8th May and set off for South America. It turned out that Willie had known what our next voyage was for a week and forgotten to mention it. He wasn't too popular, though when he told us we were loading for Avonmouth we all brightened up. Our first loading port was Rosario so I envisaged us being there for three weeks loading but they had built a state of the art loading conveyor and they loaded us with 10,000 tons of oil seed expellers in three days. At least it meant we'd be getting home sooner. The expellers were the fibre that remained after they had removed the oil and it was used in animal feed and dog biscuits and things. I had a wander up to check out my old haunts from when I'd been here on the *Clearton* but it had all changed and there was a rather nice restaurant where my local bar had been. Willie and I had a lovely steak meal there one evening. It was then down to Buenos Aires where we spent three days loading bags of bone meal which absolutely stank. We were glad to batten the hatches down and sail.

It was a three week trip up the Atlantic and it seemed to take for ever. There wasn't much work we could do either as we had run out of paint. We were supposed to get some in Durban but it never turned up. We spent the time overhauling all the cargo blocks and oiling the wires. We arrived off Avonmouth on the 28th June but had to anchor off for five days waiting for a berth. We had also run out of beer at this stage so it was a rubbish few days. When we did eventually berth I found I had to stay on another week as they couldn't find a relief for me. I was beginning to think I never get off. My relief turned up on the 11th July and I phoned home and Dad travelled down in the car to pick me up. I don't think he could believe how much stuff I had accumulated but I had been away nearly fourteen months. It was my first proper trip as Mate and I'd enjoyed it.

CHAPTER TWENTY SIX

A long leave and I join Ropners

m.v. Romanby
15th September 1969 – 11th November 1969

It was nice to be home again and as I was now on Mate's wages I was starting to accumulate a nice little nest egg. I began to think about settling down and buying a house but first things first. I needed a brand shiny new car to pose in. I really wanted a new Mini Cooper, which was the car to have, so I was straight down town to see what I could get. The Citadel Garage said they could get me exactly what I wanted in a couple of days at a good price so I put my order in. After a week or so with me chasing them every day they finally admitted they couldn't get me one and all they could offer was a Fiat 850 Coupe like the one I'd carried on the *Egton*. I couldn't believe my luck – there was even a choice of colours and two days later I was driving around in my brand new sports car.

After I'd been home a couple of weeks I got a phone call from the previous company, Headlams, and they had rechartered the *Egton* to trade down to West Africa again and would I like to rejoin tomorrow? It was tempting but not as tempting as another month's leave with Diane and driving the Fiat around.

I had six weeks leave and then I got a phone call from Ropners who operated the *Golden Comet* and had recommended me for the *Egton*. They needed a Mate for the *Romanby* which was going to be away for only a couple of months. It sounded good to me – it was nice to be wanted – and they also gave me an improved rate of pay. I joined the *Romanby* in Glasgow where she was finishing off discharging grain at the Meadowside Berth. A couple of days later on the 18th September we sailed to load a cargo of phosphate in Dakar, Senegal. The company were trying to sell the ship and this was just to fill in time while they found a buyer.

The *Romanby* was a great ship to work – everything seemed to work well and she was very easy to load with four large hatches. I knew a couple of the officers from the *Golden Comet* so I felt quite at home. It took a week to get down to Dakar and we were straight alongside and started loading. We had a bit of trouble getting the water ballast pumped out as they loaded very quickly but we managed and we sailed twenty hours later with 14,000 tons of phosphate on board. Then it was back up to the Bristol Channel to Avonmouth where we berthed on arrival and started discharge. It took a week to unload and then we shifted to a layby berth and spent a week cleaning the ship up. We were tied up beside a Spillers factory and when we went ashore we walked between conveyors carrying their Shapes dog biscuits to be packed. They smelt quite really and I was tempted to have a nibble.

After we finished cleaning the ship there was a rumour that we'd have to do another trip as they still hadn't found a buyer. A couple of days later a Greek company confirmed that they wanted to buy her so most of the crew were paid off and we just hung around trying to look busy until the sale went through. I took the opportunity to nip home one weekend and pick up the Fiat and Diane and take them back down. Diane stayed a couple of days before returning to Carlisle with bottles of scrumpy and some Cheddar cheese.

After another ten days we put the ship in dry dock so the Greeks could inspect her properly. They were happy so we all paid off on the 11th November and I loaded my car and set off home, complete with the ship's brass bell off the bridge as it was now redundant. The old *Romanby* was to be re-named *Sally*.

CHAPTER TWENTY SEVEN

A hectic leave and my one and only tanker

m.v. Border Hunter
21st December 1969 – 7th January 1970

I travelled home from Avonmouth in my little Fiat loaded down with all sorts of goodies. Ropners kept their ships well stocked with equipment so when the *Romanby* was sold to the Greeks we all filled boxes with any useful tools we could lay our hands on. I ended up with a huge range of spanners and sockets and woodworking tools. I also found a spirit level which is as much use on a ship as a chocolate fire guard. Mal MacLean, the Third Mate, lived in north of Scotland and also had his car in Avonmouth so we travelled up in convoy. He stayed with me for a couple of days to break his journey north so we had a good night out in Carlisle.

I had come to the conclusion that I needed to put down roots so being extremely romantic I asked Diane to marry me and when she said yes we set about looking for a house. I don't know how we did it but in three weeks we managed to buy a house, get all the furniture and carpets and arrange the wedding. In the middle of this Ropners phoned up and offered me a contract as Chief Officer on a really good rate of pay. The only problem was they wanted me to join a ship in Antwerp the following day! When I explained the situation the personnel manager was very understanding and said as long as I signed the contract they would leave me at home for another three weeks until mid-December. They also put me on pay straight away which helped as the bank balance was decreasing at a rate of knots.

We got married on the 6th December and had an exotic two days honeymoon in Edinburgh. We couldn't wait to set up home in our new house so we returned to Carlisle on the 8th. We stayed two days at my parents while we organised the carpets and furniture and things and moved in on the 10th.

After a week Ropners were on the phone and this time they wanted me to join one of their tankers as Mate. I explained that I had no tanker experience and didn't feel confident in taking the job. After some discussion it was organised that I would be seconded to the Lowland Tanker Company for a couple of months to learn the ropes. I wasn't looking forward to it at all but the wages were considerably more than I'd been getting so I thought it might be worth it. Consequently I joined the *Border Hunter* in Eastham at the entrance to the Manchester Ship Canal on the 21st December. She had just arrived from the Caribbean with a full cargo of bitumen. It was a real pain to discharge as it had to be kept hot, by steam coils in the tanks, to be viscous enough to be pumpable and unfortunately the weather was bitterly cold. The actual discharge went quite well and I soon got the hang of where all the valves were and where the pipes went. The bitumen smell was quite pleasant so I was coming to the conclusion that I could cope with tanker life.

On the second day the Third Mate, who had joined with me, decided he wanted Christmas at home so he packed his bags and walked off. I had been signed on as extra Mate and when there was a mad panic to find a replacement before sailing I volunteered to do the Third Mate's job as at least I would be learning everything from the bottom up. The company were over the moon and when I finally left the ship they gave me an extra £100 as a thank you. It helped pay for a carpet in our new house.

We sailed on the 23rd December and crossed the Irish Sea to berth at Whitegate beside Cork in Eire. Here we were to load heating oil so all the tanks had to be thoroughly cleaned. The tanks were washed out with hot water which was then pumped ashore into tanks. We berthed on Christmas Eve and spent all Christmas Day cleaning the tanks in atrocious weather. I was now rapidly going off tankers. We loaded the heating oil on Boxing Day and sailed in the evening back to Eastham. Discharge here was pretty slow as a pipe ashore had sprung a leak so we had to pump slowly in case it blew up completely. I hated the smell of the fuel oil and it was actually putting me off my food. I was beginning to wonder how to tell Ropners that tankers weren't for me.

After three days discharging we sailed to Swansea. It was a different grade of oil to be loaded so we had to spend a few days washing out the tanks again and pumping the slops ashore. The Mate, George, let me organise the loading and it turned out to be harder than I thought. The oil was measured in barrels so we had to work out its volume taking into account the density corrected for temperature. I don't know why they couldn't just use the tonnage. In the end I got it all worked out and the ship loaded but I was becoming rapidly disillusioned with tanker life. They certainly earned their extra money. We took the cargo from Swansea just along the coast to Angle Bay for discharge at a power station. It took just over a day to unload and then back to Swansea to load again. At least we didn't have to clean the tanks this time but the loading went pretty slowly as there was a problem at the refinery. I had a walk up into the town with the Radio Officer one afternoon. We had a couple of pints and in one bar the barmaid asked which tanker we were off. She could smell the diesel oil on our clothes. Not good.

The next morning I phoned Ropners and explained that tankers weren't for me. I didn't know how they would take it. The personnel manager was surprised as Lowland Tankers had been on to him and said I was doing really well and they wanted to sign me as Mate. No way. It was arranged that I could leave at the next port which turned out to be Tranmere on the Mersey. I paid off on arrival and made my way home vowing to stay well clear of tankers.

CHAPTER TWENTY EIGHT

Bulk cargoes across the Atlantic

m.v. Wandby
27th January 1970 – 30th August 1970

I had a longer leave than I expected as I thought I would only be home for a couple of days before I was shipped out. In the end I had nearly three weeks on full pay before I had to travel over to Wallsend to join the *Wandby*. She was a 16,000 ton bulk carrier and was undergoing her annual drydock. It was pretty quiet on board as most of the crew were from the north east and they took every opportunity to get home. It was a bit far for me to travel to Carlisle but Diane nipped over for a weekend. I also got home for a night unexpectedly. I was talking to a technician one evening who had been working on the lubricators for the main engine. He was complaining that he would have to return to finish his work the next day and it was a pain having to go back to Carlisle. I promptly cadged a lift which turned out to be a bad mistake. He was an atrocious driver who travelled far too fast and insisted on blowing his horn and flashing the lights whenever he overtook anything which was quite a lot. At least I got home pretty quickly. The return journey seemed even worse and I was really pleased to get out at Wallsend.

We sailed on the 7th February in ballast across the Atlantic to New Orleans. The *Wandby* was a proper bulk carrier which meant there were no decks in the holds and they were designed so she didn't need shifting boards to stop grain moving around at sea. It made for an easy life for me. We arrived in the Mississippi and anchored in the river for our grain inspection. The American inspectors were renowned for being pernickety but we passed no problem and berthed next morning in the middle of New Orleans and started loading maize. I was worried that they would load really quickly and I'd have a problem pumping out the water ballast but it took them two days which gave me ample time. I even managed a night out in Bourbon Street listening to the jazz. I was surprised how much it had changed from my first visit in 1962. It was getting quite tacky and commercialised but it was still a good night ashore.

We sailed on the 27ᵗʰ February with no specific discharge port but just somewhere in northern Europe. They eventually decided to send us to Gdynia in Poland which meant we had to stop off in Falmouth for a few hours to pick up some extra fuel. We anchored off and couldn't get ashore but at least we got mail and fresh stores. We then set off up the North Sea and through the Kiel Canal into the Baltic. I didn't even know the Kiel Canal existed until we went through it. Then it was another day and a half along the coast to Gdynia. We had to follow designated routes as there were still a lot of minefields. It certainly concentrated the mind when we were navigating.

Gdynia was a dreary miserable place and the discharge went very slowly. There was a thriving black market and if you had a pair of jeans you could sell them for ten times their value. If we'd known before we left the States we would have stocked up and made a killing. A filling fell out of one of my teeth and I envisaged all sorts of problems getting it fixed but in the end I got a taxi there and back to a private clinic, had the tooth crowned with porcelain, which lasted for years, all for $5. The only trouble was none of us had many American dollars so we missed out as there was a lot of bargains to be had.

Just beside our berth was a large community centre and most mornings they would bus in loads of old folks for a day out and some food. The heating system must have been on its last legs as every now and again the chimney would throw out clouds of black smoke. I was stood on deck talking to the Bosun when the Deck Boy asked what the building was. We told him it was a crematorium and in Poland they got rid of everybody over sixty as they were a drain on the economy. The black smoke was another lot being burnt. When we turned around the Deck Boy was in floods of tears so we had to back track quickly and tell him the truth.

It took nearly three weeks to discharge and they swept up all the loose grain so the holds were lovely and clean when we sailed. It saved me a job on the next passage.

We went out round the top of Denmark instead of using the Kiel Canal as Ropners didn't have another charter for us. We took a Danish pilot to guide us through the minefields so navigating was a lot easier but he kept cutting corners through designated minefields because he reckoned they were clear so it was a nervous time though we figured he wouldn't want to blow himself up. As we were passing down the English Channel we got orders that we had to load in New

Orleans again and this time for Mexico. We hit a some bad storms on the way across and got bounced about quite a lot. As we arrived at the Mississippi I opened up the hatches to ventilate the holds and was horrified to discover that the decks were ankle deep in grain and coal dust. It had fallen off the beams in the storms. I had a mad twelve hours with every available crew member sweeping it all up and lifting the rubbish onto the deck. It paid off as when we anchored off New Orleans the inspectors passed all the holds with flying colours.

We had a day at anchor waiting for a berth and then moved upriver twenty miles to a place called Destrehan to load. There was a huge bag of mail as we had received very little in Poland. I got a letter from Diane to say she was expecting which came as quite a surprise. I knew she shouldn't have come over for that weekend in Wallsend! I didn't get a chance to celebrate as I had to have a clear head for the loading but I made up for it when we got Mexico and had a real blow out. It seemed weird going to be a father because we hadn't really talked about it. But anyhow.

We loaded 15,500 tons of maize in eighteen hours and set off down the Mississippi. Our discharge port was nominated as Manzanillo which none of us had heard of. It turned out to be on the Pacific coast of Mexico so we headed down to Panama and through the canal. It turned out to be a tiny port about 1500 miles up the coast from Panama and we berthed there on the 13th May. The next day was a local holiday so we didn't start to discharge until the following day. When they did start we had to wait five hours for the railway wagons to turn up – it was going to be a long discharge! At least the weather was good, everybody seemed really friendly and the local beer was pretty good and very cheap. It took exactly the same time to discharge as it did in Gdynia but time passed really quickly. We all got to be experts at ordering Mexican food because if you got it wrong it would blow your hat off it was so hot. I never did get the hang of tequila, though, and just stuck to the local beer.

The day before we left was a national holiday called Navy Day. We were woken up at six in the morning by the band from the local navy base playing marches on the quay. Fred, the Old Man, sent down a couple of bottles of whisky as a present so they insisted on playing Rule Britannia for him (it wasn't all that good). When we went ashore in the evening the band was still wandering about playing but most of them were legless and the bandmaster was fast asleep in a bar. They had a firework display when it got dark and succeeded in setting fire to the main hotel. It was just as well the fire brigade were sober.

Our next cargo was to be a full cargo of raw sugar to be loaded 300 miles up the coast in another Mexican port called Mazatlan. We had a bit of a rush around getting the holds all washed and clean for the sugar but we managed and the inspectors passed the holds with no problems. The sugar arrived in bags by rail in a huge train, 1,000 tons at a time, pulled by a two large locomotives. The train would arrive at five in the morning and the stevedores turned up at six. They would load the bags onto the hatch tops then slit them open and throw the empty bags ashore. I thought it would take for ever but they could load the 1,000 tons by noon and the train would leave with the empty bags at one o'clock. We would close the hatches and wash off any spilt sugar and then we had the rest of the day off. Not a bad life. Mazatlan was a lot bigger than Manzanillo and a popular holiday resort for Americans. This meant prices were three times as much, though there were some quite classy bars and hotels.

The football world cup was being held in Mexico that year and the matches started just as we got to Mazatlan. We tried to organise a trip to see England play but they always seemed to be at the other end of the country. We heard some real horror stories about Mexican bus drivers so maybe it was just as well. The stevedores were great and would invite us to their union hall to watch the England matches live on television. It just happened that the crucial match between England and West Germany was on my birthday and it was a Sunday as well so we all trooped over to the Union Hall lugging cases of cold beer. The stevedores had organised all sorts of eats as well so it was quite a memorable day even though England was beaten in extra time. When the stevedores found it was my birthday they insisted I drink tequila with them. I was really ill next day and still can't face tequila but I have to admit it was a birthday to remember.

We finished loading and sailed on the 18th June. The cargo was for Baltimore so it was back through the Panama Canal and up the east coast of the States. We berthed at the Domino sugar factory in the middle of Baltimore and they started discharge using grabs and cranes. They only discharged during the day so it took them five days to unload us. It was a really rough part of town and we were told not to venture ashore alone as people were always getting mugged. We found a great little bar just outside the factory gate and whenever I see the TV programme 'Cheers' it reminds me of there as everyone seemed to know each other and they all had their favourite seats. They loved to take the mickey out of our accents but couldn't follow the Geordie accent at all. The odd thing was that it was a predominantly black neighbourhood but the customers were all white middle class.

The day before we finished discharge the new orders came through and this time it was back to New Orleans to load grain for Copenhagen. We were supposed to serve nine months on board but I was getting anxious about being home to see the baby born so I wrote off to the company explaining the situation and hoped I would be relieved in Copenhagen as I would have over six months in by then. It took a week to get down to New Orleans from Baltimore and it took us most of that time to clean up the sugar residue. It had formed puddles of sticky syrup everywhere and was a real pain to get rid of.

We got to New Orleans on the 14th July and I was over the moon when our holds all passed the 'grain ready' survey. We anchored in the middle of the Mississippi for a couple of days before our berth was ready and then went to Destrehan to load again. It was an interesting load as the Port Authority kept changing its mind about how deep we could load because the entrance to the river had silted up due to heavy rain. Eventually when we sailed we found we were just right but we passed about twenty ships anchored in the river that couldn't leave because they were too deep. I think some of them were stuck there for a few weeks until they managed to dredge a deeper channel.

It took a fortnight to reach Copenhagen and as we passed up the English Channel we got a message to say who was being relieved and I wasn't on the list. I was pretty unhappy and Lord only knows where we could head off to after discharge.

On arrival in Copenhagen we were told that our next trip was to load wheat in the St Lawrence back to Rotterdam so at least I would have another chance to get off. Fred, the Old Man, paid off and said he would mention the situation when he called into the office so I calmed down a bit. I was quite disappointed in Copenhagen because everything seemed so expensive. I went to the Tivoli Gardens and walked up to see the mermaid which was another disappointment as it was about half the size I was expecting. The weather was lovely, though, and it was very pleasant just wandering about.

We discharged into an elevator using suckers so they had us

unloaded in three days and it was off again into the North Sea. This time we went north of Scotland and through the Pentland Firth. We had the tide with us and we went rocketing through at about twenty knots. It was very impressive. We also took the great circle route across the Atlantic so we went way up north towards Greenland. The weather was brilliant and it only seemed to get dark for about an hour around midnight. We saw some amazing shows of the Northern Lights and we all tried taking pictures but they didn't really come out. Our original plan was to go through the Belle Isle Strait north of Newfoundland and I was really looking forward to it as it was supposed to be fantastic for wild life and loads of icebergs about. In the end Harry Finn, the new Old Man, got cold feet after reading the pilot books because he thought it would be too dangerous. I was well pissed off and it took an extra couple of days to go round the bottom of Newfoundland.

I enjoyed the trip up the St Lawrence. When we were picking the pilot up at a place called Escoumains the ship was surrounded by a pod of about twenty Beluga whales which are pure white in colour. They had all disappeared by the time I got my camera out though. We were ordered to load in Quebec and I was looking forward to getting ashore but it was not to be. We went straight alongside and they had us loaded and out in less then ten hours. I only got as far as the quay to read the drafts but at least we would be home sooner. There was quite a bit of mail and a letter from the company saying I would be relieved in Rotterdam so I was feeling quite happy with life.

It took ten days to get to Rotterdam and we berthed there on the 28th August. I had to stay for a couple of days to hand over to the new Mate then I caught the ferry across to Harwich. They also paid off most of the crew and as senior officer I was supposed to be in charge of them. One of them was arrested for being drunk and disorderly before we got on the ferry so I had to organise a ticket for him for the next day. There was nearly a riot in the bar on the ferry when they refused to serve them but they still managed to find booze somewhere and were in an awful state when we arrived at Harwich. I snook off quietly with the Radio Officer and caught the train up to London and left them to it. Then it was a train home to Carlisle where Diane met me looking really fit and well albeit twice her normal size.

CHAPTER TWENTY NINE

A large bulk carrier

m.v. Stonepool
15th December 1970 – 21st July 1971

It was a bit of an odd leave. The baby was due at the end of October so I had two whole months on pay before anything happened. It was good being on contract! One of the biggest downers was that I had to sell the Fiat 850. It wasn't a family car and Diane was having trouble just getting behind the wheel which she had to do on several occasions when I over imbibed. We ended up with a brand new mini with an automatic gearbox. It was quite a fun little car though somewhat slower than the Fiat.

Martin was duly born a few days late on the 8th November. I was supposed to be allowed an extra month's paternity leave and I was just sort of getting the hang of nappy changing when Ropners phoned up wanting me to join the *Stonepool* in Oxelosund on the 15th December. I had half hoped to get Christmas at home but it was not too be.

I had to catch the sleeper train from Carlisle down to London then fly out from Heathrow. I don't think I've ever been so unhappy about leaving home. Diane took me down to the station about ten o'clock at night to catch the sleeper to London and then went home with Martin. As the train left Carlisle I could see our house and thought I could see Diane in the window beside the Christmas tree we had just put up. If the train had stopped I think I would have jumped off and gone home and said sod the sea!

Things didn't improve when we got to the ship either. I wasn't really looking forward to joining the *Stonepool* as she was 56,000 tons which was three times bigger than anything I'd been on before. Loading was quite a lot more complicated as there were all sorts of stresses to be taken into account and everything seemed that much bigger. On arrival at Oxelosund the taxi dropped us a long way from the gangway so we had to struggle along the quay carrying our cases in horizontal sleet up to our ankles in wet coal dust. She was discharging pulverised coal and it was everywhere – we were filthy by the time we'd climbed on board. Our mood didn't improve once we were on board either with the people we were relieving crowing about going home for Christmas. I was rapidly going off sea life.

It took another four days to discharge the coal and then we moved back into the next berth and started to load iron ore for Antwerp. Martin Jones, the Mate I relieved, had done all the loading calculations for the iron ore which was pretty good of him so I didn't have to work all that out and we weren't required to clean the holds after the coal so life did brighten up a bit. The weather was atrocious, though, with freezing winds and continuous sleet so it was nice when we completed the load and battened down the hatches and sailed on the 22nd December.

We had Christmas dinner ploughing down the North Sea in a full gale so it wasn't much of a do but most of the crew got well and truly plastered. We arrived off the entrance to the River Schelte late on Christmas Day and had quite a problem getting the pilot on board as everything on deck was frozen solid and it took us ages to get the pilot ladder de-iced and over the side. Once we started going up the river we had to get the mooring ropes up on deck and this turned into a nightmare. Most of the crew were still incapable after their Christmas party so it ended up with three or four of us sliding around on the icy deck in the dark struggling with the heavy mooring ropes. We'd only just got them sorted and sat down for a brew to warm up when we arrived at the locks and had to go out again to make the ship fast. Eventually we got tied up on the discharge berth at six in the morning after being up all night. I'd just sat down with a large mug of tea and a bacon sandwich when Ernie Dunn, the Old Man, stuck his head around the door and said we had to have the hatches open immediately so they could start discharge. I'm afraid I lost it and told him in very un-officer like language what he could do with his hatches and if he didn't like it he could send me home. He retreated rather rapidly. Once I'd finished my breakfast I wandered slowly out on deck and routed out the soberest of the deck crew and started opening the hatches which turned out to be a major task as they were all covered in a layer of ice which had to be chipped off first. We eventually got all the hatches open by one in the afternoon and at two o'clock all the stevedores knocked off and went home as they were only working one shift that day! To say I wasn't best pleased would be an understatement.

I went back to my cabin and had a hot shower and then sat and demolished a large turkey curry that the cook had kept in the hot press for me. I washed that down with a few cold beers and put a large Do Not Disturb sign on my door and went to bed. I think I slept right through until they resumed discharge at six o'clock the following morning.

We had a really miserable time in Antwerp. The berth was miles from anywhere and we had to plodge through half a mile of mud to get to the main gate so no one bothered to venture into the city centre with all the bars. Thankfully they unloaded us in double quick time with huge grabs on shore gantry cranes that picked up fifty tons at a time. There never seemed a moment's peace as we had to load a huge amount of stores and there were all sorts of surveys going on. We were half hoping to be in for the New Year but we finished unloading and sailed immediately on the afternoon of the 30th December.

We spent the first few days washing the ship down and trying to get everything clean as there seemed to be a thick layer of coal and iron ore dust on everything. By the time we'd cleared the Channel we had got most of the muck off and could walk around the decks without getting filthy. We received orders that we were to load a full cargo of chrome ore in Port Elizabeth in South Africa so at least we were heading into some decent weather. We were also told to make sure the hatches were clean as they didn't want the chrome ore to be contaminated. This was a huge job as there were large amounts of residue from the previous cargoes in the holds. It all had to be swept up and then lifted out and dumped over the side. We had a small mobile crane on board which was in really bad condition – in fact it was a death trap. If the ship was rolling it would slide about on deck and nothing on it worked properly but it was the only way of getting the rubbish from the bottom of the holds. The work progressed very slowly and the only redeeming feature was that we headed south into some lovely weather. We had three weeks to get to South Africa and I could see it taking all that time to clean the holds so no other maintenance or painting was getting done.

I really wasn't enjoying life and for the first time since I went to sea I felt pretty homesick. The deck crew were from Middlesbrough and were a real bolshie lot and took a lot of handling. There were only a couple of decent workers and the rest used all their energy trying to avoid work. I seemed to be always on their backs and Ernie, the Old Man, wasn't much support as all he wanted was a quiet life. I

172

began seriously thinking about looking for another job preferably something to do with the sea. Things improved a bit as we headed down the South Atlantic. We actually finished cleaning the holds and got a start on chipping and painting the decks. It felt as though I was getting somewhere.

We arrived in Port Elizabeth in the afternoon on the 19th January and the surveyors passed the holds so we started loading. Chrome ore is pretty heavy so although we had seven holds we only loaded in the alternate ones to keep our stability right. This would mean three less hatches to clean for the next cargo. Yippee. The loading went very well and I even managed a couple of nights ashore. South Africa was unbelievably cheap for booze and food so I got to enjoy myself for the first time since joining. There was also a couple of letters from Diane and she seemed to be coping with a bit of help from the family. The crew had managed to drink their way through most of the beer we'd loaded in Antwerp so we stocked up with San Miguel which is one of my favourite beers. We had been drinking the Dutch beer Oranjeboom up until then and I always seemed to get hangovers from it even after only a couple.

It took three days to load and we picked up some more fuel and sailed for Japan on the 24th January. Life improved quite a bit as the weather across the Indian Ocean was fantastic and we were able to get quite a bit of work done. It took over three weeks to get to Japan and we arrived in Tobata on the 18th February. It was a large new port with brand new berths and huge gantry cranes. The Japanese were pretty well organised and whenever anyone wanted to venture up to the town they provided minibuses to take us to the centre. A big change from Antwerp.

The discharge went very smoothly and we found we were chartered to pick up another cargo of chrome ore from Port Elizabeth to Japan. On the passage from South Africa Johnny Baulk, the Chief Engineer, had been concerned about the main engine overheating and had come to the conclusion that the cooling system was clogged up so a Japanese firm was called in to flush it through with chemicals. Even I was impressed with the amount of sludge and muck they cleared out of the pipes and coolers. We finished discharge on the morning of the 23rd February and prepared to sail but when the engineers switched on the cooling water pumps every joint and gland in the system was leaking. Water was spraying everywhere in the engine room so they had to shut it down very quickly. It appeared that the cleaning chemicals had destroyed all the rubber seals and gaskets so it was a major problem to resolve as there were hundreds of different seals in the system. The Port Authority allowed us to stay alongside for twenty four hours to try and sort it out but it soon became obvious that it would take a lot longer than that. The following morning we were ignominiously towed by four large tugs into the Inland Sea to a little port called Tannoura where the repairs could be effected. It was quite an exciting trip as we had to pass through a very narrow channel called Shimonoseki and the tugs had quite a job controlling us in the strong tides.

Once alongside in Tannoura the engineers had the mammoth task of flushing everything through to make sure there were no traces of the chemical left and then dismantling the pipe work on the main engine and renewing every seal and o-ring. We had to wait over a week for the new seals to arrive as they had to be flown from Germany. I decided to take the opportunity and paint the ship's sides but it proved to be quite a task. Not only was the area to paint huge but there were some little bars with very friendly Japanese girls very close to the berth so the crew were forever sloping off for a quick drink. I never did get the side completely painted while I was on the *Stonepool*. Apart from trying to get the crew to do a day's work it was quite a nice break. I managed to have a wander around the nearby port of Moji and also bought myself a new camera and some electronic equipment. It took a fortnight to complete the repairs and we eventually sailed on the 9th March.

It was an uneventful passage to Port Elizabeth and the weather was pretty good once we'd cleared the China Sea. We did a quick load in less then two days in Port Elizabeth and then it was back to Japan. This time we discharged in Kure which is in the Inland Sea near to Hiroshima. We had to anchor off for a day as there was a big emergency in the port. A large oil storage tank on shore had split and leaked hundreds of tons of heavy oil into the port. They had been cleaning it up for weeks before we arrived but it still looked terrible. They had mobilised every available tug and fishing boat and they were everywhere scooping up the black sludge or spraying chemicals to disperse the oil. When we berthed it only took a couple of hours before people had come on board and trodden the oil into our carpets and floor coverings. None of the crew bothered to venture ashore and thankfully they discharged us quickly in a couple of days and we left port on the 27th April.

Ropners were having trouble finding a new charter for us so we anchored just outside the port to await instructions and clean all the oil off the decks. Everything was a real mess but the Japanese had given us some large drums of oil dispersant and degreasants which made the job a lot easier. The ship's agent would come out in a boat every morning with any messages from Ropners and usually some English newspapers which made welcome reading. The agent was a woman which was unusual in Japan. She was quite attractive in her forties and was really efficient.

There were all sorts of rumours about the next charter, ranging from loading iron ore in Chile back to Japan, coal from Australia back to Japan or yet another trip to Port Elizabeth and back, none of which seemed very attractive as it would be at least two months before we could even think of setting off back to the UK. After a couple of days we had got most of the oil off and cleaned the carpets and alleyways so I decided I might as well start cleaning the holds in preparation for the next cargo. It's a lot easier at anchor because the ship isn't moving around as much. On the sixth day I was down one of the holds trying to clean out a bilge when I got a message that the Old Man wanted me. As I was absolutely filthy I had a quick shower and put a clean boilersuit on and went up to his cabin. The agent was there and she had a query from Ropners as to how much grain we could load in Sydney for Europe. I went back to my cabin and got the tables out to work it all out. The agent kept popping into my cabin every five minutes to see how it was going. I assumed she wanted to get off ashore with the answers. After about half an hour I was nearly finished when Johnnie Baulk, the Chief Engineer, stuck his head into my cabin looking for a cold beer. He opened a couple of cans and looked over my shoulder to see what I was doing. He commented, "Giving them an airing then," and when I looked down my flies were completely open with all my wedding tackle hanging out to air. I'd just put everything back in place when the agent appeared again. She never said anything but seemed somewhat amused at my embarrassment. I quickly completed the calculations and off she went ashore to send the information to Ropners. Every time she came on board she made a point of saying hello much to the amusement of Johnnie.

The new charter was a bit odd as 50,000 tons of grain is quite a lot to ship at one time. On top of that all our hatches were in very poor condition and leaked quite badly. It was all right for coal or ore but not the best for grain. I told Ernie, the Old Man, to tell Ropners that we needed a lot of repairs to the hatch seals before we could carry grain but he couldn't be bothered. After another two days it was confirmed that we were to load a full cargo of wheat in Sydney for Rotterdam. We took on a load of fuel and set off.

It took fourteen days to get down to Sydney and it was a mad panic all the way there to get the holds clean and make the hatches vaguely watertight. I was sure the surveyors would fail us out of hand but amazingly we passed with flying colours. I was still very concerned about our watertight integrity but could just hope for a good passage home. The loading went very slowly as they had to rail in most of the grain. We had every night off and a weekend too. Somehow we got involved with a group of supporters of an Australian football team, the Sydney Swans, and would end up in their club drinking ice cold beer until very late. I can remember they celebrated Burns Night one evening and I don't think I've ever seen so many drunken people in kilts in one place. The odd thing is that I always thought Burn's Night was in January but that didn't seem to dampen their enthusiasm. I remember I was really quite ill the following day which thankfully was a Sunday.

One of the team that we knocked around with was a bloke in his twenties who was dying to get a job at sea but the nearest he could get was working for a ship chandler supplying the ships that arrived in Sydney. He came down to the ship one evening just as we were closing the hatches for the day. I was examining the hatch seals and muttering that we'd be lucky to even get to Rotterdam never mind have a decent cargo when we arrived. He announced that his company sold a product called Ram-nek tape which was basically wide plastic strips with a layer of tar on one side that were stuck over the hatch joints. It was the perfect answer. He actually had a sample in his car so I went shooting up to show Ernie that we had the answer but he wasn't interested especially when we worked out it would cost nearly a £1000. I got really fed up and jumped up and down and threw my toys out of the pram but he still wasn't bothered. It seemed madness to me to sail and end up with loads of water-damaged grain but it all went over his head. I didn't bother with the evening meal and went ashore with the ship chandler and I have to admit that I rather over imbibed on the amber nectar. I had the daddy of all hangovers the next morning when Ernie breezed in and announced that we were to be weather routed for the passage home. This meant that the weather on our intended track was monitored by a bunch of Germans in Frankfurt who would then send messages to advise on our best route. Ernie thought this was great and would solve all our problems as we'd have good weather all the way home. I lost my rag completely and told him he was irresponsible and that I was writing to the company to tell them of the situation and if the cargo was damaged it wasn't my fault. Ernie wandered off in a huff but never said anything. We got some mail from home that morning so I sat down and started writing a letter home. Ernie could hear me typing and assumed I was writing to the company and a little while later he stuck his head in my cabin and said he was cabling Ropners for permission to buy the tape. Bloody hurray. The answer came back to do whatever was required so we ordered the tape for all the hatches at great expense. My mate, the ship chandler, was over the moon and took me out for a slap up seafood meal and a few more cold beers.

We completed loading on the 29th May and set off round the south of Australia. We all assumed that we'd have a good passage across the Indian Ocean but our weather routers had different ideas. They sent us way south down to latitude 45° south where we endured strong head winds and heavy seas on top of which it was pretty cold. We also had problems with the Ram-nek tape as we were taking on so much water it started to wash the tape off the joints. I had to go out with a couple of crew and stamp it down again every day much to the amusement of the rest of the crew who would gather on the bridge to watch us doing a little dance across the hatch top to re-secure the tape whilst trying not to get washed off by the waves.

We were about nine days out with no let up when one of the stokers fell in the engine room and hurt his shoulder quite badly. We had to divert into Fremantle to get him some medical attention. The doctors confirmed that he had a broken collar bone and strapped him up, gave him some pain killers, and off we went again. As we had come a good way north to Fremantle we thought we'd have a decent run across the Indian Ocean but the bastards sent us way south again into the bad weather. I think if I'd have been Skipper I would have told them where to stick their advice and gone my own way. Mind you we did pass some groups of islands down there that I never knew existed. Not surprisingly they were uninhabited but the chart said they had shelter and food stores on them in case anybody got shipwrecked. I don't know who was responsible for replenishing the food or checking to see if anyone had been shipwrecked. We had another ten days bad weather and then we turned north into the Atlantic. At least the weather there was pretty good but the smell coming from the hatches didn't bode well as the grain had obviously got pretty wet and was malting so we smelt like a mobile brewery.

We eventually got to Rotterdam on the 17th July and had a hell of a time opening the hatches as by then the tape had turned solid and stuck really well. It took a full day to scrape it all off. Luckily only one of the hatches had leaked badly and they condemned a couple of hundred tons of grain. It could have been a lot worse and I've a feeling Ernie took the credit for the extra precautions. I was getting to hate the man. I had another few days in Rotterdam handing over to a new Mate and then paid off and got the ferry back to Harwich and the train home. It was really good to be home as it hadn't been my favourite voyage.

CHAPTER THIRTY

Volkswagens to the States

m.v. Norse Viking
21st October 1971 – 10th April 1972

I had quite a hectic leave and looking back packed quite a lot into the two and a half months. We'd become a bit disappointed in the bungalow as we didn't get on with the adjoining neighbours and I was a bit frustrated with the garden. Mum and Dad had been looking to move into the country and had seen a lovely little bungalow in Stockdalewath, near Dalston. We went and looked at it and decided it was for us and put in an offer which was accepted. We then quickly had to sell our own house and organise the move. Luckily the first people to view it bought it and we moved six weeks later. Everything must have gone very smoothly as I don't recall any problems.

We had about three weeks living there before I was recalled to join the *Norse Viking*. She was a car carrier designed to carry about 2000 cars and each hold was fitted with portable decks which had to be removed to carry bulk cargoes. I'd heard quite a bit about the ship and was looking forward to joining her as, apart from being very complicated, she was fitted with all the best equipment and navigational aids. I flew out to San Francisco with Jack Roddam who was going to be the Old Man. We arrived in the evening and were put up in a five star hotel near Fisherman's Wharf. We had a fantastic seafood meal but I was knackered after the twelve hour flight so I had an early night. I wished I'd had more time there because it looked a great place for a night out though I've a feeling it would have been pretty expensive.

We joined the ship when she berthed the following morning. I was relieving a bloke called Dennis Macleod who was quite a character. He was staying on board for a couple of weeks to make sure I understood how everything worked. We had two days in San Francisco then moved up the coast to Vancouver to finish off. We then had orders to load in Japan back for the States. Dennis was supposed to stay until Japan but I reckoned I could figure things out

179

so he got off just before we sailed. It was a good job he did as we spent most of our time together yarning and drinking beer so my bar bill would have been somewhat excessive by the time we reached Japan.

The *Norse Viking* was built and owned by a Norwegian company and Ropners had the contract to crew and run it for them. No expense seemed to have been spared and all the gear and equipment were the best available. I really enjoyed myself on the bridge with all the new instruments. The radar was the latest 'true motion' with all sorts of plotting devices that warned if other ships were collision risks. There was also a weather fax which produced weather maps every hour and the radio direction finder took bearings automatically. I also had to get my head around all the deck equipment as this was the first time I'd worked with cranes.

It took a fortnight to get across to Japan and by that time I'd just about figured everything out. We berthed in Nagoya late at night on the 12th November. It was an area specifically for loading cars for export and I've never seen as many cars in my life. They were arranged in rows and went as far as the eye could see. It was very impressive. We were loading Toyota saloon cars mainly, with the odd sports car and a few pickups. They started loading at six o'clock the following morning and by two o'clock had loaded and securely lashed over 2000 cars. I had been planning a run ashore to buy some of the latest camera and electronic equipment but it was not to be. We sailed at four and it would have been earlier but we had to send a posse ashore to extract some of the crew from a local bar. The cars were destined for Baltimore on the east coast of the States so we headed off towards the Panama Canal. It had again been arranged that we were weather routed by the Germans and they instructed us to steer a great circle course way up into the North Pacific. The Old Man, Jack Roddam, took one look at the instructions and threw them in the bin and headed off south into the warm weather. He might have come a bit unstuck if we'd hit bad weather but with our weather fax machine we managed to avoid any major disturbances and had a lovely trip and I got the crew painting on deck every day. Jack also kept a record of where we should have been if we'd followed orders and we reckoned we would have taken quite a battering as well as having adverse currents to contend with.

We passed through the Panama on the 2nd December and then it was a week up to Baltimore. We berthed at eight in the morning and again the discharge was really efficient and we sailed late in the evening for Philadelphia. It was quite a hectic trip as we went through the Chesapeake-Delaware Canal so it was only eight hours and we had to sweep the holds clean and remove all the decks before we arrived. We managed with half an hour to spare and we berthed early on the 9th December and started to load coal. The loading went quite slowly as the coal arrived on railway wagons which were individually hoisted up and emptied down chutes into the holds. It was pretty dirty too with the coal dust getting everywhere. We were glad to sail three days later and get the ship washed clean.

The coal was destined for Dunkerque and it was looking bad for Christmas as we were supposed to arrive on the 23rd December and sail on the 24th which meant we'd be washing and cleaning the holds on Christmas Day and then we would arrive in Bremen on Boxing Day and load a cargo of Volkswagens back for the States. There were quite a few crew changes due as well so the new crew would be unfamiliar with the equipment. I wasn't looking forward to it at all. When we were a day out we got a message that the tugs would probably go on strike on the 23rd December so we would be stuck at anchor off Dunkerque over Christmas which looked slightly better than working over the period. Ropners had sent all the relief crew over and they were waiting in Dunkerque and I also found out that Diane had somehow organised a ticket and was also there. We were about six hours away from Dunkerque and deciding where was the best place to anchor when we got another message saying the tugs would take us in provided we could get there in five and a half hours. We speeded up to the maximum possible speed and just managed to do it. We got there with five minutes to spare. Jack gave the tug Skippers a bottle of whisky each which improved matters.

We were all tied up by noon and Diane was waiting on the quay with the new crew. After a mad rush to get the old crew off so they would catch a ferry to Dover it all calmed down. It turned out that the whole port of Dunkerque was on strike until 28th December so we ended up having a great Christmas with very little going on but drinking vast quantities of booze and lots of eating. There was a Norwegian ship tied up ahead of us and they invited us all over for a fantastic smorgasbord for lunch on Boxing Day. It was beautifully laid out and they must have taken ages to prepare it. We also consumed quite a lot of aquavit. We had a bit of bother returning to the *Norse Viking* as the quay was covered in iron ore pellets so it was like walking on ball bearings which combined with the aquavit made for very unsteady progress but we managed in the end.

They eventually started unloading on the 29th December which was just as well because we'd about drunk the ship dry. There was some doubt about the next cargo as we obviously hadn't appeared on Boxing Day as required. Diane took a ferry back to Dover on the afternoon of the 30th and we sailed early the following morning. We headed up to Bremen but at slow speed as we weren't required until the 3rd January. This gave us plenty of time to wash and clean the hatches and rig up the car decks. Cleaning the holds was a lot easier than other vessels because of all the extra equipment. We had high pressure hoses and portable air pumps and the cranes were there to lift things in and out of the holds. I just wished every ship could be like this.

The weather in Bremen was atrocious with blizzards and freezing rain. We were due to start loading at six in the morning on the 3rd but surprisingly nothing happened. Eventually someone turned up and it appeared a bus full of stevedores had skidded on ice and turned over. Nobody was killed but I think they were pretty shaken up as the bus had nearly fallen off a bridge. They all refused to work until everywhere was properly gritted so we finally started loading late in the afternoon. It was slow going as all the cars were iced up and they had to be defrosted first. It was even colder when it got dark so they gave up loading for the night and came back the following morning. The cars were mainly VW Beetles and we managed to squeeze in a record 2400 somehow. We sailed on the afternoon of the 4th January. The trip down the North Sea was amazing. One minute it was clear blue skies and the next it was zero visibility in snow storms. There were quite a few collisions in the snow storms but thankfully we scooted through without mishap and set off across the Atlantic.

It was back to Baltimore to discharge again and we berthed early morning on the 15th January. I think the stevedores must have been on some sort of bonus because they worked like mad and had us unloaded by four in the afternoon albeit with one or two dented and scratched Beetles.

We got instructions to clean the holds for grain and this turned out to be a doddle as we had given the holds a really good wash out before loading the cars. All we had to do was sweep up the decks and fold up the car decks. We passed the grain inspection the next morning with no problems and then we had to anchor off for a week in the Chesapeake Bay waiting for a loading berth. Several of the crew were keen fishermen and had brought their gear with them so they were all out fishing as soon as the anchor was down. They caught an amazing amount of really big fish so it was fish and chip suppers every night. The main problem was that the fish kept falling off the hooks when they were lifting them on board so we made a platform and suspended it on a crane just above the water so that improved things. The weather was really miserable with sleet and snow but there always seemed to be someone sitting on the platform even in the middle of the night.

We went alongside on the 24th January and loaded a full cargo of soya beans for northern Spain in twenty hours. Then it was back across the Atlantic again. We were a bit further south this time as we were heading for Spain so we had some nice sunny weather for once and managed to get a lot of painting done. We berthed in Santander on the 4th February and they took four days to discharge using elevators. I think they could have unloaded us in less than twelve hours but they didn't have the storage facilities so we had to wait for rail wagons to take the beans away. Jack Roddam and I were taken ashore for a meal by the importers who were very impressed by the good condition of the cargo. It was a fantastic seafood meal but I had a hard time with the goose neck barnacles. They were the local delicacy and they were very proud of them. The trouble was every time I bit into one this orange liquid squirted out all over me. It was worth it for the lobsters though. We then were taken to a flamenco bar and were bored rigid by these ugly women being very noisy and stamping their feet all the time. At least the beer was decent. Jack seemed to really enjoy it for some reason.

After Santander we headed back to Bremen for yet another load of Beetles. It took three days so we had plenty of time to clean the holds.

They took two days to load this time and we had a lot of Volkswagen Campervans so we couldn't carry as many due to their size. We also had some brand new Porsche 911s which were very impressive. While we were in Bremen we got a visit from the people who did the weather routeing. They wanted to know why we didn't use the service. They had all sorts of fantastic literature and statistics to demonstrate their services but it ended up in a big argument when we said we could do it better. They went quiet when Jack produced his records of our trip across the Pacific. They had given Jack a lovely Gold Cross pen and pencil set and he was really pissed off when he found they had taken it back when they left. When we sailed there was a real towser of a storm coming up the English Channel so Jack decided to go round the north of Scotland. It was a brilliant decision as we had good weather and following winds nearly all the way across. Who needs bloody German meteorologists anyhow?

When we arrived in Baltimore the stevedores were on strike so we had to anchor off in the Chesapeake Bay again. Out came the fishing rods. It wasn't as good as the time before as the tide was very strong and it kept the hooks off the bottom and they could only fish for a couple of hours at a time. After two days in which they only caught a couple of small cod Jack heaved up the anchor and we moved a couple of miles north out of the tideway. It wasn't as good as our first trip but they managed some pretty decent fish so it was fish and chip suppers again. We kept getting messages saying they were going to send us to Mexico to discharge but in the end the stevedores went back to work and we berthed after waiting a fortnight.

After discharge we sailed down the Chesapeake to Norfolk and loaded a full cargo of pulverised coal for Amsterdam. It wasn't a very nice cargo as it was liable to self combust. We had to take temperatures in the holds every day to make sure it wasn't on fire. Mind you there wasn't much we could do if it did catch fire.

Luckily we got to Amsterdam without mishap and they unloaded us in a couple of days. This time it was a mad panic to get the holds clean as we were required in Emden the following day to load up with 'Beetles' again. We berthed there in the evening of the 26th March and spent all night finishing off the cleaning and preparing the car decks. We finished with a couple of hours to spare and they started loading at six in the morning.

I was being relieved and the new mate, Bob Henderson, had joined in Amsterdam. I was expecting to get off in Emden but he reckoned he needed more time to familiarise himself with the ship. The cargo was destined for the west coast of the States so I was going to have to stay on for an extra three weeks. I was not best pleased as I was already packed and ready to leap off as the ship left Emden. In the end the company got me off as the ship went through the Panama Canal two weeks later. It was quite a traumatic trip back as the first flight was cancelled because there was something seriously wrong with the plane and the pilots refused to fly it. This meant I missed my connection in Miami and as I didn't have a visa I had to spend a night in the airport waiting for the next flight. It was nice to get home.

When I left the *Norse Viking* she already had orders to load timber in British Columbia for Hartlepool so I'd left all my heavy gear on the ship with the intention of picking it up when she arrived back in the UK. Six weeks later Ropners phoned me up to say the *Norse Viking* was berthing in Hartlepool the following day so I nipped over in the car to pick up my stuff. I arrived just as they were shifting ship. As I was waiting to go aboard I noticed that the gangway hadn't been lifted high enough to clear some mooring bollards on the quay. I shouted up that they needed to pick the gangway up a bit. Bob Henderson, the Mate, was on the bridge wing supervising the operation and obviously didn't appreciate my advice and yelled, "Piss off, Jackson. You're not in charge now." Just then the gangway caught and was ripped off its mountings and came crashing down on the quay. I shrugged my shoulders and went and sat in the car. I got no satisfaction, though, as I then had to wait three hours while they rigged another gangway. Bob didn't even offer me a beer when I eventually got on board to retrieve my gear.

CHAPTER THIRTY ONE

One hundred thousand tons - the biggest yet!

m.v. Rudby
19th September 1972 – 29th December 1972

I had a very pleasant leave which was mostly spent sorting the garden out in the new bungalow. After a couple of months things were starting to look good and I had a very respectable vegetable patch going which was starting to produce some good crops. I was hoping for a bit extra leave but Ropners had other ideas. I had also been hoping to return to the *Norse Viking* as I'd really enjoyed my stint on there but it was not to be. The instructions came through that I was to join the *Rudby*, which was their newest ship, in Port Hedland in Northern Australia. It was an epic journey out starting with a sleeper train from Carlisle then a morning flight from Heathrow. It was a long flight with only a short stop at Tehran for fuel then on to Sydney. After a few hours in Sydney I caught a small ten-seater for another two hour flight up to Port Hedland. I was knackered when I got there and was really pleased to get a night in a hotel before joining next morning.

I was somewhat taken aback by the size of the ship when I went down in the morning. At 110,000 tons she was twice the size of anything I'd been on and she had just started loading iron ore when I climbed aboard so was floating really high in the water. After a struggle I managed to get myself and my bags up the near vertical gangway. The bloke I was relieving was all packed and ready to leave and I had a hell of a job getting any information out of him. His stock phrase was, "It's ten times bigger than anything else you've been on so just multiply everything by ten" It turned out he was overwhelmed by the size of the ship and had packed his hand in after only one trip. After he left I went up to see the Old Man and to my horror it was Ernie Dunn again. As previously, he had no idea what was going on so it was going to be a very steep learning curve for me. Luckily John, the Second Mate, was switched on so I got a fair bit of help there. The iron ore was loading with two conveyors at the rate of

8,000 tons an hour so I had to get my head around things pretty quickly. The cargo to be loaded was exactly the same as the previous voyage so I just used the same tonnages and tweaked the final few hundred tons to get the ship on an even keel.

The big problem was pumping out all the ballast water before we finished loading. The pumps weren't really big enough and on top of that if we didn't keep an eye on things and let a pump run dry there were all sorts of problems. We managed in the end and sailed for Japan twenty hours later at two in the morning. I managed less than an hour in bed and then I had to get up to do my four to eight watch. I was absolutely shattered what with the flight and the jet lag and I'd only managed a couple of naps while we were loading. Luckily we were straight out into the open sea but I had an awful job trying to stay awake. I got the cook to do me a couple of bacon and egg sandwiches at seven o'clock and managed to stay awake long enough to hand over to Col, the Third Mate, at eight o'clock then it was a quick shower and straight into bed only to be woken five minutes later by Ernie, the Old Man, wanting the cargo figures which I had already put on his desk. He left rather hurriedly.

I woke up about three o'clock and went for a check around the deck before going to the bridge for my afternoon watch. It was then that the size of the ship started to sink in. I'd set the crew to washing down the ship as soon as we sailed – a job that usually took a day at the most. With all the crew working and using four hoses going flat out they had managed to clean less than a quarter of the decks. With only ten days steaming to Japan it would take all that time to get the ship clean and then it would get dirty again during the discharge. Not much time for maintenance then. It also took a lot longer to get around. I was still on the focstle talking to the Bosun when I noticed I should be on watch on the bridge and it took me nearly quarter of an hour to get along the deck and up all the ladders. John, the Second Mate, wasn't too bothered about the late relief though he was beginning to think I'd forgotten about him.

I was overwhelmed by the sheer size of the ship and what amazed me was that there were tankers nearly twice our size. Fully loaded we were nearly fifty feet deep which meant we had to be careful where we went otherwise we'd be bouncing off the bottom. The *Rudby* had nine hatches and with heavy cargoes such as iron ore we only loaded in the odd hatches to keep our centre of gravity higher. Number six hatch was used for ballast water when we were empty and it held

14,000 tons of water which was an entire ship load in most of my previous ships. The distribution of the cargo was quite a science too with all the shear forces and bending moments to be calculated. We had a loading computer on board called a loadicator which, once I'd figured out how to use it, was a great help. When I came to use it I found it had been wrongly setup so Lord knows how the previous mate had worked things out.

I had just about found out where everything was when we arrived in Japan and berthed in Sakai in Osaka Bay. The discharge went very quickly using huge shore gantries which operated grabs that picked up over 100 tons every time. It was very dirty work, though, as they spilled a lot on the decks and it was incredibly dusty. We were miles from the town and I think only a couple of people ventured ashore. The discharge took less than forty hours and we sailed on the 5th July back to Australia. Again, cleaning the ship took over four days which left only five days for maintenance before we started loading the next cargo. It seemed a pointless exercise.

We were ordered to load at Port Hedland again so the cargo calculations were easy. When we picked up the pilot to enter the port I was surprised to find it was Mike Bennett who had sailed with me as an apprentice in Port Line. He was on fantastic wages and really enjoying life. He insisted on taking me out for a meal on the first night. We sat outside while they barbecued huge prawns and about half a cow for us. I was on tenterhooks, though, as the ship was loading and when they are throwing the ore on board at 8,000 tons an hour things can go wrong very quickly. Of course it was all going very smoothly when I got back but I felt it wasn't worth the risk. Mike stayed and had a couple of beers on board and nearly had me persuaded to go for a job as a pilot there. It did seem a good life.

The loading went really quickly as there were no other ships in port and they stuck an extra conveyor onto us which meant the ore was pouring on at over 12,000 tons an hour. I was running around ragged trying to get the ballast water pumped out in time. We managed in the end and sailed in the evening. Mike piloted us out and brought all the information about the pilot service and even application forms. After all the hassle I'd had loading I was very tempted to fill them out there and then.

It was ten days up to Japan and this time we had to discharge in two ports. The first was Tobata on the west coast and the entrance to the Inland Sea. The port was congested so we had to anchor off. I hated anchoring on the *Rudby* as it was quite dangerous. On the usual size of cargo ship the practice was to more or less stop and let go the anchor and it would catch on the bottom and bring the vessel to a stop. With the size of the *Rudby* the ship had to be completely stopped and the anchor was let go and then the ship slowly went astern and pulled the anchor chain out to the required length. Ernie could never get it right and we always ended up nearly breaking the chain with smoke pouring from the windlass brakes. This time was no exception and he nearly managed to pull the windlass off the deck.

The berthing was pretty uneventful after all that fun and we tied up at the discharge berth and commenced unloading. They discharged about 40,000 tons in thirty six hours and we sailed off down the Inland Sea to Sakai arriving there on the 31st July. It took two days to discharge the remainder of the iron ore and we had to leave port and anchor in Osaka Bay for a day as the company didn't have another charter for us. It looked like we were going down to Australia again but this time to load coal for Rotterdam. This meant we would have to clean the holds which was going to be a nightmare as there were tons of iron ore left in the corners of the holds which would all have to be lifted out. The only good thing was that we'd be getting close to home. In the end the agent came out on the afternoon of the 3rd August with the news that we were to go to San Nicolas in Chile to load another cargo of iron ore for Japan so we heaved up the anchor and set off. Going to sea was quite an education as I never knew Australia exported coal in any great quantity and, apart from not knowing exactly where San Nicolas was, I had no idea Chile exported iron ore.

At least now I would be able to get some maintenance done on deck as it was twenty seven days across the Pacific to Chile most of which should be lovely weather. My deck crew consisted of a bosun and nine seamen and a carpenter, who was more of a mechanic really. Once the ship was clean we set away chipping and painting on the focstle. I got really frustrated at the lack of progress. It took the crew ten minutes to walk to the focstle so for every coffee or meal break twenty minutes was lost getting to and fro. We also were having a problem with the hatch covers. They each weighed over fifty tons and were opened and closed by a system of chains and hydraulic motors. The pulleys that the chains went round had started to seize up so I decided to strip them all down and overhaul them. It turned

189

into a mammoth job and after a week we'd managed to do four pulleys and there were ten on each hatch and nine hatches!!

I had the carpenter and three of the seamen working on this so the labour available to paint was considerably reduced. It was going to be a long job and I knew how the blokes painting the Forth Bridge must feel. Anyhow the weather was good and there was plenty of cold beer and the food was pretty good too so I decided to chill and do the best I could.

We arrived in San Nicolas on the 30th August and I was pleasantly surprised. It was a really modern facility in a very pretty bay. We got most of the ballast water out before we got alongside which made for an easy life for me. The loading went really well and quickly too. They kept the ore damp so it wasn't dusty or dirty so I actually quite enjoyed the loading here. Twenty hours later we were loaded and heading for Japan. Back to the chipping and painting.

We discharged in two ports again, the first being Muroran on the northern island of Hokkaido. Discharge went pretty slowly for Japan as there was some sort of industrial action taking place because of the amount of pollution the steel works was putting out. It wasn't surprising as everywhere was a dull red colour and everything seemed to be coated in a fine red dust. The whole place looked miserable and I don't think anyone ventured ashore while we were there. It took nearly five days to discharge 70,000 tons.

Just before we sailed the ship chandler brought me a present of a large box of fresh spider crabs. They had been cooked but I hadn't a clue how to eat them. Luckily Ken Buckley, the Electrician, knew how to get the meat out and what not to eat. That night about half a dozen of us sat in my cabin with a couple of cases of cold beer, an assortment of hammers and pliers and opened them up. The original intention was to collect all the meat and have a nice meal the following day but it was so delicious that we ate whatever we managed to extract washed down by copious amounts of Asahi beer. I couldn't believe the state of my cabin the following morning. It absolutely stank and there was a huge pile of empty beer cans and bits of crab shell in the middle of the floor. It took days for the smell to go away.

We sailed the following morning for Yokohama. It was a brand new berth in the Mitsubishi Steel Works with huge cranes and they had the remaining cargo unloaded in less than twenty four hours which was impressive. It seemed to be from one extreme to the other.

It was either twenty four hours of mad panic loading or discharging followed by a month of ambling along doing very little really. As we finished off discharge the orders came through that we were going to Dampier in Northern Australia to load iron ore for the continent. This brightened everyone up as there was a good chance of getting some leave when we got back.

It was the usual ten days down to Aussie then a quick load in Dampier and off across the Indian Ocean towards South Africa. I was starting to get my head around the maintenance problem and in the thirty days it took us to get to Amsterdam I could actually see some progress. We got all the hatch opening system overhauled and painted most of the accommodation so I felt we had got somewhere. We were helped by the weather as we seemed to have blue skies and light winds all the way until we entered the English Channel. We berthed in Europort beside Amsterdam on the 15th November. I had a nice surprise as the company had paid for Diane to fly over and join me for a few days. It was a nice leisurely discharge for once as the stockpiles ashore were full and they had to make room for our cargo. They unloaded 80,000 tons and we sailed four days later for Gijon in Spain and Diane took the opportunity to sail with us. We had changed most of the crew in Amsterdam so there were a lot of new faces on board. Ernie Dunn had been relieved by Jack Roddam as Skipper. It was a pretty rough trip as we started out heading into a gale force wind which had grown to into a severe gale force nine by the time we entered the Bay of Biscay. This was where being on a vast ship had its dividends as we just ploughed steadily on while most ships were heading for port. Mind you I was surprised how much the hull twisted and bent in the huge waves but it was a brand new ship and the stresses must have been taken into account when she was built. I was a bit concerned, though, as a sister ship called the *Devonshire* had sunk the previous year in a typhoon off Japan.

We arrived in Gijon on the 22nd November and found we were the first ship to unload in a brand new facility. It was a very slow discharge as they couldn't get the conveyor system going so it all went into lorries. We also had to keep shifting the ship back and forward as they had problems moving the gantry cranes. One evening when we shifting along the Radio Officer and a couple of engineers arrived back from a drinking session ashore and tried to jump on board despite the ship being six feet off the quay. The Radio Officer fell between the ship and the quay hitting his head on the way down. We had a hard time keeping the ship off the quay while the Second Mate climbed down and got a rope round him. Unfortunately he was dead when they eventually got him out which put a real dampener on things to say the least. Nobody knew him very well as he had only just joined but he seemed a really nice bloke.

The day before we sailed the Port Authority decided to have a party on board to celebrate the opening of their berth. We spent the day cleaning the ship up as best we could. All the food and booze came from ashore so all we had to do was lift it aboard for them. It was a tremendous spread and enough booze to float the ship. It turned out to be an all male affair so Diane was most peeved not to be invited especially as she'd seen the table of food. The trouble was that by this time the ship was almost empty and really high in the water. The gangway was nearly vertical and about half the guests took one look at it and turned around and went home. Still, that meant more for the rest of us. I dutifully ploughed my way through a couple of lobsters with all the trimmings washed down with copious amounts of Cava. When it was all over and everyone and the remnants of the party had been safely put ashore I went back to the cabin clutching a bottle of Cava as a peace offering to Diane. It wasn't needed as Jack Roddam had organised one of the waiters to take some food and drink to her and the Chief Engineer's wife and the pair of them had seen off at least three bottles of cava and demolished a vast amount of food. I think they'd enjoyed the party more than we had.

Diane left the following morning to fly home and we sailed in the evening for Tubarao in Brazil. When we'd got the ship all washed down and clean I was really disappointed to see red rust streaks everywhere again after shipping the seas in the Bay of Biscay. It was disheartening as the ship had looked pretty good entering Amsterdam and it was back to square one. Anyhow we had some decent weather down the Atlantic so we just started again. We arrived in Tubarao at midnight on the 11th December and we sailed at half past six loaded with 109,500 tons of iron ore. It was amazing how quick the load was and that I managed to get all the ballast water out. It was a surprisingly clean load too as they dampened the ore to suppress the dust. It seemed odd heading back fully loaded in less than a day. I had the feeling I must have forgotten something. It was quite a decent run back and we had Christmas dinner crossing the Bay of Biscay in some reasonable weather for once.

We docked in Rotterdam in the evening of Boxing Day and my

relief arrived the following day so I handed over and left on the 29th December. Ropners had organised a flight to Newcastle so at least I managed to get home for the New Year.

CHAPTER THIRTY TWO

Another bloody trip

m.v. Rudby
19th April 1973 – 30th July 1973

I'd been home for New Year but I was getting a bit fed up with having Christmas away especially now I had a family to come home to. Diane was muttering a bit too so things would have to change. I ended up having five months at home after six months at sea and all on full pay too. Ropners had sold a ship and were overstaffed but that didn't bother me! I managed to have a really good go in the garden and got quite a productive vegetable patch going. I used to get loads of advice from the neighbours as it was beside the road and everyone had to stop give their tuppence worth. We also found out that Diane was expecting again, with the new arrival due in September so I really needed to get away to sea and back again in time for the birth. I was really hoping to go back to the *Norse Viking* but in the end I got instructions to rejoin the *Rudby* in Taranto in southern Italy. I flew down from Heathrow on the 19th April and arrived at Taranto airport at about six in the evening. There was a driver there to meet me and when I got in the car he said it was going to take a long time to get to the ship. I assumed that it was because the airport was a long way out of town but it rapidly became apparent that it was something else.

There was a huge fiesta going on with parades through the streets and all the fishing boats in harbours dressed overall. Someone from the Vatican had come down to bless the boats so all the roads around the port were gridlocked. After an hour and not having moved an inch the driver wandered off and came back with some cold Peroni beers for me and we sat on the harbour wall watching it all happening. After another couple of hours with no progress he locked the car up and took me into a little restaurant where he organised a huge pizza and more beer. I was a little bit concerned as all my luggage was left in his car but he insisted there was no problem. He paid the bill and announced that the company was paying so I had another beer. We then went and sat back on the harbour wall and watched a fantastic firework display. About eleven o'clock he managed to extricate the car and head off slowly towards the ore terminal. It was after midnight when I got aboard slightly the worse for wear. Ian, who I was relieving, had given up and gone to bed so I got the key to a spare cabin and turned in. Not a bad start to the trip.

I was woken early the next morning, though, as Ian was supposed to be catching a morning flight and needed to hand over. There wasn't much to hand over really as after a couple of hours on board I felt I'd never been away. The rest of the discharge went smoothly and we sailed the following morning for Tubarao. It was an uneventful trip across to Brazil and we arrived off the port early in the morning on the 5th May. This time it was a complete contrast to the in-and-out eighteen hour load. The port was congested and there were about twenty ships anchored off waiting to load so we found a quiet corner of the bay and dropped anchor. Ernie Dunn was the Skipper again and his anchoring technique hadn't improved. He nearly pulled the windlass off the focstle deck. We anchored off for ten days and it should have been a great opportunity to get some painting done but the weather was rubbish and I think we only had one dry day.

We berthed in the evening of the 15th May and started loading. It was an unusual cargo as not only did we have the basic iron ore but we loaded a semi-processed ore known as sinter and they had to be kept separate. My predecessor, Ian, had thankfully worked it all out so they just poured it in while I rushed around trying to get the ballast water pumped out. We managed with a couple of hours to spare. I had just developed a taste for avocados and someone mentioned that they were grown in the hills behind the port so I gave the foreman a handful of cruzeiros to buy me some. An hour later a bloke arrived in my cabin with a huge sack full of avacados. I think I could have supplied Tesco for a month with them. Needless to say I was sick of them by the time we got home and I think everyone on board was trying to grow a stone in a glass.

We sailed about noon on the 17th May and headed north towards Europe as they hadn't decided where we were going. After a few days I decided to check the cargo figures on the loading computer and record all the details. To my horror when I entered all the data I was confronted by flashing red warnings and it computed that the ship was severely overstressed and the condition should not be allowed even in port with no waves. I re-entered everything and it came up the same. It seemed that the previous Mate, Ian, must have given me the wrong figures. I beetled upstairs to Ernie's cabin and showed him the readouts. He was totally unconcerned and said not to bother him. I was really worried as it showed tremendous shear forces between numbers two and three holds. In the end I managed to reduce the strain by filling a ballast tank with water but of course then we were overloaded but at least we would sink gracefully instead of breaking in two.

Luckily we had good weather all the way back and we were ordered to discharge in Port Talbot. I couldn't understand how we were going to get in as the last time I'd been there it was a struggle to enter with a 9,000 ton ship but they had built an enormous brand new port next door. We arrived on the 1st June but had to anchor off waiting for a berth. Ernie got it wrong again but this time he put no weight on the anchor cable so we had to put the windlass in gear and pay the cable out. When we came to heave up a couple of days later we had a kink in the anchor cable which meant we couldn't pull it all the way in. I told Ernie we'd have to drop it again and see if the kink came out but we were late for the tide so he insisted we tried to heave it all the way in and of course it got jammed in the hawse pipe. We got tied up all right and started discharge and after a cup of coffee we went back up forward to try and clear the anchor cable. It was stuck absolutely solid in the pipe. We tried everything from getting a tug to try and pull it out on a wire which ended up with the wire parting and nearly taking out a couple of the tug crew. Then we fastened the other anchor to it and then dropped it to try and jerk it out but ended up with a wire jammed round the other anchor which took an hour to cut away. We were just discussing what to do next when Ernie arrived with one of the company superintendents. They looked at the chain and decided that it was nearly free and it would come clear with a good heave on the windlass. I remonstrated that it would only make it worse but was over ruled. On the second attempt there was a huge bang and the cable parted and the anchor disappeared into the dock followed by a couple of links of the cable. I walked off in disgust and retreated to my cabin for a beer. From then on it just went from bad to worse. Some local divers were employed to attach a wire to the anchor so we could lift it back on board but they could only work at low water as it was too deep otherwise. It took them two days to find the anchor as it had sunk into the mud. We were there for four days and I think I spent ninety per cent of that on the focstle trying to organise things. In the end we fitted our spare anchor and left the other one for a salvage company to retrieve. We eventually sailed on the morning of the 7th June with orders for another cargo from Tubarao.

We had changed crews in Port Talbot and picked a full crew from Cardiff. They turned out to be the laziest most bolshie shower I have ever sailed with. The Bosun was the only decent one and he had no hope of getting a day's work out of them. The only good thing was that we were returning to Port Talbot so we could get rid of them after only one trip. We got a message saying they wanted to load exactly the same as last time and when we said we had to change the amounts the charterers wanted to know why. We came up with our fuel amounts were different and in different tanks which seemed to satisfy them. I made sure I got the amounts right for this cargo and all the lights on the computer were a lovely green with not even one orange showing anywhere.

It wasn't a bad trip down though the crew did very little work and kept demanding overtime to do even less. We arrived in Tubarao on the 19th June and again it was congested so we had to anchor off for a week. The weather was good this time and I tried to get the crew painting the ship's side. I got really frustrated as if I got an hour's work out of the seamen a day I was doing well. We got a message while we were at anchor saying the ship would be dry docking after our next discharge which meant the ship's side would get completely painted by shore staff so in the end I wasn't too bothered.

Anchored just beside us was a tanker called *Sheaf Royal* which belonged to the Tyneside company Souters. I was chatting to them one evening on the VHF and was surprised to find out that the Skipper was Alan Clish who had been my best mate at sea school. It was his first trip as Captain and he seemed to be enjoying it. I started thinking that it shouldn't be too long now before I got my own ship. The extra money would be nice too!

We berthed late on the 27th June and after a pretty smooth load sailed thirty six hours later. Most of the crew had gone ashore the first night and failed to appear for work the following day, so much of the first day at sea was spent taking them up to the Old Man and fining them a couple of day's pay each. Ernie had been relieved by Colin Tingle and he was pretty strict. Not only did he fine them but stopped their beer for a couple of days. It was a quiet run north but we got warning of a bad storm in the Bay of Biscay. I was walking around the decks with the Bosun making sure everything was secure and watertight when we noticed one of the seamen tangling himself up in an air hose. He then threw a bucket of water over himself and went and lay down by the corner of a hatch. When he saw us he started groaning and said he'd been hit by a wave and he'd hurt his back badly. We both burst out laughing and left him to collect the air hose and his bucket. I often wonder how much he would have made if we hadn't caught him. Colin sent a report to the shipping office in Cardiff and we heard later that he'd been on the sick for a couple of years before from a previous 'accident'.

We arrived in Port Talbot on the 11th July and again had to anchor waiting for a berth. When we did get alongside we found that our anchor had been retrieved and was on the quay on a lorry. The next day a crane arrived to lift it on board. Unfortunately someone had given the crane operator the wrong weight and as he was swinging it on board his crane started to topple onto the ship. He had the presence of mind to drop it very quickly and it landed with a tremendous crash beside number one hatch. It was supposed to go on a frame on the focstle but understandably the crane driver wouldn't even think about moving it so we lashed it where it was and would sort it out when we got to dry dock. I was getting sick of this bloody anchor!

The rest of the discharge went smoothly and we sailed two days later up to the Mersey to dry dock arriving there on the 16th July. We lay on a river berth for three days and then entered dry dock at Cammel Lairds in Birkenhead. Diane came down to stay for a couple of days which brightened me up. We'd got rid of the Cardiff crew, thank goodness, and employed local riggers to help on deck. I was absolutely knackered working in the dock as I always seemed to be climbing ladders in the holds or going down to the bottom of the dock to check on something. The ship was programmed to sail on the 1st August and two days before, I got a message saying I was to be relieved as the ship was heading out to the Far East and they couldn't guarantee to get me home for the birth. I got off the ship just as she undocked and got home on the 30th July.

CHAPTER THIRTY THREE

Grain – bauxite – grain – bauxite – grain – bauxite - grain

m.v. Stonepool
8th October 1973 – 3rd April 1974

It was a bit of an odd leave as I'd only been away three months. I was due about three weeks leave so to stay home to see Karen born I had to take a month's unpaid leave which wasn't too much of a hardship as we'd managed to save a bit. The weather was great though I think Diane would have preferred it to be cooler as she neared the end of the pregnancy. Karen was born on the 24th September and I was aiming to stay around for at least a month to help out. Ropners used to produce a quarterly news sheet, creatively called 'Ropner News', and the latest edition arrived on about the 5th October. After studying it for a while I noticed that all the ships were in the middle of passages so I decided to make myself available for work and they would have to put me back on pay and they had nowhere to send me. When I phoned up the office the personnel manager was over the moon and told me I should join the *Stonepool* in Rotterdam the following day. It turned out that she had broken down and had to return to port and the Mate on there needed a relief. It is known as shooting oneself in the foot. Diane was devastated as Karen was less than two weeks old and I was leaving her again.

I joined the *Stonepool* in Rotterdam on the 8th October after flying over from Newcastle. I felt really guilty leaving Diane. We sailed a couple of days later in ballast for Suriname in South America; it used to be called Dutch Guinea. The ship was on a long charter to load bauxite there and take it to an aluminium plant up the Mississippi and then load grain back for the Netherlands and then back again. I felt a lot more comfortable on the *Stonepool* even though she was over 50,000 tons. As she didn't return to the UK on this charter the company had dispensed with British crews and taken a full crew from the International Pool in Rotterdam. I didn't know what to expect but they turned out to be a fantastic bunch. They were mainly ex-fishermen from north Spain and were a really happy hard working bunch in complete contrast to the shower I'd had from Cardiff on the *Rudby*. I seemed to know most of the officers as I'd now been sailing with Ropners for five years so had just about met everyone in passing. The Old Man was Mike Bradley who was doing his first trip as Skipper. I got on with him really well and he took a keen interest in everything.

We spent the first five days washing and cleaning the holds and then started on the maintenance. It was great having a good crew as you could see a difference at the end of each day.

Our loading port was Smalkalden about thirty miles up the Suriname River. We picked up a pilot at the entrance and set off up the river passed Paramaribo which was an old port on the west side of the river. The restricting factor for the river was a sand bar across the entrance and once over that is was surprisingly deep all the way up. It was odd as on one side was a thriving city and on the other side was just impenetrable jungle. Berthing was pretty interesting as the river was only just wider than the length of the ship and we had to turn around before loading. There were no tugs available but the pilot had done it loads of times and he just stuck the bow into the river bank and let the tide do the work. He made it look easy.

Once alongside we started loading the bauxite using conveyors. Loading was quite complicated as we couldn't pump the ballast out too quickly otherwise the conveyors couldn't reach the ship. It was a bit of a balancing act but we managed. We could only load 20,000 tons otherwise we couldn't get out of the river over the sand bar so we only loaded in three holds which saved a lot of cleaning later. The depth on the sand bar was constantly changing so they would only tell us at the last minute how much we could load so there was a mad rush around at the end to get the ballast out and the ship trimmed so it was level.

The stevedores provided me with a boat and driver so I could nip around and take the ship's drafts quickly. It was a tiny aluminium skiff with a huge outboard motor on the back. There was a big red sign on the boat transom saying the maximum engine should be five horse power but this thing was over fifty. The boatman insisted on showing off and nearly had me in the water a couple of times. I took to wearing a life jacket whenever I had to go in the boat which amused the boatman greatly. I couldn't understand what he was saying but it turned out he was telling me a life jacket didn't matter as the river was full of piranha anyway. We sailed early in the morning of the 24th October. A Norwegian ship was sailing from the berth ahead of us and it turned out that he had loaded three feet deeper than us for some reason. After much discussion we overtook him in case he went aground and blocked the river. We got over the sand bar all right though we stirred up a lot of mud and sand. As we looked back we could see the Norwegian ship come to a halt on the bar. He was stuck there for three days before the tides picked up and he could get over the bar. I bet there were some questions being asked on that ship.

We then set off up the Caribbean towards the Gulf of Mexico and the Mississippi River. Our discharge port was a place called Burnside fifty miles upriver past New Orleans and we berthed there on the evening of the 1st November. Just after we tied up there was a huge explosion on board. Everyone was running about trying to find out what had happened as all the accommodation was filling with smoke and the fire alarms were going off. After a while we realised one of the Junior Engineers was missing so a couple of us put breathing apparatuses on and went looking for him in the engine room. There was no fire, just a lot of thick smoke. We eventually found him unconscious up in the boiler room. He was badly burned and in a bad way. He had been lighting the boiler and it had been full of oil fumes and had exploded as he put the flame to the door. We had a hell of a job getting him out on deck and onto the shore. Mike Bradley had somehow organised an ambulance so they whipped him off as soon as we put him ashore. Everyone was very pessimistic so it was a quiet night. The next morning we got word that he was doing all right but his burns would take a lot of sorting and he would have at least a couple of months in hospital but hopefully there wouldn't be too much scarring.

After the exciting start to discharge it all went smoothly and we finished unloading at six o'clock in the evening. We moved from Burnside another forty miles up the river to a grain terminal at Myrtle Grove near Baton Rouge arriving there at two o'clock in the morning. We had to work through the night cleaning the holds and when the stevedores arrived at eight o'clock we had all but one hold clean and passed by the grain inspectors. It was a real work up and I was run off my feet trying to supervise the loading, organise the ballast water to be pumped out and make sure the last hold was cleaned properly. The inspector signed off our last hold just after lunch and with the loading going smoothly I was able to sit down and enjoy a couple of cold beers. The rest of the loading went smoothly but the ship was too big to load a full cargo so we sailed on the 4th November and shifted downriver to load the last 5,000 tons. This berth was at a place called Ama directly across the river from New Orleans and it was a bit frustrating seeing all the neon signs and not being able to get there. It took them two days to finish off loading as there was a problem with the grain elevator. It made life easy for me and we eventually sailed in the evening of 6th November. I was pleased to see that Ropners had spent a lot of money repairing the hatches since my last tour on board but we still made doubly sure they were watertight by using the Ram-nek tape everywhere.

It took seventeen days to get to Rotterdam and we berthed at a brand new silo in an area called Botlek. The discharge was quite slow as they were commissioning all the conveyors and pneumatic dischargers. We had to take on board six months' stores whilst we were there and it all arrived in a huge lorry on the second day. It was a nightmare to load, as we had to hand carry it along narrow catwalks to a platform from which we could lift it on board. It took the best part of three days to get it all on board and stowed away. While we were discharging the engineers were overhauling the main engine and discovered a problem with one of the turbo chargers so when we finished unloading on the 29th November they towed us up into Rotterdam and we tied up to buoys in the middle of one of the harbours while they sorted it out. We had to wait a few days for some new bearings to be delivered and fitted and eventually we sailed in the evening of the 2nd December.

It was a repeat of the previous voyage though the weather wasn't as good crossing the Atlantic. We arrived back in Smalkalden on the 14th December and it was quite nice to be greeted like old friends by the loading foremen. The loading went very smoothly and we sailed after two days. This time we had a variation in that we had to load an extra 10,000 tons in Port of Spain in Trinidad on the way to the States. This only took us twenty four hours and we were on our way again. We were quite pleased to get away from Trinidad as there was a real anti-white regime there and we were told it wasn't safe to venture ashore. The whole place had a really bad atmosphere.

We arrived back in Burnside at ten o'clock on Christmas morning and anchored in the river just off the berth. We had a lovely Christmas dinner with nothing much going on so we were all able to relax and have a few drinks. We actually stayed at anchor for another three days though we were nearly sunk on the second day when a huge string of barges loaded with grain broke adrift further up river and the tugs only just managed to stop them colliding with us.

We went alongside in Burnside at breakfast time on the 28th December and they had us unloaded early the following morning and we set off up river to Baton Rouge. I was amazed at the strength of the river. It knocked our speed down from thirteen knots to seven and it took us over seven hours to do the fifty miles. The Skippers of the old steam river boats must have been really good at ship-handling manoeuvring the old stern wheeled paddle boats. Mind you the blokes driving the tugs with fifty odd barges in tow did a pretty mean job. We anchored just south of Baton Rouge and spent a day getting the hatches cleaned and passed by the inspectors. We then had to wait for four days as our cargo wasn't ready. We all managed to get ashore and have a look around as it was a really picturesque old town and the night life was pretty lively. I actually spent my money on something useful for once and invested in an electronic calculator. It cost nearly £30 and had only the basic four functions and was about the size of a house brick but I thought it was amazing. It made a huge difference when working out the grain stability calculations. It used to take well over an hour and I was now able to knock one out in about ten minutes once I got it sussed.

On my way back to the ship I had to wait quite a while for a launch to take me out to the ship anchored in the river so I wandered into a scruffy little bar where I could see the launch jetty. I got talking to some locals though they spoke in some weird patois French and were very hard to understand. They ended up giving me a box of fresh crayfish they had just caught. When I got on board I gave them to the cook to sort out. I thought he would just freeze them but he turned to and cooked them. They were in a hot garlic sauce and were absolutely delicious. I sat out on deck and polished the lot off washed down with a few cold beers. It wasn't such a bad life.

That night we were woken up at two in the morning by a huge bang followed by shouting and engines revving. A tug coming downriver with twenty or so loaded barges had lost control on a bend and ended up colliding with us. By the time we got up the tug and barges had been swept way down river but we could hear on the radio that they were having a hard time collecting them all together. We checked around expecting to find quite a bit of damage and maybe even a hole in the side but there was only a small dent in the starboard bow and a bit of paint off. The barges weren't so lucky as at least two of them sank.

We eventually got alongside on the 3rd January and loaded 40,000 tons of maize in forty eight hours. We then shifted down river to New Orleans and loaded 15,000 tons of soya beans. We berthed close to Canal Street but I was too busy so didn't get a chance to go ashore and we sailed very early the following morning. Mind you from the state of those who ventured ashore I was pleased I'd stayed aboard. Johnny Baulk, the Chief Engineer, had been enthusing about a local drink called a sazerac which he reckoned was the best ever. It is peculiar to Louisiana and is apparently very moreish. The lads must have drunk New Orleans dry of sazerac as they returned aboard very much the worse for wear. The hangovers lasted a couple of days so we all steered well clear of it on future visits.

It was an uneventful trip back to Rotterdam and we berthed on buoys in the middle of the Waalhaven on the 22nd January. It was a slow discharge as they used floating elevators and unloaded us directly into barges which took the grain inland up the River Rhine. I loved watching the barges as they were all beautifully turned out with immaculate paintwork. It must have been a hard life, though, as they never seemed to get a break and were always on the move.

As we were tied up to buoys it was a pain to get ashore as it meant catching the ferries at set times or paying a fortune to get a water taxi. I managed to get off a couple of times and was taken out for meals. It was nice going to a port regularly as we got to know the agents, chandlers and stevedores personally and it felt good to be greeted as an old friend whenever we arrived. We also knew how the port worked so generally the cargo work went pretty smoothly. The Old Man, Mike Bradley, paid off and Colin Tingle took over. I'd sailed with him before on the *Rudby* and we got on well so I was looking forward to another decent trip.

It took ten days to discharge and we sailed again on the 1st February and headed off in ballast for the Caribbean. We ran into a storm as we cleared the Channel and without asking anyone Colin Tingle decided to fill our wing tanks with ballast water to make the ship more comfortable in the heavy seas. The wing tanks were tanks high up on the side of the ship under the main deck. They could also be used to carry grain and we had left them set up for that with all sorts of timber and sacking packed in the corners. The tanks filled all right but it became a different matter when we tried to pump them out a week later. The suction pipes and valves became blocked with sacking and wood. We managed to empty all but two which we couldn't pump out no matter what we tried. Then someone had the brilliant idea of using our breathing apparatus, which was for entering smoke filled compartments, as a scuba kit. It worked and we took it in turns to dive down and unblock the pipes. We must have been mad as it was dark with zero visibility and the air demand valve on the breathing apparatus kept sticking so we had to rush to the surface for air. We managed in the end and got the tanks pumped out but I dread to think what Health and Safety would have said about it. Colin gave us a couple of cases of beer for our efforts and it was a really good feeling afterwards, when we'd cleaned up, sitting in the sunshine drinking cold beer on the deck.

We arrived in Smalkalden on the 13th February and the cargo was a repeat of the last trip with us topping off in Port of Spain in Trinidad. As per the previous visit none of us ventured ashore. We used to get quite a few salesmen coming on board hawking souvenirs and local goods. One bloke had some bottles of top quality rum which was really smooth and tasted great so some of us invested in a couple of bottles each even though it wasn't cheap. Most of us were going to try and take them home. After we sailed the Chief Steward decided to sample his bottle and was most put out to find it tasted like petrol. It turned out the bottles were filled with some cheap alcohol and sealed up so we'd all been had. A lesson to be learnt.

After Trinidad it was back to Burnside to discharge where we arrived on the 23rd February. It was the usual quick discharge and then we shifted down river to anchor off New Orleans and clean the hatches. There had been a bit of a drought over the last few months so the Mississippi was at a really low level. Consequently the barges loaded with grain were unable to get downstream so all the silos around New Orleans were empty. This meant there was a huge backlog of ships waiting for grain and it was an amazing sight seeing them all at anchor for miles down the river. The grain inspectors were being really strict and failing the holds for cleanliness. This meant they didn't come on charter until they had passed so it was saving the shippers millions of dollars. Inevitably we were failed but due to a misunderstanding and to my great delight the inspector failed the only hold that had been cleaned by shore labour. This meant the shore gang had to return and clean their hold again and I could relax on deck with a cold beer. The inspector passed the hold first thing next morning so we were on charter and making some money for the company. We were stuck at anchor for two weeks which was a bit frustrating as we could see all the lights ashore but the ferries were far too expensive.

On the 14th March we moved up river and berthed at Myrtle Grove again near Baton Rouge. We could only load half our cargo, though, as the river had silted up near the entrance so they sent us out to Houston in Texas to finish off loading. We had problems there as well with the low water levels and ended up being stuck on the bottom and having to get some extra tugs to pull us off. We sailed on the 19th March and set off back across the Atlantic. Just for a change they decided to send us to Hamburg for discharge and we arrived there on the 2nd April. Just before we arrived Colin got a message saying I was being relieved so I was paid off the next day and flew home to Heathrow hired a car and set off north. It had been a five month trip and it actually seemed to have passed very quickly.

CHAPTER THIRTY FOUR

The Pacific iron ore run

m.v. Rudby
28th June 1974 – 30th January 1975

I got home in early April which was a lovely time of year to be home. Karen was just six months old and to start with had a hard time coping with the strange bloke wandering around the house. Martin just seemed to accept things. I spent a lot of time in the garden and produced some pretty decent vegetables. I was half hoping to go back to the *Stonepool* as Terry Jones who relieved me had been told he would only be doing a couple of months and then was being promoted to Captain. It all looked good on paper but just after my birthday on the 14th June I got a call saying I was going to the *Rudby* again. I was joining it in Valparaiso in Chile so it took a few days to organise a visa.

I flew out on the 25th June with Captain Tims, Ropner's Marine Superintendent, as the ship needed some repairs and he had to oversee them. We landed in Santiago late in the afternoon and were transported in style by limousine to Valparaiso. I was glad I was with Captain Tims as if I'd been on my own I'm sure I'd have had to take a bus. It was an interesting trip to say the least. I really enjoyed seeing the countryside but they were having some sort of revolution and there were soldiers and road blocks everywhere. We got stopped numerous times and had to get out and have our papers checked and I got really fed up having to open my cases for inspection. There was a countrywide curfew making it illegal to be out on the streets after dark. Needless to say, with all the delays at the road blocks, it was getting dark as we arrived on the outskirts of Valparaiso and our driver was getting increasingly nervous. When we were stopped at yet another roadblock he ended up having an argument with the soldiers and it looked pretty serious until an officer appeared. He spoke really good English and had trained at Sandhurst. He apologised profusely and organised an armed patrol to escort us to our hotel. It was quite impressive and only in the hotel did we find out that there had been a big gun fight on the same road two days previously resulting in quite a few soldiers being killed. Ignorance is bliss! We had a couple of days in the hotel waiting for the ship to arrive but we didn't venture far though it seemed to be a very pleasant port. We were taken out for a couple of lovely meals by the shipyard who were going to do the repairs and I was introduced to Chilean wines which I really enjoyed.

The *Rudby* arrived on the 28th June but she had to anchor outside the port as she was too big to enter the breakwaters. We went out by tug and had a hell of a job getting on board as there was a huge swell and the ship was really high out of the water. I was sure I was going to lose a suitcase into the water but we managed in the end. The damage to be repaired was to a bulkhead between numbers two and three holds which had become distorted and broken away from the deck at the bottom. It took them a week to force it back to its original position with huge jacks and then it was rewelded. Captain Tims spent quite a bit of time trying to work out why it had happened. I had a pretty good idea it was caused when the ship had been seriously overstressed when I'd been on board a couple of years earlier but I didn't dare mention it.

Eventually on the 8th July it was all passed by the insurance surveyors and we sailed up the coast to Huasco to load. There was only one loading berth and it was occupied by another ship so we had to anchor off for two days. Loading was a real pain as it was an old berth and there was only one loading conveyor so we had to move the ship back and forth to load the different hatches. They always seemed to want us to move in the middle of meal times or just after everyone had gone to bed. We eventually got the mooring lines organised so that we could shift the ship with just four people which made life easier. They finished loading late on the 13th July but we had to sail 100 miles south to Guayacan to load the final 20,000 tons as the port of Huasco was too shallow for us to load completely. Guayacan was much more modern and we loaded in less than eight hours and then set off across the Pacific towards Japan.

It was a really slow trip as the *Rudby* hadn't been dry docked for over a year and the hull had become heavily fouled with weed and shell. We were supposed to do over eleven knots but we were lucky if we did ten and it wasn't doing the engine much good either as it was constantly overheating as the cooling water system was also clogged. The passage across the Pacific was pretty tedious really as our track didn't take us near any islands and we rarely saw any other ships. Still, the weather was usually pretty good.

We arrived in Mizushima in the Japanese Inland Sea at nine in the morning on the 16th August. It was mayhem. A team of divers arrived to start scrubbing the hull with machines to remove the weed, six months' stores appeared on the quay in a fleet of lorries and vans, discharge started and I had to organise ballasting the tanks, a barge tied up alongside with 3,000 tons of fuel and about half the crew were relieved so we had to show the new arrivals around the ship. I was soon wishing for the tedium of the sea passage. The discharge was completed pretty quickly and the divers seemed to have done a pretty good job removing the weed. The only trouble was they had removed a lot of paint as well so the ship's side looked really rough.

We sailed at six in the morning on the 19th August and by the evening we had sailed out of the Inland Sea and cleared the Japanese coast and set off for another thirty days across the Pacific to Chile. It was an uneventful trip with pretty good weather all the way over. Cleaning the weed off the hull seemed to have been a success and we knocked over a day off the passage time arriving back in Huasco on the 15th September. The loading was identical to the previous occasions so that went pretty smoothly. It was getting a bit monotonous, though, and there was nothing to go ashore for, so only a few of the hardier souls ventured the three mile walk to town.

It was a slower than usual load as they were having problems with their conveyor belt but we sailed early in the morning of the 19th September and headed south to finish off in Guayacan. We had to climb down a ladder to a platform near the water to read the draft marks and I'd just climbed down and was writing the draft in my notebook when something black and white went zipping passed just below the surface. My first thought was killer whale and I shot up the ladder at a rate of knots. When I stopped and looked back I was amazed to see a huge flock of penguins tearing about chasing a shoal of fish. The water was really clear and it was fantastic seeing them twisting and turning after the fish. I ran up to my cabin to get my camera but when I got back there was no sign of them but talking to the loading foreman he reckoned they were always around. I later identified them as Magellan penguins though the book reckoned they didn't get that far north.

It took nearly a day to load as the shore terminal didn't seem to be in a hurry. We sailed on the 20th September and set off for the long drag across the Pacific. The weed and shell on the hull had already started to grow back but it wasn't enough to affect our speed. This time our discharge port was Chiba in Tokyo Bay and we arrived there early on the 21st October. As soon as the ship tied up we would be boarded by a gang of Japanese draft surveyors whose job it was to calculate the amount of cargo we had on board. They used to drive me to distraction as they would work to six or seven decimal places and in the end would fiddle the figures so we had at least 100 tons less cargo than the Bill of Lading. I was so fed up of this that this trip I had actually loaded an extra 200 tons of cargo which didn't show on the Bill of Lading. They took the readings and made the calculations and then sat around in a huddle muttering in Japanese and sucking their teeth. After an hour they came up with a figure of twenty tons less than the Bill of Lading figure but I disagreed, showed them my calculations and insisted there was slightly more. There was a lot of head shaking and muttering and they set about recalculating it all again. After six hours I had to admit defeat as they were still sitting in my cabin, drinking my beer and changing figures but we agreed on five tons less so they didn't lose face. I decided I wouldn't do it again.

It took just over three days to discharge. The Old Man, Fred Carter, was relieved by Alex Dekonski who I hadn't sailed with since my first trip with Ropners. I was hoping he had mellowed and improved with age but he hadn't and he was soon throwing his weight about and being a pain. The only good thing was that a new Second Mate, Ron Dodd, had also joined and he had been told by the company to understudy me and he would be promoted and relieve me. I had been promised Christmas at home this time so I figured if they relieved me next time back in Japan I would just get home in time.

We left on the 24th October to head back to Chile and it became obvious that the weed and shell had grown back on the hull as our speed was right down. I soon realised that if I wasn't relieved in South America I wouldn't be home for Christmas. I pointed this out to Alex, the Old Man, and he promised to send a telegram and make sure the company was aware. I then concentrated on making sure Ron was up to speed and could take over as Mate. Ron had spent most of his time with Bank Line, which operated old fashioned tramp steamers, and hadn't done much on bulk carriers. He was fifty odd and though a very good seaman couldn't cope with technology and had a hard time with our loading computer. We spent a couple of hours a day going through old cargoes and trying new ones and he became pretty proficient in the end. As the trip progressed it became obvious that Alex disliked Ron intensely and always seemed to be having a go at him. Alex kept asking me if I was sure Ron was up to the Mate's job and I always assured him that Ron was more experienced than me.

About a week out from Chile I suggested to Alex that Ron should take over as Mate which would make for an easy handover but he would have none of it and insisted I carried on which pissed me off somewhat. Two days before Chile we got a message saying there would be no relieving so I would have to stay back to Japan and miss yet another Christmas. I was more than a little bit peeved and ended up having a good old shouting match with Alex. I think I won because he went out of his way to be pleasant for the next few days which wasn't normally his style.

The load went really smoothly and we set off back for Japan on the 24th November. One good thing about the trip across the Pacific was the weather. It always seemed to be calm seas and blue skies which actually got a bit monotonous in the end but it meant that the deck maintenance always progressed at a good pace. Being on the four to eight watch I always had a kip in the afternoons between one and three. It was very therapeutic especially after a couple of cold beers at lunch time.

One afternoon about halfway across the Pacific I was more than a bit annoyed to be woken and told the Old Man wanted me on the bridge. I decided it must be pretty serious for him to dare to interrupt my kip. It appeared the Radio Officer had just received a message from a radio station in Hawaii warning all ships of a large tsunami moving south east across the Pacific. There had been an earthquake somewhere near Tahiti and it had triggered this wave which they estimated was over forty feet high which was no mean wave. They also had it travelling towards us at eighty miles an hour which took some believing. Nobody had ever heard of a tsunami so we got the books out and did some hurried reading. We calculated we had about eight hours before it arrived so the crew were galvanised into action checking all the watertight hatches and getting everything that moved off the deck and stowed away. We also lashed all the stores and other equipment so it wouldn't move. It took us until six o'clock before we were satisfied and we knocked off and had the evening meal. Everyone was pretty quiet as we had no idea what to expect but being on a huge ship gave us a better chance than most.

I finished my watch at eight o'clock and had a final check around the decks with the Bosun. We had received another update which meant we'd hit it in two hours at ten o'clock. Nobody went to bed and some even dug their lifejackets out from under their bunks. We sat around and knocked back a few beers. Just before ten most of us went up to the bridge where they had the radar going. We figured that a forty foot wave would show up pretty strongly and give us some warning. After a couple of hours staring out to the north west we all got rather bored and reckoned the Yanks had got it wrong so most of us headed for our beds leaving instructions to be called if the wave did eventually appear. I was woken as normal for my four o'clock watch and when I arrived on the bridge we had reverted to our normal sailing routine. The radio stations were still giving out the wave's position and it was now well behind us which didn't seem to make sense but at least it had livened up a day for us. When I went to record the weather conditions at six o'clock I was surprised to note that there was a blip on the barograph chart just after ten the previous night which showed the ship had indeed been lifted up about forty feet. As we were in very deep water it meant the wave hadn't really developed and had just been a huge mass of water beneath the surface. It took us all next day to unlash everything so I ended up losing a day's deck maintenance which was a bit of a pain.

As we approached the Japanese coast I again started to pack up my gear and hand over the reins to Ron as I was sure I would be flown home as soon as we docked and at least I'd have New Year and a belated Christmas dinner at home. Two days before Christmas there was a message from Ropners wishing us all a Merry Christmas and saying that there would be no reliefs in Japan. I found out later that the personnel manager had phoned Diane the same day to wish her a Happy Christmas and give her the news that I had requested to stay on for another month. It wasn't the best phone call because Martin had pulled the kitchen table over onto himself and trapped his hands just as Diane had found that all the icing on her lovely Christmas cake had all fallen off so when the call came she burst into tears. I wasn't the most popular bloke around! I found out much later that Dekonski didn't want to promote Ron so he'd sent a message to Ropners without my knowledge saying as I'd missed Christmas I would be willing to do another couple of months on board. The Radio Officer heard me muttering and told me about the message but I couldn't do anything about it without dropping him in the proverbial.

We arrived in Mizushima on the 28th December and after a pretty quick discharge we sailed again for Chile on the morning of the 31st. Ropners had organised for the divers to come and scrub the weed off again. This time they had more powerful scrubbers that worked off boats alongside. They certainly took a lot of weed off as the water all around us was turned into a thick green soup while the cleaning was going on. It seemed to have worked as we were back up to speed again when we set off.

It wasn't a bad trip across and it went pretty quickly. A week before Chile we got a message saying that four of us were being relieved on arrival. This time I got packed and handed the job over to Ron before we docked. Just after we tied up the Old Man came running into my cabin with a message from the charterers saying they wanted to change the loading figures and he wanted me to work it out. I told him I'd handed over to Ron but he insisted I should work it out as he didn't trust Ron. We ended up having a huge shouting match. It nearly came to blows which would have been a good way to end the trip.

I never did work his bloody figures out and we got off the ship the next morning. It was quite a trip home. We had a four hour taxi ride to a small airport where we caught a dilapidated old plane down to Santiago. When we arrived there nobody seemed to know anything about us but eventually we got booked into a hotel. They said we'd have to wait at least four days as all the flights out were full. At least the hotel was pretty reasonable with good food and it appeared all the drink was paid for so we set about taking advantage of the situation. I was woken about five the next morning by someone hammering at my door to tell me a taxi was waiting to take us to the airport. We were all severely hung-over and we couldn't find George, the Chief Steward. His room was empty and his bed hadn't been slept in. Feeling rather guilty we decided to leave him and took the taxi to the airport arriving just in time to catch the flight. He eventually turned up two days later in the UK – it seems he'd been enjoying himself in a brothel. The aircraft was run by a local airline and was extremely overloaded. There were four or five passengers sitting on deck chairs in the aisles and baggage was everywhere. Thankfully it got us to Miami where we transferred to a Pan Am flight to Heathrow. I hired a car and drove home though I should really have stayed in a hotel for a night. I nearly put the car in a ditch a couple of miles from home as I didn't realise the roads were so icy. It was good to be home, though, and I swore I'd never sail on the *Rudby* again.

CHAPTER THIRTY FIVE

Working ashore

m.v. Bridgepool
10th July 1975 – 15th July 1975

It was lovely to get home again. The trip on the *Rudby* had seemed to go on forever. A couple of weeks into the leave Karen was found to have a problem with her hips which entailed an operation with lengthy stays in hospital and being in and out of plaster for about six months. There was no way I was going back to sea while all this was going on. I told Ropners about it and said I would take unpaid leave at least until things were sorted out

I got a job as a ganger with Laing Offshore who were laying a gas pipeline from Scotland down through Cumbria to the Midlands. I was put in charge of eight blokes, a bulldozer and a JCB complete with drivers. We had to lay 'riprap' which was basically making a temporary road over boggy areas using sawn trees. It was rubbish to start with as four of my team were idle deadbeats but being a new man I had to put up with them. I quite enjoyed the organising side of the job. We were paid by yardage and I soon got the hang of things and started making pretty good money. Word got about that we were doing good yardage and I was approached by several blokes wanting to join my gang. I managed to get rid of the deadbeats and ended up with a really good team. This resulted in even more yardage and even more money. I was beginning to like this! We had a system where we would unload the timber from the lorries straight away even if it was in our meal times. The lorry drivers liked this as they weren't hanging around so we always had loads of timber when we needed it. We were all sitting having a late lunch one day when the agent and some managers stopped by. They demanded to know why we weren't working and I explained that we'd worked through our meal hour. They insisted that lunch had to be taken between twelve and one and then drove off full of importance. I wasn't going to take any notice but the next day one of the lorry drivers pointed out that a couple of managers were sitting in a Landrover on the next hill watching us through binoculars. This went on for a week and did my head in. It slowed us down which meant less money at the end of the week. The next time the managers drove past I went and confronted them. They were adamant that we had to have our breaks at the set times even though it was less efficient. I decided I was fed up and packed my hand in the next day much to the disgust of my gang who had to be split up.

I then applied for a job in the port control at Milford Haven. It was a brand new state of the art facility and I rather fancied it. It also looked a lovely part of the world to live in. I got an interview but it was on the day of Karen's operation so I phoned up to explain and see if I could change it and was told very bluntly that if I didn't turn up for the interview I wouldn't get the job. Needless to say I didn't go and I heard later that it was a terrible place to work with all sorts of back biting and unpleasantness. That's all right then.

The next week Diane happened to mention that John, who had the local dairy farm, needed someone to help with the haylage harvest. I ended up working for John for about three months. I thought it would be an easy life sitting driving a tractor all day but it turned out to be really hard work. I don't think I've ever been fitter or felt better. The money wasn't great but we seemed to manage pretty well.

The first week in July I got a phone call from Ropners that they needed a mate to move one of their ships from Middlesbrough to Hartlepool as they were laying it up. As it was only for a week I said yes and travelled over and joined the *Bridgepool* on the 10th July. She had just come out of dry dock and was all nicely painted up. She was very similar to the *Wandby* so it was easy to find my way around. The Old Man was Terry Jones and he was having to go back to being Mate again once we'd laid the ship up. It didn't look good for promotion prospects. It took one or two days to sort the ship out and we shifted the few miles to Hartlepool on the 14th July. It was then a matter of making the ship nice and secure and we all paid off and went home the following day.

Karen had her last plaster removed the week after I got home again and a couple of weeks later we took her in for an X-ray and were told she'd need another operation in a few months time. I then had to decide what to do job-wise. Ropners had bought another ship the same size as the *Rudby* and I knew I definitely didn't want to spend my life on that sort of vessel. I'd been keeping in touch with John Bannister, who was an old school friend, and he had joined a new Arab company called Kuwait Shipping Company. It looked too good to be true with newish general cargo ships, fantastic rates of pay, five month trips and good promotion prospects so I decided to give them a try. I went down to Liverpool for an interview and was very impressed by the set up. The only negative thing was that the ships spent most of their time in the Arabian Gulf but it was a part of the world I hadn't been to so I thought I'd give it a go. They offered me a job and said they would be in touch in a couple of weeks so I returned home to tell Diane the good news. She wasn't too happy with me returning to sea but I couldn't stay at home forever.

CHAPTER THIRTY SIX

Working for the Arabs

m.v. Al Rumaithiah
28th August 1975 – 4th November 1975

I knew I had to go back to sea pretty soon as we were starting to use our savings because farm labourers weren't among the highest paid. On one hand I could go back with Ropners which was a reputable family company and I had made a lot of friends there but I hated the large bulk carriers and promotion prospects were virtually nil. The other option was to start anew with Kuwait Shipping which had no reputation but the wages and promotion prospects were brilliant. Another factor I had to take into account was that Karen would have to have an operation in mid November so I only wanted to do a two month trip at the most. The problem was solved almost immediately when Ropners rang to say they would like me to rejoin the Rudby in the Far East and they couldn't guarantee to get me home for Karen's operation. The next day Kuwait Shipping called to offer me a job on one of their newer vessels. When I explained the situation with Karen they said that they would fly me home in time for the operation. I also had another week at home and they put me on pay straight away. It was a no-brainer really.

I'd been at home for eight months and it was a huge wrench to leave but I flew out to join the *Al Rumaithiah* in Dubai on the 28th August. I arrived in Dubai early evening and was taken to a five star hotel for the night. I took advantage and had a fantastic meal of lobster with all the trimmings and half a bottle of very expensive wine and retired happily to bed. I got up early next morning and had breakfast expecting to be taken to the ship first thing. By mid morning there had been no communication so I tried to get in touch with the agent. The girl who answered the phone knew nothing about me but said she would find out and ring back. At three o'clock after a rather pleasant lunch I was starting to get worried and rang the agent again only to find the office had closed for the day. It was turning into a bit of a nightmare but the hotel receptionist assured me that the bill was taken care of and I should relax in the bar. Eventually at six in the evening a taxi arrived to take me down to the ship. It turned out that there had been a party on board the previous night and the Chief Steward had dropped down dead in the early hours and in all the confusion I had been forgotten.

First impressions were not very good. Everyone I met seemed to be pissed or well on the way. The air conditioning had broken down and the temperature was up in the forties. They were discharging cargo and it appeared that the wrong cargo was being unloaded and one of the cranes had obviously broken down though nobody seemed to be trying to repair it. This didn't bode well at all. After a while Tom Weale, the Mate, appeared – he'd been ashore at the hospital trying to sort the paperwork to repatriate the Chief Steward's body. At least he was sober though pretty upset as the Chief Steward had been a close friend. We got the cargo problem sorted and he found an engineer to repair the crane so things settled down. His flight was first thing next morning so we were up until pretty late as he handed over to me. I got to bed about two in the morning but it was so hot it was impossible to sleep. I was rapidly going off the Arabian Gulf.

When I got up next morning Tom had already left so I had breakfast and a wander around. Apart from the air conditioning being broken and the temperatures being in the upper forties it wasn't all that bad. The Indian deck crew were working away painting the ship's side oblivious of the heat. This was my first experience with a full Indian crew and I was pleasantly surprised. The first thing I had to learn was the hierarchy because it seemed it was very easy to insult them without realising it. Instead of a Bosun the head crewman was the Serang and his second in command was called the Tindal. Next in line were the Seacunnies who were essentially the helmsmen at sea and the watchmen in port. It was a very cushy number and they were usually bone idle but always handy for organising tea and toast in the middle of the night. The engine room and catering department were similar to European ranks but we had an extra cook to cook solely for the crew called the Bhandary and he had a sidekick called the Bhandary's Mate. At the bottom of the pile were the Topazes who were 'untouchables' and their job was to keep all the toilets and public places clean. If I needed a job doing I had to send for the Serang or Tindal who would delegate the job and I wasn't expected to give orders direct to the ratings. The system actually seemed to work very well.

After the previous night's hiccup the cargo discharge was going along smoothly. The only problem appeared to be that the Chief and Second Engineers were alcoholics and were dragging the rest of the engineers down with them. We were waiting for a new motor for the air conditioning but their way of keeping cool was to down as much cold beer as possible in the shortest time. I could see this was going to be a right pain.

After four days we sailed having discharged all the Dubai cargo apart from one huge wooden crate which was buried under 500 tons of Bahrain cargo. I was pretty concerned as it was going to cost a bomb to ship it back but no one else seemed worried and reckoned it happened all the time. Our next port was Abu Dhabi which was only ten hours steaming away. We anchored off for a day due to the congestion but went in the following morning as we had priority cargo on board though I don't know what it was. I think it was a fiddle to get us in ahead of all the other ships.

The Gulf seemed to be one huge construction site. Everywhere you looked they were building something and the ships were queuing up outside every port with even more construction materials. It was nice to be back working with general cargo and we had quite a few heavy lifts of 100 tons which made life interesting.

The motor for the air conditioning finally arrived and the engineers stayed sober long enough to get it working again so at least we got a comfortable night's sleep. It took a week to discharge and we sailed on the 12th September up to Kuwait. I couldn't believe my eyes when we arrived off Kuwait. The bay was filled with hundreds of ships at anchor all waiting to discharge. It looked like we could be stuck there for months but again we were taken in after a day at anchor with our priority cargo. It turned out to be equipment for the new hospital but as soon as that was unloaded we had to sail even though there was still 2,000 tons of Kuwait cargo still on board.

Our next port was Bahrain where construction seemed to be more restrained and there were no ships waiting so we went straight alongside and started discharge. I quite liked Bahrain as it seemed more westernised than the other ports. It was very pleasant to wander ashore in the evening and have a couple of pints of draft beer in one of the numerous bars. All the bars had themes from genuine Irish with Guinness on draught to Dickensian London Pubs with Watney Red Barrel. All were staffed by genuine buxom barmaids from the correct area. It was all very civilised. Discharge went on at a very leisurely pace with only one gang working most of the time. It was probably just as well as the cranes were always breaking down and it was a right pain trying to get the engineers to put down their can of beer to fix it. The *Al Rumaithiah* was only a couple of years old but it was like going back ten years with the technology. She had been built in Russia and all the equipment was very dated and required a lot of maintenance to keep it operational. The accommodation was comfortable though and all the senior officers had huge fridges to keep the beer cold.

On the last day of discharge we uncovered another 100 tons of Dubai cargo in addition to the huge wooden crate we had been unable to discharge while we were in Dubai. The company organised a tug and barge so we discharged it all into the barge and off it went to Dubai at great expense. I was sure there would be recriminations but nobody seemed bothered and I gathered it happened a lot. We sailed on the 8th October and steamed the twelve hours up the coast to Dammam in Saudi Arabia. I thought there were a lot of ships in Kuwait Bay but there must have been twice as many anchored off here. It looked about the total world fleet of general cargo ships. It took ages to find a spot to anchor. I couldn't figure out if Maurice, the Old Man, was either a brilliant ship handler or hadn't a clue what he was doing and was very lucky. We threaded our way through all the ships actually passing so close that we had conversations with the other crews as we passed until he found a nice spot just off the harbour entrance. I later came to the conclusion that although Maurice was a fantastic bloke he had absolutely no idea about ship handling and lived a charmed life.

We didn't have any priority cargo for Dammam so we had to lie at anchor for three weeks waiting for a berth. It was pretty boring with nothing much to do but listening to the talk on the VHF radio. Some ships carrying cement had been there for months and the cement was going off which didn't sound the best organisation in the world.

We eventually berthed on the 27th October and started discharge. It was surprisingly efficient with the operation being organised by a squad of Liverpool dockers. They certainly earned their money as it was unbelievably hot for the first few days we were alongside. Being Saudi Arabia all the booze was locked up as soon as we entered port so there was a complete change in the attitude of the engineers. The longer we were in port meant the longer they were without beer so the cranes were actually fixed before they broke down. It took six days to discharge the cargo which was mostly constructional steel and not very interesting. The ship was starting to get pretty empty now and we sailed on the 3rd November back up to Kuwait with only 2,000 tons on board.

We arrived off Kuwait the following day and there seemed even more ships at anchor and we got instructions to anchor. The following morning we were told that we'd have to wait at least a month there. I was getting a bit nervous about getting home for Karen's operation but in the afternoon we got a message that my relief had arrived and would come out by boat the following morning. Sure enough the next morning a launch dropped Alan Rattray on board and said I had two hours to hand over and they would be back to pick me up. It was a mad panic trying to pack and hand over to Alan at the same time but at least there wasn't much cargo to tell him about and he had a month at anchor to learn about the ship. He was, like me, brand new to the company, and had come from P&O so it was quite a step down but he wanted promotion and liked the high wages even more. I was taken ashore just after lunch and caught a plane home in the early afternoon. I couldn't believe the action as soon as the plane took off. As Kuwait was a dry state the first priority was to serve everyone booze and that was the major preoccupation all the way back to Heathrow. There were some pretty sorry states by the time we landed. As we were arriving late at night I booked a hire car to get home so I only had a couple of beers on the flight. I had a great drive home through the night with hardly any traffic and had to wake Diane to let me in at five in the morning. It was nice to be home again.

CHAPTER THIRTY SEVEN

The Arabian Gulf again

m.v. Al Odailiah
29th December 1975 – 28th April 1976

I'd only been away a couple of months so was only due about a fortnight's leave. Karen had her operation in the second week and everything went well. My big problem was that I really wanted to be home for Christmas this time but I'd run out of leave by the end of November. In the end I phoned Kuwait Shipping and explained the situation and said I wanted to go off pay and I'd be available after Christmas which didn't go down very well at all as obviously they were counting on me going back early December. In the end I had a lovely Christmas at home with the family but the company insisted I join the next ship as soon as possible and I flew out to Kuwait to join the *Al Odailiah* on the 27th December. At least I'd got a Christmas at home though.

The ship was fully loaded and lying at anchor in Kuwait Bay in the midst of the hundreds of other vessels. I had a night in a hotel and then was taken out by launch the following morning. I relieved Jake Scallan who gave me a lightning handover in about quarter of an hour as the launch refused to wait any longer and he would have ended up spending New Year in Kuwait which was not to be recommended as alcohol was still prohibited there.

The *Al Odailiah* was another Russian built ship but of a different design to the *Al Rumaithiah*. She had twin holds and eleven cranes which made her ideal for the huge variety of cargo and the numerous discharge ports. She had just arrived from Japan and had yet to discharge any cargo so I spent quite a bit of time with the cargo plan working out where everything was. With the huge congestion at all the Gulf ports the company had devised a plan whereby when a ship arrived in the Gulf it would go around all the ports and register and then anchor off Kuwait waiting until its turn came up at one or other of the ports. It must have been a nightmare to organise as obviously some of the ports had longer waiting times than others and if the ship wasn't there when it was called it went to the back of the queue which could mean a long wait at anchor. The *Al Odailiah* had registered everywhere so we sat there and waited for orders. The Old Man was Pete Walton, an old hand from Liverpool who was a real character. All the other deck officers were either Indian or Arab and it was my first experience with foreign officers. They were a really nice bunch and all very professional and easy to get on with.

After being at anchor for a week we got instructions to take on fuel and water at Mina, just outside Kuwait Bay, and head down to Dubai as our turn was coming up there. We still had to anchor off there for a week before getting alongside but at least the weather was nicer. In Kuwait it was always cool with sand blowing in the air while off Dubai it was a lot warmer and cleaner. We eventually berthed in Dubai on 13th January and started discharge. The ship had loaded in the Far East and I couldn't believe the diversity of the cargo. There was a huge amount of electronic equipment and white goods from Japan and tons of cartons of clothes and shoes from Taiwan and Hong Kong. We also had ten large mobile cranes to unload which was pretty tricky as we couldn't work out where their centre of gravity was when we fixed the slings and I was sure we were going to drop one but it all went OK in the end. I got pretty fed up with all the pilfering of the cargo but couldn't seem to stop it. The stevedores would turn up in scruffy clothes in the morning but when they went ashore in the evening they were pictures of sartorial elegance in their new suits and shoes which they had extracted from the cargo. I tried putting my crew down as watchmen but they came up dressed even smarter so I gave up on that.

We sailed on the 20th January up the coast to Abu Dhabi where we had to anchor again for another week waiting for a berth. We berthed on the 26th and were completely overwhelmed by the huge labour force that boarded. I think they had about twelve gangs on board as they organised a couple of shore cranes as well. Normally ships worked with five or six gangs at the most with each gang consisting of eight or nine labourers, a hatchman, two winch drivers and a foreman. There seemed to be people everywhere with loads swinging through the air in all directions. The cargo was mostly materials to build a sports arena with everything from the rows of seats to the sprung wooden flooring and even the shower cubicles. It was loaded directly onto lorries and taken straight to the site which was about five miles away. It was a really efficient operation supervised by a team of Japanese who made sure nothing was damaged. After eighteen hours of pure mayhem it was all discharged and the Japanese were over the moon that the only damage was some paint scratched on the seating. It turned out that they had to erect everything and have the arena ready for a tournament in five days so they definitely had their work cut out. We sailed in the evening back up to Kuwait Bay to wait at anchor again. It was either a feast or a famine regarding the work.

This time we had to wait for three weeks before we entered port. It went surprisingly quickly. There were several other Kuwait Shipping vessels close by so we put the lifeboats down and went ship visiting and swopped films so we had a film show just about every night interspersed with barbecues. The company sent a launch with the mail every other day so it was quite a pleasant existence. Eventually our turn came and we berthed on the 21st February. The ship was again flooded with labour and the cargo was quickly discharged. We had to be on our toes though as all the stevedores were interested in was discharging as quickly as possible regardless of damage to the cargo or their own safety. It was a wonder there weren't any accidents and I was quite pleased with our outturn as the cargo seemed pretty unscathed and no one had been killed.

We sailed after three days and headed down to Das Island which is a small island off Abu Dhabi. It was almost completely covered by oil drilling equipment and refineries. There was no actual port so we had to anchor close in to the shore and discharge into barges. The labour came out with the barge and stayed on board until the cargo was discharged. They slept where they could find a quiet corner. There were three extra hands with the labour gang. One was their cook and the other two were fishermen. Their employers had provided them with bags of flour, a few spices, a couple of fishing lines and an old oil drum cut in half as a cooker and they were expected to cater for themselves. The cook would start to cook chapattis first thing in the morning and although not the most hygienic they were delicious. We used to swop tins of condensed milk for them. The fishermen caught an unbelievable amount of fish which were either made into a fantastic fish curry or exchanged with our cook for meat and vegetables. It was a great system and really seemed to work.

It took them three days to unload the cargo which was mainly drilling equipment and steel pipes and we steamed back up the Gulf yet again to Kuwait Bay but this time we only anchored for a day before going in to discharge 500 tons of steel pipes which had been under the Das Island cargo. This took less than a day and then we were back out at anchor again to await our turn at Dammam. After a week we got instructions to head down to Dammam as our turn was coming up so we picked up and steamed south arriving off Dammam on the 14th March. Again there were hundreds of ships in the anchorage and it looked as though it was going to be a nightmare finding enough room to anchor safely. Just as we approached the edge of the area we heard the Port Control on the VHF radio calling up another of our ships to heave anchor and come inside the port. Pete grabbed the VHF and asked them where they were and when they told us we nipped in and dropped anchor in their spot just as they left. Ace. Pete was well chuffed but we weren't able to celebrate as the Saudi customs boarded us straight away and sealed all the booze and they also confiscated all the girly calendars much to our annoyance. We only had to wait five days before we got called in to the port. It took them a week to discharge the remaining cargo which was all construction materials and quite a lot of roofing slates from China. It seemed odd because most of the buildings had tile roofs but no doubt somebody wanted to be different.

We sailed on the 26th March with instructions to proceed to Europe to load which suited me down to the ground as it usually took a month to load so I would be able to get off before the ship set off back to the Gulf. We passed through the Suez Canal on the 5th April and as we approached the English Channel got instructions to go to Tilbury to a layby berth and await further orders. We tied up on a river berth just beside the Tilbury Passenger Terminal on the 17th April. This was a bit of a pain as we had to keep tending the ropes as the tide went in and out but we got a routine going in the end which seemed to work. It was quite pleasant walking down to the terminal for the papers in the morning. We spent the time painting out the holds and after a week the ship was looking really good. Pete Walton was relieved by Jack Wilkie who was another old hand and easy to get on with. Eventually orders came through that we would start loading in Antwerp on the 1st May and also the good news that I was to be relieved on the 28th April before loading commenced. Diane travelled down with Martin in the car to pick me and my baggage up. Frank James took over from me on the 27th April so we stayed the night in the Seamen's Mission and travelled home the next day.

CHAPTER THIRTY EIGHT

Supercargo with the Greeks

m.v. Feax
23rd July 1976 – 8th December 1976

I had a very pleasant leave lasting nearly three months with my vegetable garden flourishing and Karen fully recovered from her operation. I did the odd day's work up on the farm but my heart wasn't really in it. Halfway through July I got a call from Kuwait Shipping and they wanted to know if I'd be interested in working as a supercargo for a few months. That meant I'd be working as Cargo Superintendent on chartered-in ships to supervise the cargo operations and act as liaison officer between the ship and the company. It was quite a responsible position and it meant I'd be meeting and dealing with the agents and shore personnel in all the different ports and would be fantastic experience if I ever got promoted to Captain. I jumped at the chance and got instructions to join the *Feax* in Antwerp on the 23rd July. I got the night sleeper down to London and caught an early morning flight to Antwerp then a taxi down to the ship. As soon as I got aboard I was involved in a heated argument with the Captain about who should prepare the holds for the cargo. It wasn't a good start but I eventually got things sorted and we started loading. I had a preliminary plan for loading but it soon became obvious that I'd have to change things drastically as information came in about the cargo. I was beginning to wish I'd never agreed when salvation appeared in the form of Baz Vieveen, a Dutch stevedore who had been assigned to help me. He'd seen it all before and soon had things back on track. He was a real character with a great sense of humour and I brightened up considerably when I found out he'd be helping at all the continental ports.

The *Feax* was a very basic standard design with five holds and old-fashioned cargo handling gear even though she was pretty new. The Skipper was called Captain Andreas who owned a large lump of a Greek island with quite a few properties. Most of the crew actually lived in his houses so he had absolutely no problems with discipline.

He had a really negative attitude and I found him hard to work with. This coupled with the fact that I knew no Greek, apart from 'calamari' which I though meant 'good morning' but turned out to be Greek for squid. When they finished cargo for the night I went ashore with Baz and we demolished a fair few pints of draft Stella Artois and had a meal because the food on board was inedible.

Next morning started badly with an argument about which hatches to open. Baz appeared about ten with a hangover and a couple of bacon sandwiches. I was moaning on about my problems and Baz grinned and said I should use the magic word, "BONUS." He said all we needed to do was let the crew know that it was my job to write a report on them and it was on this report that their end-of-charter bonuses were calculated. He managed to tell the crew this sometime in the morning and the change was unbelievable. They couldn't do enough for me. I even had a special meal made as I couldn't eat the stew they were having for lunch. Life looked better.

We sailed in the evening and headed up to Bremen arriving there in the early hours of 26th July. We spent two days loading special cement-lined steel pipes. They had to be handled really carefully to avoid damaging the cement and I was dreading discharging them in the Gulf. Once the pipes were loaded and secured we shifted up the coast to Hamburg. I went up in Captain Andreas's esteem when I phoned the Hamburg pilots before we sailed and organised the pilot to join in Bremen. This meant we went straight up the Elbe instead of messing about changing pilots at sea. We berthed in Hamburg on the 28th July and started loading large crates of machinery which kept me busy. Baz turned up mid morning with all sorts of changes to the cargo. It appeared we had to load four complete escalators in Rotterdam for a shopping centre in Kuwait. They were each over twenty tons and sixty feet long complete with glass sides and everything. They had to be under deck and we couldn't load anything on top of them so we had to rethink most of our loading plan. We adjourned to a little café Baz knew and after a superb lunch of numerous different German sausages washed down with copious amounts of Becks beer we sorted it out. I was really enjoying this. It took a couple of days to load the machinery and we spent most of the last day securing it. I had a bit of an argument with Captain Andreas because we had to weld lashing points to the ship's side to secure things but he was only half-hearted and gave in quite quickly.

After Hamburg it was down to Rotterdam where the main cargo

to load was the escalators. We spent the first day loading general cargo in the other holds and the next day was Sunday so there was no work. Baz lived just outside Rotterdam and he turned up mid morning and took me up to his house. It was a lovely day and in the afternoon we had a walk along a canal stopping off for the odd beer. In the evening his wife had made a huge meal and then Baz took me back to the ship. It was a very pleasant way to spend a Sunday.

It all kicked off on Monday morning when we started loading the escalators. It was really windy and they were blowing about all over the place as soon as the crane picked them up. On top of that they were bigger than we'd been told as they had brackets sticking out at each side. Eventually after much swearing and cursing we had them loaded and securely lashed. Baz then had a brilliant idea. We had twenty tons of blankets in cartons which we were having trouble finding a space for. We stowed these all round the escalators to protect them. We spent the rest of the day loading the remainder of the general cargo and sailed at midnight on the 3rd August.

The next port was Liverpool which was two days steaming away. It was quite nice sailing on a ship with no responsibilities and just watching the world go by. The crew had started calling me Captain Bob which I thought was pretty cool. The Second Mate was a great bloke in his late sixties. He had no qualifications and was a hopeless navigator so I used to go on watch with him and help him out. He tried teaching me Greek but without much success. We berthed in Langton Dock in Liverpool early on the 5th August. Once again the cargo on the quay bore no relation to what I was expecting but this time I had to sort it out myself. There was a huge variety of stuff to load but it was mainly cartons of tinned food and about 100 tons of bottles of Vimto. It appeared the Arabs couldn't get enough of it. I got it sorted quite easily in the end. The loading went at a very leisurely pace with only one or two gangs working and only during the day. The main bugbear was that I couldn't get home easily and only managed one weekend in the fortnight we were there.

The ship was scheduled to finish loading in Valencia and as it would take six days to get there I was hoping to go home for a couple of days and fly out but it was decided to save money and I had to travel out with the ship. We sailed from Liverpool on the 19th August and set off south. Again, once I'd updated my cargo plan I had nothing to do so I volunteered to do a bridge watch and let Georgis, the Second Mate, off to work on deck. It worked well and Captain

Andreas even gave me a case of beer for my efforts. I was a bit unnerved when we went through the Straits of Gibraltar, though, as they insisted on ignoring the traffic lanes and charged though against the flow of traffic. We got through unscathed and berthed in Valencia on the 25th August. Here we only had to pick up crates of tiles so the loading went pretty easily and took only two days. I packed my bags and got off just before the ship sailed. I had to explain to Captain Andreas how the registering was done in the Gulf as he had no idea what it was all about. I spent the night in a really nice hotel down by the beach and completed the cargo plan of everything that had been loaded. The agent picked me up after breakfast and arranged for the plan to be photocopied and sent out to all the discharge ports. He also took me to a Lladro shop where I was able to buy Diane a lovely figurine at a discount price. After a leisurely lunch I got a taxi to the airport and flew home.

When I got home I was told it would be about six weeks before I had to rejoin the *Feax* in the Gulf. I thought I could cope with this – one month working and six weeks off. No wonder some people volunteered to work as a supercargo all the time. I had another lovely leave, for once actually enjoying some of the vegetables I'd planted.

I was a bit disappointed when the company phoned up and said the *Feax* was soon going alongside and I'd have to go to oversee the discharge. I flew out to Kuwait on the 15th October and spent the night in a hotel. You have to give the Kuwaitis ten out of ten for ingenuity as there was a real shortage of hotel accommodation so they dredged out a dock and floated an old cruise liner in and then filled the dock in around it. They connected up some services and there was a ready made up-and-running hotel. They even seemed to have employed some of the old crew to work there. Next morning I went up to head office to see what was going on and was surprised to find that somebody had actually got it right and the ship was berthing the following day so I organised myself a launch out and joined the *Feax* out at anchor in Kuwait Bay. The crew were over the moon to see me and find out they were going alongside as Captain Andreas had been unable to get any information from anyone and they were fully expecting another month out at anchor. They were very short of fresh water and stores as well so the news was very welcome.

We went alongside the following afternoon and started discharge. I thought I was going to have an easy life wandering around watching the cargo being unloaded but it was not to be. The crew were supposed to adjust the position of the derricks when it was necessary to unload another part of the hold but there was never anyone about when it needed to be done. I complained to Captain Andreas but even the mention of the magic bonus had little effect. In the end I had to write him an official letter complaining about the situation so a bad atmosphere developed on board. The food was still abysmal and I used to invite myself aboard any nearby Kuwait Shipping Company ship for meals whenever I could. There were always a few cold beers provided as well so life wasn't all that bad. It took ten days to discharge all the Kuwait cargo and though I say it myself I was very pleased with the condition of the cargo and the way it was discharged. I even managed to unload the escalators in pristine condition though I did hear later that one had fallen off its lorry when it was being delivered. I had taken to adjusting the derricks myself with the help of the stevedore foreman just to avoid all the hassle.

We sailed on the 28th October and headed off down to Dammam in Saudi Arabia where we had two days to wait at anchor before our berth came free. On the first night I couldn't sleep so about two in the morning I got up and made myself and mug of tea and wandered out on deck to drink it. I was surprised to see Captain Andreas and several of the crew messing about on the deck beside number two hatch. Being nosey I ambled up for a look. All hell broke loose. They were taking cases of food from the cargo to use as ship's stores. Captain Andreas blustered and said they had found the cases on deck and were returning them to the hold so I stood and watched as they returned all the cases to the hold and closed the hatch. It was considered a very serious offence to pilfer the cargo and could even result in the sacking of the personnel involved. I was at a bit of a loss as to what to do so I made another mug of tea and retired to my cabin. Next morning the change in the atmosphere on board was unbelievable. Captain Andreas decided I should move into the owner's suite rather than my own little cabin. It was a huge cabin with a bedroom and dayroom and its own little galley with fridge and everything. The fridge was also fully stocked with beer and soft drinks. I rather liked this. We berthed in the afternoon and I nearly got arrested as I'd forgotten about the beer in the fridge which I should have put in the bond. For a while I thought it was a ploy to get me off the ship but I don't think they were that devious. When we started discharge Captain Andreas announced that there were two seamen on call twenty four hours a day to adjust the derricks if ever I needed them. The midday meal was a sort of seafood dish with large prawns fried with mushrooms and aubergines on rice which was about the only meal I really liked on board. I decided that I could manage like this so didn't mention the cargo pilfering to anyone. It was my secret weapon.

Discharge only took four days and again everything seemed to go well. I just had to mention derrick and someone would appear to adjust it. We sailed late on the 6th November and steamed the six hours down to Bahrain. We had to only wait a day at anchor before berthing. The discharge went pretty slowly as they only had a couple of gangs working. It made for an easy life for me and I would wander up to the British Club in the afternoons. It had a swimming pool and bar and meals at pretty reasonable prices. I met up with quite a few expats who were working there so even managed some intelligent conversations instead of struggling to speak Greek. There were some jobs going as Pilots and Assistant Harbour Masters with fantastic rates of pay and conditions and I did a little bit of investigating and was more or less offered a job. After a week there, though, I decided that, nice as it was, the expat mindset would do my head in. Six years later the whole set up was arabised and all the Europeans sacked so I'd made the right decision.

We sailed from there up to a brand new Kuwaiti port called Shuaiba which was just outside Kuwait Bay. It was in the process of construction and very basic but we only had to discharge the special cement-lined pipes from Bremen. The labour they sent to do the unloading was very inexperienced, in fact I don't think half of them had seen a ship before. There were special clamps to discharge the pipes but they were heavy and awkward to fit. We started discharge at four in the morning and I assumed once we had shown them how the clamps worked it would be an easy. After an hour I decided to grab some coffee and a bit of breakfast and I'd just sat down when I heard all sorts of shouting. I found that as soon as I'd gone the labour had started using ordinary pipe hooks as they were a lot easier to carry around. The shouting was an inspector on the quay refusing to accept two damaged pipes. After I'd placated him and remonstrated with the stevedores we resumed discharge but the winch drivers were useless and kept banging the pipes against the coamings and the ship's side resulting in even more damage. I was rapidly loosing my cool when Captain Andreas suggested using the crew as winch drivers. After that things went pretty smoothly and we managed to get the rest discharged without serious damage by two o'clock in the afternoon.

We sailed shortly afterwards to Kuwait Bay to anchor and wait for our turn to come up at Doha. We had a hell of a time finding somewhere safe to anchor as not only was the bay really crowded with ships but it was blowing a hooligan from the northwest and visibility was down to zero. We eventually found a spot but it was pretty close to some other ships and we were all swinging about wildly in the wind. I had a shower and sat and consumed half a case of cold beer accompanied by a huge plate of toast and Marmite because I couldn't cope with the stew that the crew were eating.

Next day was pretty bad with strong winds again and Captain Andreas was getting really agitated about the closeness of the other ships. I think he had been up all night with the engines ready on stand by. I couldn't understand why the company insisted we anchor in Kuwait Bay so I made a radio telephone call to the office and explained the situation but no one seemed really interested. The weather got worse all day and Captain Andreas was turning into a gibbering wreck. As I was going to bed I heard the engines start and went up to the bridge to find we had started to drag anchor. I told Captain Andreas to pick up and go and anchor off Mina al Ahmadi out of the wind. He didn't want to as the company had told him to anchor in Kuwait Bay but in the end I gave him the instructions in writing so he was over the moon. We picked up and steamed round the corner and found a nice quiet spot. Captain Andreas was so pleased that I'd organised it he gave me a bottle of malt whisky as a present. We had another four days at anchor before we got instructions to proceed to Doha and we arrived off there early morning on the 23rd November and told to anchor yet again for a few days. In the end it was so busy there that we had to go in and anchor inside the port and discharge into barges which was pretty slow.

The ship was now nearly empty so I started ringing head office in Kuwait to find out what I should do next. I had heard on the grapevine that there was another supercargo job coming up on an Indian ship that was loaded and due to start discharging around the Gulf Ports. I'd also heard that it was a nightmare with things breaking down and incompetent officers and crew so I was hoping I wasn't sent there. Nobody seemed interested in me so when the discharge was completed on the 8th December I prepared to leave the ship. It was quite emotional leaving the ship in the end and the old Second Mate gave me a hug and burst into tears. Even Captain Andreas seemed sorry to see me go. He brightened up when I gave him his malt whisky back as I wasn't allowed to take it ashore.

I went ashore with the labour on a barge and booked myself into a five star hotel at company expense. After a swim in the pool, a fantastic seafood meal and a few cold beers I turned in for a relaxing night's kip. Next morning I phoned head office in Kuwait to find out what to do next and how to dispose of the large box of ship's papers and documents I still had in my possession. After being passed from one department to another I got to talk to one of the engineer superintendents who said I should quietly sod off home and ask questions later. No sooner said than done. I got a taxi to the agent's and organised sending all the papers by courier to Kuwait and the agent got me a ticket on a plane to Heathrow leaving in a couple of hours. I had a quick phone call to Diane saying I was in Doha and on my way home. It was a confusing call as she thought I was in Dover and couldn't figure out how I'd got there. Then it was a taxi to the airport and just about straight onto the plane and on my way home.

I got home on the 9th December and had a feeling I was going to miss yet another Christmas at home as I'd only been away five weeks. I phoned the office in Liverpool the following morning and they were most surprised that I was home as I was supposed to do the supercargo job on the Indian ship. After some discussion they decided to send someone else and I was transferred to the personnel department to find out my next employment. Jean, the personnel manager, somehow worked out I was due a month's leave and told me to send in any claims for expenses and they would be in touch the first week in January. Yippee – two Christmases at home on the trot and on full pay too. Life was good.

CHAPTER THIRTY NINE

Back to the Gulf yet again

m.v. Farwaniah
8th January 1977 – 28th May 1977

It turned out to be a great leave and a fantastic Christmas and I'd just about recovered when Jean from Kuwait Shipping phoned on the 5th January and told me that they wanted me to fly out to Kuwait on the 8th and join the *Al Farwaniah* as mate. It was an early morning flight from Newcastle so Diane took me across the previous evening and I stayed in the airport hotel. I joined the ship alongside in Shuwayk, which was now the official name for the port in Kuwait. I was beginning to think I was spending most of my life in or around Kuwait. The ship was halfway through discharge and they seemed in a hurry as they had every crane working plus a couple of shore cranes. It looked chaotic but actually it was going pretty smoothly. I relieved Pete Roberts who had been told he was going to be promoted to Skipper when he got home. The Old Man was Pete Laurie who was doing his first trip as Skipper. They both reckoned I was well up the list for promotion especially as I'd done my supercargo bit. Pete Roberts enjoyed a drink or two so by the time he'd handed over we had emptied his fridge of beer and I'd forgotten most of the stuff he'd told me. We poured him into a car about five in the evening and off he went to the airport.

It took another sixteen days to discharge the Kuwait cargo and then we sailed down to Bahrain to unload the final 500 or so tons. It was mainly drilling equipment which was really awkward and hard to handle and had to be loaded directly onto special lorries. It took us three days and then we sailed on the 28th January in ballast back to Europe.

As we passed through the Straits of Gibraltar we got our instructions to proceed to Liverpool to load the majority of the cargo and we arrived there on the 16th February. It was a really diverse cargo with everything from toilet pans and baths to tinned food. There was even gardening equipment which seemed odd as there were very few gardens out in the Gulf. The company had employed some locally based cargo superintendents to oversee the loading and they had prepared the stowage plan so it looked like an easy life but it was not to be. The superintendents were virtually useless and their main occupation was to try and drink the ship dry before it left. I had to completely revise the plan otherwise we'd have had a lot of damaged cargo when we arrived in the Gulf. The sanitary ware was shipped in flimsy wooden crates and the initial plan had them loaded in the bottom of the hold with hundreds of tons of tinned food on top which would have completely destroyed the lot. The loading went on at a very leisurely pace with no work at night or on the weekends. I managed a weekend at home and Diane came down for another.

I caught a bad dose of the flu and was laid up for a week. I would crawl out of bed in the morning and give the crew their orders and then go back to bed. The cargo supers would sit in my dayroom drinking my beer and reading newspapers and the only communication I had with anyone was when they stuck their heads in to tell me the beer had run out. Eventually we sailed from Liverpool on the 29th March having been there nearly six weeks. I was really pleased to get away as it was frustrating being so close to home and not being able to get away. We sailed up to Glasgow where we had some heavy lifts to load.

They were building a brand new dry dock in Dubai and we had the job of carrying out the dock gates which had been made in the Clyde shipyards. The gates were massive and weighed about 150 tons each and there were four of them. We were supposed to load them using our heavy lift derrick but after a lot of manoeuvring and cursing it became apparent that the derrick was too short to lift them off the barge. A large floating crane was hired in and soon had the first two lifted on board and we started to secure them. We had a crew from Sierra Leone on the *Al Farwaniah* and it was the first time I'd sailed with a crew of that nationality. They were a happy bunch and generally pretty switched on to things.

I was leaning on the rail talking to the Bosun and he observed that the way the gates were loaded we wouldn't be able to unload them with our derrick in Dubai. I said they would just have to use a shore crane again to which he replied that he didn't think there was a heavy lift crane in Dubai. Mmmmmm. I wandered over to the cargo super and casually pointed out the situation and asked if he knew of a heavy lift crane in Dubai. After a lot of muttering he went off to enquire and half an hour later came back waving his arms and stopped the loading. We still had two gates to load with one of them already hanging on the floating crane. We landed it on deck and then had to wait for nearly two days while the powers that be tried to decide what to do. It eventually turned out that there was a floating crane in Bahrain that could sail down to Dubai and do the job at great expense. So on the morning of the 3rd April we loaded the last two gates and secured them and set off to finish off loading in Marseille. As a final gesture the cargo super gave me the proposed loading plan for Marseille which when I looked at it had us loading most of the cargo in number four hold which now inaccessible as it had four very large dock gates sitting on top. When I pointed this out he shrugged his shoulders and headed off to the pub. We sailed off down the Clyde and it was an amazing evening with absolutely no wind and the sea like glass. The islands of Arran and Ailsa Craig looked fantastic as we cruised past.

On the trip down to Marseille Pete Laurie and I composed a letter to the company listing all the problems and extra costs that the cargo supers had caused us, not mentioning the vast amounts of beer consumed on expenses. It came back to haunt me later on in life as whenever I asked for a superintendent to help out I was told that I had said they were unnecessary. I think I made a rod for my own back.

We berthed in Marseille on the 9th April which was a Saturday and they announced that the loading wouldn't start until Monday so we had a lovely leisurely weekend off. The local agent took Pete Laurie, me and Alex, the Chief Engineer, out for a meal in the evening. We went to a fantastic little restaurant down in the old port. He insisted we had the bouillabaisse which was the speciality. It looked bloody horrible with fish eyes and gooseneck barnacles floating in it but suitably fortified by copious quantities of red wine I managed to consume most of mine. Actually it was really tasty but I don't think I could have eaten it sober. We finished off with some sort of sweet pancakes which the waitress set fire to at the table. Alex burnt his mouth quite badly as he tried to eat his before the flames died down. The agent wanted to carry on to a night club but the three of us were burbling so he poured us into a taxi and we went back to the ship. I was pretty glad we had the Sunday off as I was feeling pretty fragile. In the afternoon Pete and I had a quiet stroll around the old port and the marinas, bought the Sunday papers and after a couple of cold beers to settle our stomachs wandered back on board. Very civilised.

The stevedores boarded first thing Monday morning and we were expecting all sorts of problems as we had hardly any space to load anything. The head stevedore appeared with the cargo lists, full of apologies that half the cargo hadn't turned up. The main part of the cargo was supposed to be a consignment of twenty Exocet missiles in special containers but there was a problem with the paperwork and we weren't allowed to load them. The rest of the cargo was mainly a selection of assorted vehicles from armoured cars to forklift trucks and small mobile cranes. Even with these we ran out of space and had to load most of the forklifts on top of the lock gates. It took us a while to secure them but eventually everything looked good and we sailed on the 13th April and set off for Suez.

It wasn't much of a trip down the Mediterranean as we sailed out into a really strong Mistral that bounced us around for a couple of days. It was quite interesting, though, as Pete took us through the Bonifacio Strait between Sardinia and Corsica and then down through the Straits of Messina. The weather eased for a while but blew up again after Malta. We heard on the radio that another of the company ships ahead of us had lost two valuable boats off the deck. One of them was going to be the new pilot boat for Kuwait so somebody was going to be unpopular. We slowed down a bit to stop the heavy rolling but everything seemed to stay where it had been put.

We arrived at Suez on the evening of the 17th April and transited the following day clearing the southern end late in the evening. Our first port was supposed to be Dubai with the dry dock gates but they were covered up with twenty or so forklifts for Kuwait so after a flurry of telegrams back and forth it was agreed we nip up to Kuwait first and unload the vehicles. We had a pretty good passage and arrived in Kuwait on the 29th April which was a Friday and all the offices were closed so we anchored in among the hundreds of other ships. There seemed to be more anchored there every time I went.

The following morning a large flat-topped barge was brought alongside by a tug. We queried it with the tug Skipper and he confirmed that it was for us and he would be back at nine in the evening to take it away. Pete got on the phone to head office and asked what was going on and was told that it was all arranged for the ship's crew to discharge the vehicles as there was no labour available. It was no great hassle but it would have been nice to have been told as we could have unlashed everything first thing in the morning. I found the Bosun and gave him instructions to start unlashing. After half an hour I noticed that very little had been done and the crew were all standing around muttering. The Bosun then approached me and said they wanted extra pay to unload the cargo. I beetled up to see Pete and we frantically looked through the crew contract but couldn't find any mention of cargo handling. Pete went back on to head office to ask and was told there was no extra and it was part of their duties. I went back to the Bosun and the crew promptly went on strike and sat in the crew mess refusing to come out.

After an hour's arguing we were getting nowhere and the tug would be coming back for the barge in the evening. I left them to it and started to unlash the forklifts myself. Then Frank, the Second Mate, and the two electricians appeared and gave a hand. We soon had all the lashings off and after a quick discussion decided to unload the cargo ourselves. I drove the crane while Frank and the Electrician slung the forklifts and the Second Electrician was on the barge unslinging and parking them. It went like a dream apart from the Second Electrician getting a bit cocky and nearly driving one into the drink. We had the job done in less than three hours and stowed the crane and everything. Pete had spent most of the time arguing with the crew and trying to sanction an extra payment from head office. Just as we finished they gave him permission to pay the crew a bonus but we'd done the job by then. Pete gave the four of us a couple of cases of beer each so we were all well pleased but the crew wasn't too happy.

The tug came and collected the barge and we sailed at ten o'clock to Mina Al Ahmadi to take on fuel and fresh water. It took about six hours and then we were off down to Dubai. Just before arrival at Dubai we got a message from head office asking if a consignment of empty Coca Cola bottles destined for Abu Dhabi were available for discharge. It turned out they were in number two hold and accessible so they diverted us to Abu Dhabi just to unload the bottles as it appeared the local bottling plant had run out of bottles and there would be no Coca Cola in the Emirates until we arrived. We anchored off at noon on the 2nd May and a tug with barges and a couple of gangs of stevedores arrived shortly afterwards. It appeared that running out of Coca Cola was a situation to be avoided at all costs.

We had just settled down into the discharge when we were called up by the *Al Jabiriah* another company ship that was anchored close by. It seemed that were in even more dire straits as they were running out of beer. Pete agreed to transfer some of ours but insisted they organised the transport. Soon a gang of them arrived alongside in their lifeboat to pick up the beer. The group included Pete Roberts who I had relieved and had now been promoted to Skipper. Also in the team was John Bannister, my old school friend, who was Second Engineer. They were all slightly inebriated and promptly adjourned to our bar to continue drinking. After a couple of hours they were all well away but we managed to get them and fifty cases of beer into the lifeboat. Just after they set off their engine stopped as it had run out of fuel but instead of refilling the tank with diesel they mistakenly filled it with battery acid. There was a really strong tide running and they were rapidly swept off along the coast. I volunteered to take our lifeboat and rescue them but Pete was very reluctant as our lifeboat engine was notoriously unreliable. We tried to get the tug to go and bring them back but they weren't interested so we lowered our boat and went in pursuit.

I had strict instructions to tow them back to the *Al Farwaniah* and it would then be their problem to get back their own ship. It took about half an hour to retrieve them and by this time we were closer to the *Al Jabiriah* than our ship so I towed them back alongside their own ship. We left them under the davits being picked up but ten minutes after we left we heard shouting and looked back and the boat was again adrift but they had left Minty Medwin, the Third Engineer, hanging on a wire. There was no way he could get on board and it turned out there was a sizeable shark cruising around in the water below him. His wife had come out on deck and witnessed this and was having hysterics on the boat deck. There was nothing for it but to return and rescue Minty which we did and then set off to retrieve their lifeboat yet again. Pete Laurie was watching all this from the bridge of the *Al Farwaniah* and was not best pleased. We got back to the other boat and our Electrician threw them a line which they were too drunk to catch and it got wrapped round our propeller. Things were not looking good. We had to take turns diving down and trying to cut the rope off with a knife while the others looked out for sharks. We eventually got it clear and towed them back to their ship. This took over an hour against the tide and it was starting to get dark but we got there in the end and we made sure they were securely hooked on before we left as their team had made serious inroads into the beer by this time.

It was well dark by the time we got back to our own ship and the engine was starting to make funny noises so I was really pleased to get back and secure the boat in its davits. I was then confronted by a very irate Skipper berating me for disobeying his orders.

It also turned out that the only crane that could discharge the bottles had broken down. The wire had jumped off a sheave and jammed solid. It took me another two hours to free this ending up covered in oil and grease. It took them another three hours to finish unloading and we sailed at one o'clock in the morning. I was completely knackered and collapsed into my bed only to be woken at half past three to get up and do my bridge watch. We were steaming at reduced speed as we weren't needed in Dubai until ten o'clock so it was really boring and I had a hard time staying awake. The seacunnie was kept busy making mugs of strong black coffee which resulted in me being hyper by the end of my watch.

I managed a couple of hours kip before we berthed in Dubai. We then found out that the floating crane hadn't arrived from Bahrain though it was due the next morning. We spent a leisurely day unlashing the dock gates and I even managed to get another few hours kip in the afternoon. The crane came alongside first thing next morning and had the gates off in no time and we sailed just after lunch back up the Gulf to Shuaiba in Kuwait to discharge some drilling pipes.

We arrived in Shuaiba on the 9th May and started discharge straight away. Pete Laurie was relieved by Trevor Williams who had also just been promoted to Skipper. He had joined the company a month before me so promotion prospects were looking good as the company were still expanding and building new ships in Korea and on the Clyde.

It took us two days to unload all the drilling equipment and then we sailed to Kuwait Bay to anchor to wait our turn in Abu Dhabi. While we were there we took the opportunity to overhaul the lifeboat engine. It was a complete wreck inside and the engineers couldn't understand how it ran at all. It had been a lucky escape down in Abu Dhabi and I was glad Pete Laurie wasn't there or he'd have had a fit.

We had ten days at anchor and while we were there the *Al Jabiriah* arrived in the anchorage and we could hear them on the VHF radio trying to get more beer as they had run out again. They didn't even bother to ask us.

241

We sailed on the morning of the 21st May and headed back down the Gulf to Abu Dhabi where we went straight alongside and started discharge. Trevor appeared in my cabin in the afternoon with a message that I was to be relieved the next day even though I hadn't done the usual five months. He reckoned they needed to get me home to promote me but I didn't know whether he was kidding. The next morning my relief, Brian Bartlett, appeared. He had been in the company for quite a while and had considerably more experience than me and had been hoping to be made up to Skipper but they had told him they wouldn't need any new Skippers for a while so that dashed my hopes.

I handed over to Brian but they couldn't get me a flight until the next day so I was put up in brand new hotel for the night. When I got to the airport the next morning the check-in girl said they had a problem and the plane was overbooked. I was expecting to have to wait a day but she upgraded me to business class for free. That was the way to travel. It was free booze and everything so I was quite chilled by the time we landed in Heathrow. In fact I was so chilled I had to catch the sleeper train home instead of driving as I'd planned. I remember I had a terrible hangover when Diane picked me up from Carlisle station in the early hours.

After nearly three months leave I got a call to attend the office in Liverpool. It appeared my next employment would be as Captain and they needed to explain the paperwork and introduce me to the office staff. It was exactly twenty years since I started my Pre-Sea Course at South Shields and now I'd made it. It was a fantastic feeling made even better when Diane sewed the shiny new braid onto my uniform.

Printed in Great Britain
by Amazon.co.uk, Ltd.,
Marston Gate.